Now That You're Out of the Closet,
What About the Rest of the House?

What about

DISCARDED

now that you're out of the closet,

the rest of

the house?

LINDA HANDEL

SOURCEBOOKS, INC.®
NAPERVILLE, ILLINOIS

This publication is designed to provide accurate and authoritative information in regard to the subject matter covered. It is sold with the understanding that the publisher is not engaged in rendering legal, accounting, or other professional service. If legal advice or other expert assistance is required, the services of a competent professional person should be sought.—*From a Declaration of Principles Jointly Adopted by a Committee of the American Bar Association and a Committee of Publishers and Associations*

Published by Sourcebooks, Inc.
P.O. Box 4410, Naperville, Illinois 60567-4410
(630) 961-3900
FAX: (630) 961-2168

First edition published 1998 by The Pilgrim Press. Paperback edition published 2000 by Sourcebooks, Inc., by arrangement with The Pilgrim Press.

Library of Congress Cataloging-in-Publication Data
Handel, Linda, 1944–
    Now that you're out of the closet, what about the rest of the house /
    Linda Handel.
      p. cm.
    Includes bibliographical references.
    ISBN 1-57071-652-8 (alk. paper)
    1. Gay men—Psychology. 2. Lesbians—Psychology. 3. Gay men—Life skills
    guides. 4. Lesbians—Life skills guides.
  I. Title
  HQ76.25.H354 2000
  306.76'6—dc21

                                         00-044037

Printed and bound in the United States of America
BG 10 9 8 7 6 5 4 3 2 1

Contents

Acknowledgments

There are many, many people who helped me take this book from dream to reality! My heartfelt thanks to the following:

To Josh and Jenna, for their insight, encouragement, love, humor, and loyalty.

To Mom and Bea, for gallons of soup, and years of support and love.

To Dr. Charlie Assad, the best and most patient therapist, who guided me down this path with unwavering faith.

To Jean Chapin, Bill Eyman, Nancy Mullen, Rose Randall-Hicks, and Cynthia Wilcox for unconditional and constant friendship at every turn, and for a very long time.

To Paula Sperry, for her love, support, suggestions, stories, companionship, chiropractic skills, fun, and pride in me.

To Gina Bartolomucci, who started the best lesbian club in town—DeVille's.

To the volunteer staff at *Options* magazine, and especially to Gary Richards for allowing me to develop my style.

To Sean Bresnahan and WSBE-TV, where our show received an Emmy nomination.

To Brian Jones for his fabulous "marriage for all" logo.

To Raymond Beausejour for sharing his gift of photography.

To Ann Waterman, the best publications consultant ever, who encouraged me from the beginning, pored over every word, and never let me down.

And finally—
To all my clients who can't be named but were my greatest teachers and inspiration.

Note: The stories in this book are not about any one person, but are a conglomerate of many stories, ideas, and people melded together. Any resemblance to any specific person is a combination of coincidence and the wondrousness of human nature in all its forms.

Preface

I like to tell my clients that "no *uh-huh* therapy goes on in this office." That makes them smile. It also makes them think.

Just as when they choose to go to a therapist, people pick up a self-help book because they need help putting their own situations in perspective. Something needs fixing, or at least changing or acknowledging, but they may not always know what or why. That realization is a wonderful first step—but in order to really make progress, they have to be prepared to stand up to their problems and *do* something about them. And that's the rationale behind this book. What are the questions that gay and lesbian adults face? What are their fears? What are their unique wants and needs, and is it always easy to know the difference? As a therapist, I know the "talk" perspective—but as a lesbian, a mother, a partner in a relationship, and someone active in the community, I also know how it's lived.

Now That You're Out of the Closet is intended to be, above all, a *helpful* book. It provokes thought, and it prompts action. It analyzes and offers solutions. It does not coddle; but neither does it lecture or judge. It *empowers*. Its direct, down-to-earth method is the one that has been the key to my successes as a therapist, counselor, gay/lesbian spokesperson, and devoted friend for many, many years.

Within these chapters, we examine the full range of life concerns—from the lingering childhood issues to families, dating, sex, work, and love, to disturbing adult issues such as self-hatred, homophobia, intolerance, and abuse. My goal is to help the reader understand both the universal aspects and the uniquely gay and lesbian perspectives on these issues in a way that is always direct, open, and honest. Together we'll face—and overcome—such seemingly insurmountable barriers as the "self-esteem robbers," same-sex meanness, long-term socialization, and coming out to our parents and our children. Together we'll deal with our images and our stereotypes—our Uncle Anns and our Aunties and our self-proclaimed "aging queens." We'll address our fears, and our courage. We'll get far beyond our former closet to the rest of the house and its future.

In summary, the book is geared toward establishing balance. In confronting life's issues, there's a lot of laughing and a lot of crying. People have to grieve their losses, but then they have to cut those losses, and cheer their successes! In this way they can learn to normalize their lives.

Now That You're Out of the Closet is a timeless, sensitive, and organized way to do just that. Welcome!

LINDA HANDEL

"The Weather Outside Is Frightful/ The Fire Is So Delightful"

A Special Introduction by Bill Eyman

Now That You're Out of the Closet, What About the Rest of the House? Where was Linda Handel in 1958? in 1973? in 1981? Those are my milestone years. I could have, would have used it. The most powerful tools we have for overcoming isolation and self-denigration are information and connection with others. "I'm alone (and I deserve it)." "I'm bad/crazy/nonexistent—that's what people who know more and have more power say, so it must be true." These beliefs have a long and enduring history among those of us who know ourselves to differ from the sexual and gender norms of our society. Increasingly, over the last two generations, many forces have conspired to help us break the barriers that have imprisoned us in self-isolation, doubt, rejection, and hatred. Our world is, in many ways, more open, informed, resource-rich, and connected. Linda is a powerful ally in our development toward wholeness, both personal and communal. Her own life experiences, her work as a therapist, and her amazing insights have prepared her admirably to offer us the gift of this book.

If you grew up in a "dark age," you'll rejoice in having survived and grown into the light. You'll wonder how people made it through when access to information and connection was nearly impossible. And you'll thank Linda for her courage, wit, and fluency in writing this book.

For most of us, it has never been easy being anything other than heterosexual, but it used to be simpler. Most of us made, and lived, our decisions privately. If we chose to follow our sexual/gender–identity destinies, we found or created our own safe places—our own acquaintances and friends, our bar, our vacation spot, our publication, our therapist, perhaps our softball team. If we came out, we did so to trusted friends and family. A few of us went beyond these boundaries and became more visible. Over the last generation, after Stonewall, we collectively transformed our relationships with ourselves, and the world at large has responded. Sexual and gender identity are now mainstream public issues. Everyone knows something about gayness, or thinks they do, and most of us know someone who is openly, or obviously, gay. Issues abound, and everyone's got an opinion. It's no longer simple. Hence the urgent need for this book.

What does this mean to me, as a gay resident in this world of new challenges? Once we focused only on the closet. Now, if we choose to have a fuller and more open life, we concern ourselves with the entire house. Out of the closet and into the bedroom? Not anymore. It's not just a question of who we sleep with (and have sex with), but how we live our whole lives. Enter the living room (or the parlor, to us New Englanders). You have endless choices about who you invite over—into your life—and they're not limited to "gay." They're now lesbigay, bisexual, transsexual, transgendered, queer—and straight. Many of our clearly identified nongay friends and colleagues have moved in from the tolerance/acceptance zone, and they now want to be in our lives actively and wholly. They want to learn about us, and from us.

Enter the study—or these days, perhaps the home office. A dizzying array of publications, organizations, networks, and Web pages beckons us. We're not alone! "The love that dare not speak its name" has become "the love that won't shut up." Even if we wanted to avoid gayness as a public phenomenon—and some of us do look fondly on those simpler, more private days—we couldn't. Doing the family books at your desk or on your PC? There are gay-friendly banks, financial advisers, software. Planning retirement? Think about domestic partner benefits, gay retirement centers . . . even gay funeral directors.

Enough of that! On to the recreation or family room. There are gay characters on every channel—routine, increasingly average people,

not oddballs, tragic figures, or comic heroines. There are gay magazines for many tastes—politics and fashion, of course, but travel and
education, too. (When will *Gay Mechanics Galore* premiere?) Books,
books, books. Novels. Gay history. Queer history. Memoirs and biog-
raphy. Gay wellness and medical advice. Lots of travel. Videotapes and
CD-ROMs—hundreds of selections, and not just porn, but adventure, romance, sports, drama, comedy. Sports? Yes, the Gay Games.
Out. Very "out" professional athletes.

The garage. Did you buy that car from a gay dealer? Did you
choose the brand because the company is known to be gay-affirmative?
What do your bumper stickers say to the world? Want recreation equip-
ment in your trunk? You're in a queer bowling league? Your lesbian
soccer team competes openly with the full range of other mainstream
teams? And your camper—are you off to a new gay resort in Ohio?
Why not? Off with your partner and gay friends to the place you camped
as a kid, where the likes of you no longer arouse even a whisper.

Soup's on! The kitchen, the dining room, the deck. Gay-inspired
cuisine—nothing new, but now you *know* the chefs are gay because
they tell you. And the guests! Your lover. Mom. Your ex-lover. Your
closeted cousin. Two straight friends. (Yeah, you're gay. So what?) Two
gay friends (one married, with family, as mainstreamed as one can be;
the other a queer, front-lines activist). Years ago, they'd have all been
gay, and you would have talked about nothing else but gay, gay, gay!
You have that option tonight, too, but it's just as likely that you'll talk
about life more generically, because you're all becoming more and
more aware of common ground. Aberrations that separate are out;
and differences are to be valued and respected. Of course, that doesn't
happen in everyone's house, but it can happen in yours, and we can
learn how to deal with the others.

Up to the attic and down to the basement. The junk of our lives
and the archives. (Later on, the psychological junk.) Now in our years of
blossoming, however, that old stuff—family pictures, memorabilia of our
straight-appearing years, etc.—takes on new meaning, less painful, more
understandable in the context of our lives, which are now cohering.

Off to bed. Tonight, with a partner. Long-known? Committed?

Recent acquisition? Fun and casual? Think of the tools you've got (yes, the playthings, too, but mostly the psychological tools). You're living in an era of unprecedented resources for relationships. You've got therapy. Support groups. The Internet. A world library of literature. Friends with experience, support, and advice. Talk shows (not all of them sensationalist). Your capacity to make informed, if often confusing, decisions is a new phenomenon in the world. You work things out together, and when you hit the bump in the road, neither of you balks too much at seeking help.

Off to be alone? Your thoughts and dreams are yours. Yes, you're human. Yes, the world's still a confusing, often dangerous place. Yes, you're still hated by many for who you are and often have little official protection. But your private thoughts and dreams tonight are different. They're about the many safe and comfortable places you've found and created. About your plans to be "more you." About weaving your personal and vocational lives closely together. About how you're going to help others learn about the new world of diversity that's emerging. About the fun you're going to have this weekend.

You sleep. The whole house is yours.

CHAPTER ONE

Somewhere Over the Rainbow . . .

BOOM! You have just landed—with a resounding thud—in the Land of Gay and Lesbian. Congratulations, and welcome. As you dust off your skinned knees and your bruises, you may be a little nervous about what lies behind that door you're about to open, so I've provided a guide. No, it's not Glinda the Good Witch. Actually, it's more like a floor plan, designed to guide you through the rest of the house, now that you're out of the closet. My house landed just down the block from yours a few years ago, so I can still remember the jolt; and believe me, that floor plan came in handy! Now, as a therapist, a counselor, a mom, and an ambassador of Gay and Lesbian Land, I'm here to help you straighten out (sorry!) a few things on the inside of your house so that when you open that door you'll experience the fabulous gay life you now realize you're meant to have.

Coming out of the closet to yourself was quite a process. Like a great tornado, you were spun around and around in the dark. What was clear to you before was suddenly swept away. The forces of nature took over. You felt totally out of control. How could you feel so right and so totally confused at the same time? Now it's as if you have awakened from a great sleep, and things feel strangely at peace. But there are questions. Many, many questions.

Before the storm came, do you remember looking for something? Something wasn't quite right. Something was missing and you didn't know what or why. For all you knew, it might have been your sanity!

Now, since your exit from all you thought you understood, you realize that what you were looking for is a guidebook or an owner's manual for this newly emerging lifestyle. I looked for one, too, when I was in your ruby red slippers, not only for myself but for the multitudes of clients who come to me hoping for the premier edition of "How to Live as a Gay Man or Lesbian . . . the Condensed Version."

So let's get started. We've got some cleaning up and sorting out to do. In this first chapter, I'd like to peek into some of the musty old rooms and take a look at some of the work that lies ahead. As you read, I'll guide you in a way that not only feels comfortable for you but also allows you to fully emerge into your very own definition of this wonderful lifestyle. Always remember one thing: No matter what you choose to do or believe, there are as many different kinds of gay people as there are people. There's plenty of room for all types and styles. You'll still be you, and even more so when you get it all sorted out. We don't call it "gay" for nothing!

In this book I address all kinds of relationships. Many of us feel especially vulnerable—what can you do about this? When is it appropriate to come out to your parents? Your children? Those at work? Even to your husband or wife of twenty-plus years? How is a gay or lesbian relationship the same and at the same time different from nongay relationships? Same-sex couples have no established guidelines and so few visible role models; but, believe it or not, this can be an advantage. There are no societal patterns for you to fall into as a couple. It's fun to make up your own ceremonies and rituals to celebrate your relationship. You can arrive at a balance of intimacy of love and have a wonderfully successful long-term committed life together as you learn to bridge your differences.

We'll explore your self-worth and help you gain a foothold even as you're running scared. I'll help you unlock the skeletons in the closets of your relatives' homes, where others of your breed lived entire lifetimes either shunned, in secret, or unnoticed. Who do you think those relatives are? What were the skeletons? Problems with partner abuse, dating, and codependency aren't exclusive to the gay and lesbian lifestyle, but they do tend to have a somewhat different gay slant. In the dating chapter, I'll help you to find others like yourself in appropriate places. And wouldn't you like to know how it's even possible to get a date with the object of your affection? Then, of course, I'll have a word with you about not clinging to this individual just because you fear that finding another gay person on the planet is nearly impossible.

You find that you're attracted to your lover's ex-lover. How could this be? It can be so confusing. But she is really cute—and aren't you lucky that your girlfriend continues to have such good taste or she wouldn't be with you! We'll look at differences between gay men and lesbians with respect to those who have addictions. That's one thing that doesn't change if you're gay or lesbian, except that you may find yourself drinking less after coming out because you no longer have to dull your feelings with alcohol. On the other hand, we're going to address your internalized homophobia and how addictions may come from the painful experiences of rejection. But you won't get left hanging, because as long as you're willing to keep your feelings from overpowering your judgment, you can learn to make clear decisions to change addictive behavior.

Whether you're sixteen or sixty, being blasted right out of the comfort zone of the straight world is both exciting and scary. New things, feelings, sensations, and awareness are pouring out of you now. But where are the role models? You may not identify with the effeminate talk-show guest, and the butchy dyke at the post office may offend you, possibly even more because of your new self-awareness. The thought of hiding your life away from these folks may seem like a good idea. You may be just as scared of them as you are of the anticipated straight rejection. Yet somehow you admire their courage in just being themselves. It might be time to examine your own homophobia and broaden your range of friendships. Maybe these gay icons who are so outspoken in society are heroes to you. But what about that hunk at the gym? Could he actually be . . . ? He sent a friend over to ask if I was married. I am (oops, I was). Now what?

If you feel lonely or misunderstood, you're probably right on schedule. What about sex? Why do we feel shy? What if we're having a problem? Who do we talk to? What do we read? All those men in the magazines—we don't look like that. And for women there's the eternal bookstore problem of finding a well-illustrated book on sexual techniques. Oh, those self-doubts! It's time to go into that room and vacuum up those culprits!

My grandmother didn't raise her grandchildren to be shy, and my clients don't come to me for just a nod and an "uh-huh." Being opinionated tends to run in my family and in my practice, so I hope that with Grandma's style of humor and caring, combined with my many years as a counselor and therapist, I can provide some answers and direction for you. One thing is certain, now that you've uncovered a new part of yourself. Take a good look at the task ahead of you; and before you open the door to step out into this brave new world, make yourself comfortable and at ease within your own house. You already sense that there's no turning back. Dorothy, you're not in Kansas anymore. Opie, you've left Mayberry, too.

THE HOUSE

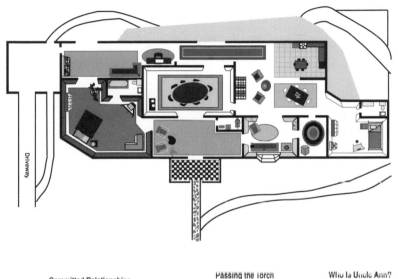

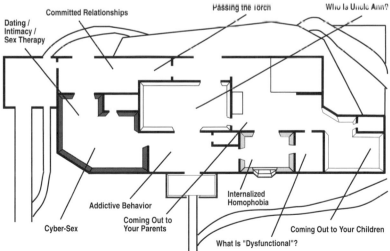

Dating /
Intimacy /
Sex Therapy

Committed Relationships

Passing the Torch

Who Is Uncle Ann?

Cyber-Sex

Addictive Behavior

Coming Out to
Your Parents

What Is "Dysfunctional"?

Internalized
Homophobia

Coming Out to Your Children

Driveway

CHAPTER TWO

"Nowhere to Run, Nowhere to Hide" (A Lesson in Self-Worth)

Sex addiction . . . romance addiction . . . addictions to relationships or people . . . problems with food, anger, or drink . . . low self-esteem . . . terrible childhood . . . it doesn't matter what you name your behavior, or what caused it. Until you're willing to stop the destructive activities and go through the inevitable pain of taking responsibility, you're bound to keep repeating yourself.

Do you feel you're on a losing track with someone? Do you continue to stay in an unsatisfactory or abusive relationship out of fear of being alone? Are you just plain grateful that anyone will have you? Do you derive your self-esteem from attachments to other people, rather than from yourself? Are you out of control with substances? Do you think your rage is justified? Are you waiting for someone to rescue you? *Or,* are you ready to invest in your own self-worth? If the answer to this last question is yes, then congratulations. People *can* go from victim to survivor and love it.

When I hear a client say the words "It works! It really works!!" I know that my task is nearly done. Unfortunately, this revelation doesn't happen in just a few weeks, or in just a few tears. The people who get to this point are brave, have guts, and stay with their plan even when all seems hopeless. These are the ones who are willing to look their "poor me" in the face and make it go away. They have taken charge, and taken responsibility for themselves. It's true that they'll never be the same, but why would they want to be?

Changing your patterns and taking control of unhealthy attachments, addictions, and compulsions takes time. It's uncomfortable, but it *is* possible. You need to be willing to be alone in order to reflect on your personal goals. You need time to see what actions to take, such as how to replace your old behaviors with new ones, *and to practice them.* The best part is just to sit back and finally feel great about the new you.

But be warned! Just *knowing* what your patterns are isn't enough. Getting in touch with your *feelings* is important, but that's not enough, either. In order to build your "good mental health" bank account (your self-esteem), you need to *take actions* that build. You have to be willing to take personal risks to look and act differently. You may have to give up friends who don't support your new strengths. After all, you're taking away the very thing—your misery!—that probably started those friendships and kept them going. You have to make sacrifices.

You need to understand what the long-term negative impact will be if you don't take healthy chances and make healthy choices starting today. Finally, you must take responsibility instead of blaming your current unhappiness on your past and all the people who hurt you. Those hurts may be substantial, and they shouldn't be minimized—but they don't have to be what drives your life today.

This commitment to yourself takes courage. Are you brave enough to start taking charge of yourself and stop blaming others? Great! Take a few moments to write down five new behaviors that are positive changes. Include some safeguards stating what you'll do if you start to slip back. Some good examples might be:

> "I am not going to engage in any romantic or dating relationship for the next ten months."
> "If I feel myself slipping, I will read my journal to remind myself that I have work to do."
> "I will take a yoga class and ballroom dancing to replace my old patterns and have some fun doing new things."
> "I am going to plan my next vacation and not complain that I never have anything to do."

The bottom line is, "Stop being a victim." Did you ever notice that you can always find somebody at the bar who'll support your victimhood? Our culture seems to love victims. We identify easily with their pain because we've all had problems at some point that have made us weak and sad. People instinctively project their hurts onto the victim, but this doesn't do anybody much good. There comes a time when we simply have to move on from past abuse. Yes, the pain will always be there in one form or another, but it shouldn't drive you to irresponsible behavior and then be used as an excuse.

Comedian Flip Wilson used to do a skit in which he would say horrible things to people and then hold up his hands and declare, "The devil made me do it!" This is a popular phrase because most people can relate, humorously or otherwise, to wanting to avoid taking responsibility for their actions. Even O. J. Simpson appealed for sympathy by claiming that Nicole abused *him*. Clearly, being a professional victim does work for some people.

Think about what happens when two of your friends break up. One of them is acting out, crying at parties, and looking "down" every time you see her at the club. Friends gather around to lend sympathy and "poor you" talk. They listen to the war stories of the old relationship and how badly she was treated. They can all "relate."

On the other hand, the ex-girlfriend, who is probably just as hurt, doesn't get the sympathy cards because she appears to be taking care of herself. She isn't outwardly needy. She's not out enlisting people to take her side. As a matter of fact, she's probably looking after herself with the help of a therapist or a good friend.

Why does victim behavior get so much sympathy? Our society attempts to program young girls to be nurturing and understanding. They're encouraged to be peacemakers, non-confrontationalists, and helpers who never get angry. While these may be good qualities, there have to be limits. When is enough enough?

What's missing is teaching children appropriate boundaries. Wouldn't it be a good life skill to learn, in our early years, to recognize when a friend is taking advantage of your kind nature? Or when you're being used by a friend so he doesn't have to solve his own problems? If we learn these boundaries, we won't support a friend's bad behavior just because she "can't help it."

Another issue that touches both men and women is the shame you feel when you screw up. When you do something wrong, isn't there a part of you that wants to blame someone else? Or lie? It's easier to rationalize, "I beat my boyfriend because my father used to beat me," than, "My behavior is wrong. I need to stop. I need help." History does not have to be destiny! Taking full responsibility for yourself is a very adult behavior, and being accountable is often extremely hard. It's especially difficult when you're surrounded by people who don't give you the reality check you need, such as, "Your drinking seems to be getting out of hand," or "I know you've been hurt, but don't you think it's time to move on?"

The victim, who is out of control, may be deciding that it's easier to drink (or to eat, lie, do drugs, gamble, steal, hit, attach to someone) than to deal directly with some painful event. If there's one situation where it's okay to have a guilty conscience, it's when we're acting out like this. Our culture seems to support the notion that "I don't have to feel guilty if I don't want to." This kind of thinking, if carried to excess, could eventually lead to our becoming a country full of sociopaths! Feeling guilty about your problem behavior may be just the impetus you need to get help. Justifying poor behavior *after the fact* is no substitute for taking a courageous step beforehand. Your conscience can often help you decide what is the right thing to do. (I'll bet you never thought you'd hear a therapist say that there are times when guilt is a good thing to have!)

Here are some first steps you can take to stop running away from yourself and back to old addictions and bad behavior:

1. Write down your repetitive, negative behaviors.
2. Write down your reachable goals.
3. Identify the consequences of your repetitive behaviors.
4. Figure out what faulty beliefs are limiting your growth. Often they come from your past.
5. Determine what is the truth.

6. Decide on your first steps toward meeting your goal, and stay with them for a while. They may turn out to be right or wrong, but you'll never know until you try.

7. Decide how you want to feel, and do what you have to do to get there. What are the stumbling blocks to your having a more positive life? What reasonable things can you do to move forward? Remember, doing what is brave will make you feel better about yourself. You are in charge of your feelings.

Here's an example of how someone might do this exercise:

1. Repetitive behavior: "I make myself a cocktail and call the chat line every time my lover goes out with his friends from work."

2. Goal: "I will stop calling the chat line."

3. Consequences of calling the chat line: "I feel guilty because I know I'm just trying to get back at my boyfriend. I get very high phone bills, and I have to hide them. I feel like a liar. I feel bad about myself. I do things for my boyfriend I wouldn't normally do, to try to make myself feel better. It isn't right."

4. Faulty beliefs based on personal history: "When I was growing up, my father used to go out drinking with his friends after work. He used to come home drunk and beat my mother. I was really scared of him. One day he never came back. The same thing is going to happen to me. I had no control over the situation when I was little, and I have no control now."

5. The truth: "My boyfriend never gets drunk, never beats me, always tells me where he is, always comes home when he says he will, and tells me he loves me."

6. What am I going to do? Idea: "I'm going to tell my boyfriend how I feel, and let him know I'm working on it. This is *my* problem. I'm going to come clean about the chat line and ask for forgiveness. I'm not going to make excuses for my bad judgment. When my boyfriend goes out again, I'll make plans to go out with my friends. Or I'll do something that's constructive and not destructive. I will not drink alone. I will stay with my feelings and know where they came from."

7. How do I want to feel? "I want to feel good about myself. With better self-esteem. More in control of my behavior. I can do this because I am in charge of myself!"

Clearly, this person is on the right track!

One of the most common complaints I hear from clients is that they can't do anything right in their lives because they have no self-esteem. "I think I have a problem with self-esteem," they say. "When I get some self-esteem, I'll be able to do the right thing." Sounds like self-esteem is something you can bring home from the mall. Some people actually do try to purchase self-esteem by surrounding themselves with outrageous material things and exhibiting show-off behavior. Guess what? This doesn't work. You don't get self-esteem by thinking about it or accumulating things! You can only get self-esteem by taking positive and courageous actions.

Each positive and healthy action you take, however small or unnoticed, will add points to your "good mental health bank account." As that account grows, so do your feelings of self-worth. Then, when a rainy day comes along and you make an all-too-human mistake, you have a little savings to see you through. You'll have had some practice in taking responsibility for yourself. You'll be able to get back on track quickly because you have something in reserve.

At first, this process may feel uncomfortable because you aren't used to admitting to mistakes and taking action to correct yourself. This discomfort is actually a good sign! It means you're changing old habits. If you find yourself being too comfortable in a situation, it's probably because you're in an old pattern. Step back and evaluate what's going on. Call a friend. Review your list. Sweat it out. You are worth it!

Congratulations. You've taken the important first step: You've decided you'll no longer run and hide!

CHAPTER THREE

So Who Else Is Gay in Your Family? (or, Who Is Uncle Ann?)

I want to take you for a walk down Commercial Street in Provincetown on a rainy day in August. (Provincetown is a Cape Cod town known to many as a gay/lesbian mecca.) All the tourists who have come during their week off are muttering under their breath about the lousy service and the crummy weather. You know the feeling. Then, just as you're passing the U. U. church, you see a sight that makes you smile: Three young men, dressed exactly alike, are walking in perfect sync, and blocking the cramped, narrow street. They're sporting blue T-shirts with the sleeves meticulously rolled up to a crisp line across their shapely biceps, and perfectly pressed white shorts with matching white sneakers. They're adorable! But look again. You also see three identical faces with clear, blue eyes . . . shiny, white, toothy smiles . . . and perfectly trimmed, identical hairstyles. Wouldn't you love to know the location of the water supply that made those gorgeous, gay triplets?

Well, I saw this sight, and it got me to thinking. Over the last three years alone, I've counseled at least sixteen people who are twins. Of the identical twins who are gay or lesbian, their twin sibling is also gay or lesbian. Of the gay or lesbian fraternal twins, however, the twin sibling has been straight.

At first, I was curious about why I was attracting so many twins. (Perhaps because I'm a Gemini?) Then I started seriously hitting the books to see what studies have been done on gay and lesbian twins. Here's the scoop. In 1952, a researcher named F. J. Kallman found that of 85 sets of identical twins in which one was gay, the other was also gay; and of 85 fraternal twins in which one was gay, less than half of the twin siblings were also gay.[1] In 1991, J. M. Bailey and R. C. Pillard found that among sets of identical twins in which one was gay, the likelihood of the other being gay was only 52 percent.[2] With the fraternal twins, the likelihood of the other being gay was 22 percent. My big conclusion, which would have saved them all a lot of time and trouble, agrees with a man named Hirschfeld, who in 1931 observed that "homosexuality seems to run in families."[3] We knew that.

Now it seems that researchers everywhere are trying to find a genetic basis for homosexuality. There are studies dealing with terms that most people can't even decipher. For instance, do you really want to know the lurid details about phenotypic similarities? Or probands? Neuroendocrine theory? Testosterone deficiency? (Who'd want to be in that study?) LH secretion? Blah. Is CAH or INAH-3 the reason you're gay? Who knows? We do know that if you're gay, someone somewhere in your family tree probably is too. Does anyone really know why? No.

Certainly, research is important, and it provides clues to some complicated puzzles. However, many people have their own reasons for wanting research to identify a genetically based and concrete reason for homosexuality. For example, if a genetic cause is found, gays and lesbians might be considered a "legitimate" minority. After all, if we didn't choose our sexuality, the implication is that we're not intentionally acting this way. We should then be given minority status and all the civil rights that go with it. This sounds good—but unfortunately, with a proven genetic theory come serious risks.

The fact is that homosexuality has been with us since the beginning of time—and any scientific proof that we can't help being gay or lesbian may be a double-edged sword. If homosexuality is shown to be genetic, what will become of the gay population with the advance of genetic engineering, combined with the stealth politics of the right wing? After all, today it's genetically perfect red ripe tomatoes; tomorrow, perhaps, the elimination of the gay population? We all know that there are precedents for sick minds to persuade masses of people to act without morality.

And what if research finds that sexual orientation is "alterable"? If the data shows that you're deficient in hormone levels, there are testosterone injections just waiting for you in a procedure that's already been tested. Electroshock therapy was used on a friend of mine to "cure" her lesbianism when she was a teen. Then there is aversion therapy, religious conversion, surgery to your sexual organs, and other gruesome tortures I've already witnessed.

Part of the medical establishment actually supports mind-altering treatments. Until recently, being gay or lesbian was considered a diagnosable, psychiatric "condition"—a mental illness. What's next in the hotbed of drug therapy? I can hear it now: "Honey, did you give Junior his sexuality drug today? He's acting a little more Nelly than he did yesterday. Poor thing just can't help himself."

Many psychiatrists still think being gay is a treatable disease. The causes of this disease, of course, are overinvolved mothers, distancing fathers, immature sexual response, and all that psyche jargon. Interestingly, though, Freud did not consider homosexuality unnatural. In fact, Freud's view maintains that there are homosexual tendencies in all people and that homosexuality is not an illness but "a variation of sexual function."[4] I jump ship, though, when he calls homosexuality "a certain arrest of sexual development." Why did he have to go and say that, after he was so right on?

My all-time favorite theory about why some women are gay comes from friends who watch way too much TV news. Apparently, it was reported that a mother's hormone level during gestation is the determining factor in producing lesbian children. (These same friends claim they had a testosterone bath at birth. Is that why they play softball, drive Jeeps, and wear those funny, spiky hairstyles?) By the way, scary as it might sound, this is a bona fide theory, and the cure it promotes is to give women steroid shots during pregnancy to prevent them from giving birth to YOU, a lesbian.

What are some other theories as to why you are gay or lesbian? Some of my clients think they're lesbians because of sexual abuse by someone of the opposite sex. There is absolutely *no* evidence that sexual abuse causes homosexuality. Statistically, three out of five girls are sexually abused by a man before the age of thirteen; and the logical conclusion of this theory would make these girls grow up to be lesbian. If three-fifths of adult women are lesbians, I'd like to know where they all are!

By the way, having "good" heterosexual sex can't convert you to being straight, as many of society's ignorant seem to believe. Actually, this misguided attitude has been responsible for more than one rape and murder of a lesbian who rejected the advances of some unbalanced straight man prone to violence.

Can you "catch" homosexuality? I recently attended a panel discussion of college students and young adults whose parents are gay— that is, who have a father or mother who happens to be gay or lesbian. The young people were all straight. And, by the way, they were also very well adjusted and productive members of society. These children of gay parents felt loved and respected, and had no pressure on them to be gay. They were close to their gay as well as their straight parent. This is not to say that there weren't regular conflicts, but sexuality was not one of them. If it were true that you could catch being gay from someone through contact, having a gay or lesbian parent would have been a pretty foolproof way to get the gay bug!

Still, there is often a family *connection*, or a frequency of occurrence within families. One of the first questions I ask a new client is, "Who else in your family is gay or lesbian?" After the initial shock of the question, I hear about a cousin . . . a grandmother whose best friend lived with her and slept in the same bed for forty years . . . six siblings of which only one was straight . . . a mother who should have been . . . a nephew who will be in a couple of years . . . and an older brother who never married but adopted children.

This brings us finally to Uncle Ann, whom we mentioned in the chapter title and you're probably wondering about. Who is she? See if you can recognize her in her many forms. She's the family member no one has anything nice to say about. Not only is her personality abrasive, she's domineering. She's not pretty or "feminine." Because she's pushy, she's been converted from Aunt Ann to the infamous "Uncle." The silent message here is that only men are allowed to have these traits. If Ann were more "girlish," she would've been more accepted.

But Ann goes on to play the trumpet in her own band; and although she isn't particularly attractive to her family, her girlfriend seems to like her well enough. But, to a kid growing up and questioning her own sexuality, the silent and soon-to-be-voiced negative messages about Uncle Ann are subtle and yet clear and easily picked up.

Let me tell you about my friend Marisa, who is related to Uncle Ann. When she was a little girl, and a bit of a tomboy, Marisa wanted to play the trumpet more than anything in the world. Her mother forbade it. The more Marisa was forbidden, the more desperately she wanted to play. She begged and she pleaded. "Why, why, why can't I play the trumpet? It's all I want to do!" "No," was the succinct and constant reply. "But I didn't want to play the clarinet, or the piano, or anything else," Marisa recalls now. "I felt it. I wanted to play a horn as I imagined the angels in heaven did. I wanted the clear tones to become part of my inner song."

Little Marisa cried and begged for several years. Her greatest love was music, and she dreamed of hearing the trumpet as her voice in her unforgiving environment. But her mother stood firm. Why? "Aunt Ann plays the trumpet, and you will *not* be like her. And that is that."

And that *was* that for Marisa. If she played the trumpet like Aunt Ann, her family figured, clearly she would grow to be like her in all the other "bad" ways. The eventual result was that, in Marisa's impressionable child's mind, Ann came to represent the enemy who kept her from her dream of sounding like an angel. Many years later, Marisa was finally given permission to learn the trumpet, but by then her dream had turned to bitterness and she no longer wanted to play. To Marisa, Aunt Ann had become nasty Uncle Ann—and, perhaps paradoxically, she had also set the stage for Marisa's future attitude toward her own sexuality. Ann had developed her tough exterior in order to sustain her identity in a family that would rather she disappeared, and the lesson she unwittingly taught Marisa was, "Be silent about your sexuality in front of those who may also turn you from aunt to uncle."

Marisa finally came out in her twenties, and still has mixed emotions about her "uncle." Of course, Ann never wished her young niece any harm—their family's preconceptions and prejudices lie behind the actions of both.

It's sad that my friend never did get to play the trumpet, because she would have been good at it. And it's too bad that families create an "Uncle Ann"—or an "Auntie Fred"—as someone not to value, someone not to be like. When you finally break away from your family's repressive hold and become like that person in the way your family feared most, you may find that it's difficult to learn to like that part of yourself. Learning to like yourself regardless of your family's approval is your challenge, and it's a big one.

Frequently I hear clients tell stories of an eccentric old cousin who lived at home with Grandma and ended up becoming her care-taker. These stories contain a silent family message that says, "Isn't Cousin George wonderful? He never burdened us with his sexuality." There may be others somewhere in your family tree who evolved to become caretakers of their elderly siblings or parents rather than evolve within their sexual orientation. These relatives may be your "gay" link.

Society is predictable in its treatment of gays and lesbians. When the political and social environment is more free and open, so is the sexual expression of its citizens. During such times, homosexuality *seems* to be on the upswing. The truth is that members of your family tree were able to be more openly gay or lesbian without fear of being burned at the stake, at least publicly. It is a fact that being gay or lesbian is *not* a rare occurrence. Sexuality may develop later for some people because of family taboos, as in the case of my friend who was related to Uncle Ann. Or sexuality may never be revealed, leaving you at a loss to find a gay relative in your family history.

Here are some interesting questions that might help you crystallize the relationship between your sexuality and your family:

- Who in your family could be gay or lesbian? Who definitely is?
- Do you think a person can be "converted" into being gay or lesbian by gay family members?

- How are other gay or lesbian family members thought of or treated?
- Do you think you can change your sexuality?
- What would you say or do if a younger member of your family came out to you?
- If you are a gay identical twin with a gay twin sibling, how are you two different? Did your family treat you each differently? How did your twin deal with his or her homosexuality as compared to you? How about if you are a fraternal twin? What if your twin sibling is straight?
- How did the other gay or lesbian family members treat you?
- How did the presence of other gay or lesbian family members affect your upbringing?
- Would you have come out sooner, or later, based on what you saw happening to other gay or lesbian family members?
- What lessons did you learn from observing the way other gay or lesbian family members were treated?

Now, close your eyes and slow down. You are who you are, and it's very important that you accept that. The alternative can be very dangerous. I once heard a rabbi speak about accepting gay and lesbian family members. Apparently, when he was a new rabbi, one of his congregants came to him to ask if there was a prayer for her gay son who had committed suicide. She was grief-stricken and guilt-ridden that she had not been accepting of her son when he told her of his homosexuality. He had drifted away from her and sent letters home reporting about "the cure" he was working on with a "therapist." The result was that this young man took his own life rather than disappoint his mother when he couldn't fulfill her dream.

The rabbi recited, in ancient Hebrew, a prayer and a blessing for forgiving ourselves, accepting ourselves, and loving our children for who they are. That this prayer is ancient signifies to me that the quandary of being "different" from our parents' expectations rings true throughout time. We are not on this earth to be the perfect child or the answer to our parents' dreams. We're here to be who we are, just as our family members are who they are. Through self-acceptance we can be at peace with our sexual orientation, and hope that those we care for will accept us as well.

CHAPTER FOUR

What Is "Dysfunctional"?

Are you in touch with your "inner child"? (Please don't groan yet.) Are you "reclaiming" your life? (Hold on . . .) Are you in a "codependent relationship"? (Okay, go ahead and groan.) Self-help jargon is *everywhere* these days, but the word "dysfunctional" has a special place in my heart. I was once given a T-shirt for my birthday that depicts two smiling people in an otherwise empty auditorium with an overhead banner that reads, "Welcome ACONP Members." Most of us wouldn't have guessed that this stands for Adult Children of Normal Parents.

What does "dysfunctional" mean? Why does this word strike a chord with so many people? Why do people love to use "I can't help it—I came from a dysfunctional family" as an excuse for their poor behavior as adults?

Elie Wiesel, renowned philosopher, biblical scholar, Holocaust survivor, and writer, stated in a 1994 lecture that there are precedents in our culture for dysfunctional families.[5] He pointed out that Adam and Eve, the "first family" of the Bible, had two sons, and one son killed the other. This is not a happy family situation. And where did everyone else come from if Adam and Eve were the only people on earth? Obviously, Wiesel points out, there was an odd relationship between Eve and her sons, and their children with each other. What's *that* about?

Another great Bible story concerns Isaac, who thought his father Abraham was taking him up the mountain to sacrifice a ram. Isaac kept looking around for the animal and asking his father where it could be. Abraham lied to his son. There was no ram because Abraham's intention was to sacrifice his son on a pyre of wood that Isaac himself had collected. Isaac willingly lay on top of the altar and was about to have his throat slit when an angel appeared, and Isaac was spared. Was Isaac outraged with his father? Not according to the Bible. To further complicate this story, many scholars now estimate that Isaac was at least thirty-five years old when this happened.

Can you remember a time when one of your parents seemed to sacrifice you? Did you go along with it somehow, pretending to yourself that this was okay? How old were you? Does this still happen to you? Do you remember being lied to as a child? Were you made to feel less significant than a sacrificial animal? How many dysfunctional family behaviors can you identify in just these two stories? What are the parallel stories for you? How are you still carrying around the results of being sacrificed for your parents' poor behavior? I see examples of these sacrifices when clients, both men and women, tell me how their mothers knew they were being molested by the "new dad," but the child went unprotected. I hear stories of how parents kicked out or tormented their gay or lesbian teen because being gay is "against our rules." Your example may not be this dramatic, but I can assure you that your family "dysfunction" is affecting your life today!

Family dysfunction seems to be part of the human condition. Not only are there many different types of dysfunction, but there are different degrees as well. As an adult you tend to repeat the patterns of your family because those are the behaviors most familiar to you. You're comfortable with the old ways, and people like feeling comfortable. This comfort zone, or familiar emotional place, however, just leads to your repeating what didn't work for you when you were growing up.

No matter how far away you move from your family, your experiences are still shaped by your past. Your internal system, formed as a child, forecasts the way you'll respond to yourself, your family, and your adult relationships, no matter where you are.

Do you think your parents failed you? Do you find yourself being angry or making excuses for the way you were treated? Sometimes these feelings are completely justified, but sometimes they are not. There are times in everyone's childhood when we were ignored or when we felt that our parents were being unfair. This doesn't mean your family was dysfunctional. Sometimes parents have to act for the greater good of the family and cannot base their actions on your individual needs. Sometimes your family might have failed you completely when you really needed them. The key word here is "sometimes." This doesn't mean your family was dysfunctional.

If you saw your parents come home intoxicated from a party, or they were too busy to get dinner ready sometimes, or they had to miss a school function, this is not dysfunctional. If, on the other hand, your parents were drunk regularly, rarely prepared meals, or promised to come to your school functions but never showed up, that is dysfunctional.

Like many parts of life, the degree and the constancy of our experiences are the key. If your feelings were consistently ignored, if you were abused, if your boundaries were continually violated, or if you were regularly called "little fag" like one of my clients was from the time he could remember, these may be the very areas where you have problems today.

In the book *Growing Up Gay in a Dysfunctional Family,* author Rik Isensee lists sixteen traits common to dysfunctional families.[6] One or more of these traits may apply to you. See how you respond to this list, and make a note of what is true in your own experience. Don't be surprised if you check off more than one.

According to Isensee, dysfunctional families:

- *Are intrusive:* They walk in on you in the bathroom, constantly. They read your diary, listen in on your conversations, and in general ignore your right to privacy.
- *Stereotype gender roles:* Boys play ball, and girls play dolls. They call you a sissy if you're a sensitive boy. They don't go to your softball games if you're a girl. Family members are expected to perform

according to society's prescribed roles, and any deviation is grounds for ridicule or punishment.

- *Violate trust:* They tell your secrets, make fun of you, or don't show up when they say they will. The adults are dishonest with each other, have extramarital affairs, or act irresponsibly financially.

- *Are inconsistent:* They laugh at you one day and punish you the next for the same behavior. You never know from day to day what will happen to you because of their moodiness. You find yourself rising and falling with their behavior.

- *Give mixed messages:* They tell you that you come first but treat you otherwise. There may not be enough food on the table, but there is always alcohol or a new car for them.

- *Are chaotic:* There's no food, or meals, or bedtime, or clean clothes, or money to pay bills. The electricity is shut off because the bills weren't paid. Your shoes were always too small, and the garbage is piling up in the back hall.

- *Are rigid:* They overdiscipline children, always say no, or are overly religious or self-righteous. If you frequently wonder whether someone is mad at you, or you constantly feel that you did something wrong, overdiscipline is probably involved.

- *Are isolative:* There are no friends for parents or children, or no goodwill toward others. You spend time at other children's homes because they aren't welcomed in yours. You feel you can't tell anyone about your life or something terrible will happen to you at home.

- *Are secretive:* "Why is Mom in the hospital? Where is Daddy?" They won't tell you. Your father ran off but no one told you he wouldn't be home. For years you wonder what happened but you would never ask. Family secrets are revealed to you after you're grown (such as "the man who raised you isn't your natural father," and you always wondered why he treated you differently from your other siblings).

- *Lack open communication:* Nothing of emotional content is really discussed. If something is bothering you, chances are you never talk about it with your family. You only talk to people outside your home, if at all. You might act out while growing up, as a cry for help.

- *Suppress feelings:* They act like things are fine when they're not. If you have a feeling it's not important, because only the adults count. If you're scared, they make fun of you. If you're beginning to have same-sex feelings, home is the last place you'll talk.

- *Exhibit uncontrolled rage:* They engage in physical and/or verbal abuse toward you, each other, and your siblings. You never know what might set this off or when it will go off, and you wonder if it will ever stop or how far it will go. This is not the environment in which to come out as gay or lesbian.

- *Deny addictive behavior:* They pretend that a case of beer a night is not a problem. The problems created by drinking, gambling, drugs, sex addiction, or overspending are ignored as the family deteriorates. No one seems to draw a bottom line, and everyone is a "victim."

- *Scapegoat children or weaker members:* They blame a powerless family member for all the problems. "If it weren't for you ..." Scapegoating occurs when people project their weakness and poor behaviors onto others and blame them rather than taking responsibility for themselves. If you're a "different" child, chances are that you are picked on or abandoned by at least one of your parents.

- *Give children adult responsibilities:* The older siblings are responsible for raising the younger ones. Sometimes you may not even know this has happened until you're grown up. One client once told me that if she knew she was raising her younger brothers she would have done a better job. Both brothers became drug addicts.

- *Have children who develop phobias or illnesses to distract their parents from their intolerable behavior:* For example, if the adults drink, one of the children may develop severe asthma. The parents don't drink when they take the child to the doctor, so the child continually has attacks to keep the parents from drinking. (The child manages all of this subconsciously, having no other means of control.)

This list is overwhelming, I admit. What's important to remember, though, is that most of us have had some dysfunctional experiences in our families at some time in our lives. It's when there's a *prevalence* of addictive behavior, uncontrolled rage, suppression of feelings, or emotional abandonment that there's deep trouble. Unfortunately, a child usually has no frame of reference as to how an open and functional family is supposed to feel compared with his or her own. Family, to a child, is all that exists. When that child grows up, he or she may be very unhappy and never know why, except that it's the way he or she always felt.

Many clients report to me that, when they were growing up, their role-model families were on television—the Cleavers, the Nelsons, the Bradys. This is because many of them would much rather have been part of a TV sitcom than experience the craziness and misery of their own childhood. The family has amazing power; and within that overpowering framework, destructive families defeat the physical and mental health and well-being of the child.

If you find yourself having the same kinds of problems over and over, getting into relationships with the same kinds of people, and doing and saying the same things, you may need to make some personal changes. How do you change life patterns deeply ingrained from your past in order to create a different future?

As with any major change in your life, the first step is to recognize that you keep getting into the same situations and that they're not working. Either your relationships are short-lived, you drink too much, you're constantly apologizing, you can't tell what your feelings are, you find yourself lying or unable to speak up for yourself . . . whatever the pattern, you need to have a certain awareness. Some would say you have to get out of denial and take responsibility.

Take a minute and be very honest with yourself. Write down three behaviors that you do consistently that may fit into this category. Are you secretive? Do you blame others for your own mistakes? Do you always have to be in control? Do you fly into rages? Do you tell people one thing and then do another? Do you operate in extremes, where things are either all good or all bad? What are you currently doing that was done by your family when you were growing up? Is this something that worked in a healthy and productive manner? If not, then why repeat it?

Now think about the impact of your behavior on you and on others in your life. When you're in an uncontrollable rage, do people want to be with you? Is your lover scared of you? Do you keep losing good jobs or good friends? Do you never seem to have enough money to buy that house or that car? Are you disapproving of people if they don't think like you do? If a friend makes a mistake, do you dump him? Then it's time for a reality check!

You lost a lot as a child if your parents were only there for themselves. You have the right to be angry and sad. Take some time to grieve having had no childhood innocence. Sadness is often replaced with a sense of anger at the loss. Some people feel that they wasted so much of their adult lives because they didn't realize sooner how their childhood had influenced their adult behavior. Most people don't dwell on this very long, though, because they're anxious to get the best from the rest of their lives.

How do you get the best? Start by visualizing what you want and writing it down. Put the list away in a safe place, and promise not to look at it for at least a year. Then pick one of your three behaviors that seem to get you into trouble, and problem-solve how to behave differently the next time. Be clear, because you may have to keep adjusting. If you are quick to blow up in a rage at people at work or at home, write down each time it happens for a week and what the circumstances were. Now you have a baseline. The following week, make a major effort not to blow up at all. Make a note of times when you felt the rage about to come on, and how it felt to be in control of yourself. Think about how it felt for you to be yelled at, and how others feel about you. Reflect about the person who yelled at you growing up and whether you want to be like that person or want to be thought of with distaste. Do the same with the other behaviors you want to change. *This will take time and energy,* but remember: *you have more control than you initially thought.* After all, you're an adult now, and you are in charge of how you behave.

Don't expect others to respond favorably to your new behavior for quite a while. You may be changing, but they're used to the old you, and they're just waiting for you to go back to your old ways. You may find that you're being set up to act the same old way because people are confused and don't know how to be around you. At least when you blew up at them they knew what to expect. You did some damage by having uncontrollable rages. You scared your lover, if she stuck around. It will take some time, and lots of talking and effort, to feel the new behavior taking hold. But it's well worth the trouble!

It takes about thirty or forty tries before a behavior becomes a new habit. At first you'll probably feel uncomfortable. If you try this technique and don't feel you're having much success, don't give up hope. Have a replacement behavior ready—for example, "Instead of uncontrollable rages, I will _____." The blank could be to take a walk; leave the room; close your eyes and take five deep breaths; or say "bring it down" to yourself. Don't you wish that the important people in your early life would've honored you enough to take the time and effort to change in this way?

This technique will help you deal with your adult response to the dysfunction in your family. It's important to understand, though, that making changes in yourself is not a simple task. For some people, complex patterns of family abuse need to be explored with the help of a counselor. Others may simply say, "I'm not going to do this anymore," find the support they need, take responsibility for themselves in the here and now, and succeed in breaking the cycle of family patterns of dysfunction.

Issues about growing up gay or lesbian in a dysfunctional family and a homophobic society need to be addressed specifically as you examine your family patterns. Were you made to feel different? Did you try too hard to be like everyone else but still feel "other"? Did your family make homophobic remarks? How did you respond then? How do you respond now? Did people make fun of you? Did you act macho when you really wanted a Barbie? Did your parents go to your softball games? How accepting are your parents of differences? Were you made to feel ashamed of your sexuality? Did you take the blame for your parents' problems because you "disappointed" them?

The more you get in touch with yourself, the more your abilities for intimacy and happiness will evolve. If you use the excuse "I'm from a dysfunctional family and I can't help myself," you may not be ready to become truly intimate and happy. If you say, "No matter what happened to me, I don't have to make the same mistakes," you're ready to have a more fulfilling and intimate life.

Good luck with your quest to find your true self!

CHAPTER FIVE

Intimacy: "Put a Little Love in Your Heart"

What do we know about intimacy, anyway? If current research is to be believed, we know very little. Adjust that for what we know about gay and lesbian intimacy, and we're in the sub zero range!

There are books on the shelves about intimacy, but most of them are for folks who have addictions and issues with codependency. None of these books specifically addresses intimacy as it relates to gay men and lesbians. There are books on gay and lesbian relationships, but none that delve into the barriers to intimacy for same-sex committed couples, or same-sex friendships, for that matter.

When I was very new to being a therapist, I made the fatal mistake of asking a heterosexual male client to think about what intimacy meant to him. The man was newly married and already involved in an affair with a woman he had met on a business trip. I never saw this client again! Since that day, I'm very cautious about broaching the subject of intimacy so directly or so soon into therapy. *The feeling that something so important is missing can be a devastating thing to face.* Until then, I had never realized the power of that issue.

Gay men are constantly asking me why they don't have the intimacy that lesbians do. They *want* to be able to sit and talk about things. The difference is even visible at the clubs. The women's bar in my city, named DeVille's, has tables arranged for conversation, and also has games and a really good jukebox. DeVille's always has a birthday party, or a ballroom dancing lesson, or a small concert, or a political lecture going on. There is dancing and a pool table, of course, but in another room. The men's bar, on the other hand, is smoky and pounding with house music. Its offerings include Leather Night, Uniform Night, Dominance Night, Teddy Bear Night, White Knight, and other predatory themes. Men who come to the women's bar are expected to behave better than that, and they appreciate the difference. Some gay men tell me it's easier to meet other gay men in a lesbian bar than in their own clubs.

One gay male couple I counseled on intimacy issues called to thank me for "making them lesbians" because they were now processing their problems instead of throwing things and yelling. They felt much more intimate, they said. They also broke up shortly after the call. Especially with gay men couples, it seems that intimacy is quite a challenge to maintain.

But are intimacy problems exclusively male? Far from it. Lesbian couples, by contrast, frequently confuse intensity with intimacy. Because of the patriarchal nature of our culture, women often have difficult issues with their sense of self and knowing how to operate separately from others. When two women in a relationship share this same socialization, they may have a more intense relationship than two men do—but is this really intimacy? And is this intensity helpful or harmful to the relationship?

The intensity may seem appealing at first, but it can be all-consuming and actually create a barrier to real intimacy in lesbian relationships. Intensity is often short-lived; and frequently, when it disappears, the couple is left wondering what to do next. Or they may be so fused together with intense feeling that they have a hard time breaking up when they really need to. In my office I keep a toy snake that has one body and two heads—it's a metaphor that's always understood by lesbian couples who come to me for counseling for this type of relationship.

Same-sex couples have few or no couple role models. Unless you happen to have a gay or lesbian relative who is willing to share his or her experiences with intimacy, where can you get information about this important aspect of your life? There is practically no published material on gay or lesbian intimacy. In the indexes of several gay books, all the references on intimacy have to do with sex, or communication skills. What does that mean? Are talking and listening skills the definition of intimacy? Is sex really intimacy? In many popular lesbian books, discussions on intimacy go right into fusion and the intensity of the relationship. We know that's misleading. It's time for you to find the direction away from what is always stated and toward what can be.

Let's give it a try. What is intimacy, really? *Intimate* comes from a Latin word meaning "innermost." Innermost what? Innermost feelings and thoughts? Can you act your innermost? Is too much innermost a problem? Here's a definition by example: Intimacy occurs when your lover needs to cry like a baby and be held for no apparent reason, *and* when you can stay with those feelings without question, and without laughing at them or feeling threatened.

When you're feeling your feelings and not just talking about them, you're being intimate. When you're taking responsibility for yourself, rather than blaming your lover for your feelings, and you're being honest, you're being intimate. When you can see your lover as separate from yourself, you're being intimate. And when you see your lover as being equal—not better or less than yourself—that is also being intimate.

Anne Wilson Schaef's book *Escape from Intimacy* contains the best definition of intimacy I've seen to date: "True intimacy is a process that grows over time. It is a process of knowing and being known, and it requires openness and willingness from each person involved. Intimacy has no techniques. In spite of how-to books that tell us all we have to do is follow the manual, intimacy cannot be orchestrated. It starts with the self, knowing the self and being present with the self."[7]

Aha! Back to that "knowing yourself" business again. Well, what did you expect? That getting into a relationship would solve all your problems? I'm reminded of an old Chinese expression: "He who knows himself knows others." If being intimate means knowing who you are, you may have a challenge in front of you.

The other day, my son called from college. He met a girl he really likes. "How do you have a relationship with a girl, Mom?" he asked.

He went on to say, "You have some experience in that area, so I thought you could talk to me." After I wiped my eyes, I gave him what turned out to be a list of do's and don'ts. Be a friend, I told him, and be open about what is important to you. Be clear about what you can and cannot do—set the boundaries. Be honest. Don't try to "fix" or change a person. Don't sacrifice to your detriment, and don't run away when your girlfriend does the same with you. Above all, don't expect your relationship to be perfect or the answer to all your prayers.

That ought to keep him busy for a while! In essence, I was telling my son that he's going to have to find out who he is in order to be intimate. It's not an easy lesson to learn, but it's well worth the effort.

How do you find out who you really are? Do you find that you're missing in action? For women, the "true self" has historically been defined in terms of being with another. That "other," of course, was always a man, and this is where lesbian relationships can get off track. Women are socialized in a male culture, and are programmed to please—that is, to be ready to conform and be less significant. That's when women are told that they're doing a good job. A very strong-willed woman I know was told by her psychiatrist, "If you want to be in a good relationship with a man, you'd better just shut up." Well, she tried for a very long time. Then she came out.

For a lesbian—and, I believe, for any woman—instead of looking to a relationship for self-esteem and for the answer to where and who you want to be, it's necessary to look at yourself as only yourself. Write down your goals for the next year and the next five years. Where do you want to go? How will you get there? What do you want to be? What is your boundary style? Are you a sacrificer? A minimizer? A caretaker? Do you do these things at the expense of your own good? Do you expect someone to take care of you? How do you act that out, even subconsciously? What are the messages you learned from your mother on how to be a partner in a committed relationship? What was her role in the family? How are you like her? How are you like your father? What do you want to change? Challenge yourself to be mindful of how *you* are, and stay with your feelings instead of fusing to another. You'll then be on your way toward a more intimate and open relationship.

Men, I find, are frequently lost in the realm of intimate relationships. If your father was absent more than he was present in your childhood, you probably got the message that it's women's work to put emotional energy into a relationship and to basically do all the functioning and even overfunctioning to keep the family connected. Emotional functioning is considered a "sissy" stereotype. Males are rewarded for making the sale or getting the promotion, not for maintaining the couple. Money frequently becomes the power base through which men have control over the family; and money, competitiveness, and power issues are just as much a problem for gay men in relationships. For example, the partner who has less earning power may find himself burdened with an unfair share of the chores.

Distancing is another socialized behavior men have learned to use when things get too close and uncomfortable. Instead of staying with the growing and uncomfortable feelings of closeness, men may seek new relationships. Sexual acting out is one way that men distance from having to learn about themselves in a relationship.

As a gay man, how do you get to know yourself so that you can develop intimacy skills? Since men are conditioned to function independently, you need to define how you see yourself in a relationship. Do you know how to share? On a scale of one to ten (ten being the highest), what is your comfort level in talking about your feelings? Can you stay with the discomfort and work toward an eight or nine? When you feel the urge to distance yourself from an emotional discussion, are you able to stay with your feelings and acknowledge the difficulty you're having? Do you want to run away? What do you fear about opening up? Do you feel trapped when you think of a long-term intimate relationship? What is your definition of supportive? What was the role your father took in the family? Your mother? Which one are you more like? What characteristics of each do you like or dislike? Be aware of your urge to leave when you feel that being intimate is becoming truly uncomfortable—then identify where that feeling is coming from. Make yourself stay with the feeling, and with yourself, in order to learn how to know yourself better.

If you're a lesbian, make sure you're taking care of yourself in the same wonderful way you've learned to take care of others. If you're a gay man, use your skills of independence to move toward your partner instead of away from him.

For both men and women, learning about yourself can be a challenge; but clearly this knowledge is essential if you're going to be intimate with another. I recommend that you keep a journal, recording when and how you catch yourself acting out the pattern of your socialization. This is where the trouble lies in same-sex relationships *when both partners are operating by the same rules.* Do this with your lover, or by yourself. Use the information to change the pattern of your behavior, and intimacy may find a place in your heart.

CHAPTER SIX

How to Date and Be Gay About It (or, How to Be a Road Runner on the Path of Life)

Once upon a time there was a little kitty cat. Every day Little Kitty would go out into the backyard and chase his tail around and around—all day long. Every day Big Grandpa Cat would sit up in his tree and observe the kitty, until one day he couldn't stand it anymore.

"Hey, you! Kitty!" he shouted. "What in the world are you doing chasing your tail and spinning around all day long?"

Little Kitty looked up at Big Grandpa Cat and said with great importance, "I heard that happiness is at the tip of my tail, and I'm going to catch it."

Big Grandpa Cat blinked. "Hey, you! Kitty! All you're doing is spinning around and around. Didn't it ever occur to you that as you walk along your path, happiness will follow you wherever you go?"

Thus another road runner is born!

And so it goes with dating. Talk about complicated! Talk about universal. As you go spinning around and around, trying to find the perfect mate, you forget about the process of moving along in your life. You're not being open to the possibilities of what might follow if you take your path forward instead.

This doesn't mean you shouldn't get some dating basics down as you journey. As I was researching information on dating, I found the usual gobs of material for heterosexuals, such as *Guerrilla Dating Tactics: Strategies, Tips, and Secrets for Finding Romance.*[8] Of course, there are only dribs, drabs, and Ellen DeGeneres's coming out, and no specific books about gay or lesbian dating. I combed fifteen different volumes and found a total of about twenty pages on the entire subject.

Most of what I did find was pretty repetitive: the usual stereotypes about lesbians who "merge" and move in together after the second date, and gay men who run away from intimacy and always have sex before they have relationships. These images are wearing pretty thin. I don't know about you, but it seems to me that we can either fall into stereotypical traps or explore our potential to be different. Don't you think it's time to develop our own gay and lesbian style of dating and put the "expected" behavior aside?

Now, let's see what this gay and lesbian dating is all about. I'm not talking romance here. That's easy. I'm not talking about sex, either. That's too easy! I'm talking about meeting, asking out, and enjoying another person's company without flipping out in a panic or worrying about what your family might think. What happened to the concept "to go out"? How does it happen that you translate this immediately to "committed relationship"? Sometimes a good friendship may be the end result of special times, and that's fine.

Dating is one of the hottest topics in my office. People fear rejection. A single date becomes so serious that no one has any fun. After the age of thirty, too many gay men worry that they're over the hill and get seriously depressed. Women in their mid-thirties are just beginning to bloom professionally, and they don't want to slide from one relationship to another as they did in their twenties. But what's the alternative?

This brings to mind the developmental issues about dating. For example, when you were a teenager you probably dated heterosexually. This is pretty common behavior and nothing to be ashamed of. But now you know who you are. You're twenty-one, thirty, or forty-nine and maybe just coming out. Where does that put you age-wise with respect to dating experience? Basically you're starting the dating process all over again, but hopefully you'll mature at a faster rate! It's actually great to learn dating gay when you're older. Relax! You're getting a second chance to do it right this time around. Pretend you're in one of those science-fiction movies where your brain gets switched with your kid sister's but no one knows! Eventually your emotions and body will get back together, although it might not seem so now.

Joking aside, you can already see that you've skipped the developmental stages of holding hands with your same-sex lover at the prom. If you had the good fortune to know you were gay or lesbian in high school, you probably had to be pretty secretive about it. In any case, you can see that your adolescence was no training ground for what you need to be doing now. Back then, boys did the asking and girls did the waiting. You were unsure of your sexual identity or in denial. I can see why it's so much easier now to get lazy and forget the whole thing!

Then there's the "Where do I meet others like me?" problem that faces everyone who is gay or lesbian. This is a problem not to be minimized. Heterosexuals have the same issues of meeting potential mates, but they don't live in such a small community. As gay or lesbian, even if you live in a major city there are still very few resources for meeting people. I know gay men and lesbians from Provincetown whose therapists have instructed them to date off the Cape because the community is so limited. What I hear from clients is, "I joined a softball team to meet some new people. After the first two games, that's over with. Now what?" Well, now play and have fun!

"How can you tell if someone likes you before you ask them out?" This is a favorite question. Often the popular method is to quickly form a committee of seventy-five close friends who make endless "discreet" phone calls to get a feel for whether Sue will go out with Mary if Mary asks her. By the time Mary actually does the asking, seventy-five people have already invested in the "relationship," and poor Sue is still obliged to act as if she didn't know a thing.

Often there's such an overriding fear of rejection that we reject ourselves first and save our potential dates the trouble. We have our friends surround us for a safety net to be sure we won't be hurt or humiliated if we ask someone out and they turn us down. This reminds me of traveling in packs, which is definitely *not* the way to get out and meet potential dates!

Other questions are, "Why am I always attracted to men/women twenty years younger than I am? Can that work? Am I asking for trouble?" "What do I do if someone makes a move on me?" "Who pays for the date?" "When do I tell this person (1) I take Prozac; (2) I'm in a twelve-step recovery program; (3) I have a good friendship with at least four of my exes, including my ex-wife; (4) I'm dating several other people; (5) I'm HIV-positive or have herpes?"

You may also be coping with the painful realization that you haven't dated in ten years and now you're single again. You feel out of it. You don't see yourself getting out there and being vulnerable after all this time. You feel lost in a sea of youth. These feelings of being so out of place often keep people for too long in relationships that are abusive or have gone sour. In these situations, you need to take time to heal before you even consider dating.

Friends want to fix you up. You write personal ads but don't mail them in. Friends write personal ads for you. You go to therapy. You devise an interview process so that you know what to explore with someone for future dating. "Looking for someone to fill the position of person to date. Must have the following qualifications . . ."

Here's a real-life story of someone who was finally ready to date after a series of painful relationships. Cindy was fixed up with a woman she really liked. They started to date. Really date. They shared some nice times walking along the beach. They talked about sad and happy times. They went to movies and didn't even hold hands or share a kiss. Because of therapy and her own good sense, Cindy finally felt emotionally healthy enough to date without jumping into the future or committing to forever after only three dates. Although Cindy was strongly attracted to this new woman, she chose not to become physically intimate. Then, six weeks into dating, her new friend tested positive for HIV. I can't even comment on how devastating this was for both of them.

Cindy suddenly found she had little understanding or support from the friends who had invested their efforts into creating a couple. After considerable agonizing, she decided to discontinue the dating aspect of the relationship, although she tried to remain a friend. More than anything, Cindy had to come to realize that, for her, six or seven dates does not make a long-term relationship. She had to come to terms with her painful decision, and then she told her new friend she didn't feel she could handle allowing the relationship to deepen, given the circumstances. This is a true story but it is not that uncommon. Just replace the circumstances with something that you would find hard to deal with for the rest of your life, and see if you wouldn't make the same difficult decision. Cindy was so grateful to have learned the lesson of patience and self-understanding. She has stopped beating herself up for being "selfish" (as she was accused of being) and is learning to live with her decision. Many gay men won't even date someone who is HIV-positive, and they have a lot of guilt for that decision as well.

In other instances there's something I call the "false advertising syndrome"—or is there ever truth in advertising who you are? Is the person you're dating truthful about who he or she is? Typically, people put their best face forward on a date. You wouldn't be caught dead in old sweats and a ripped T-shirt. Your date may never admit to hating the art museum you chose to take him to on a second meeting. Everything seems so perfect. This is the make-believe date with a fantasy partner. If you can hear refrains from songs that encourage codependence—"I'll go anywhere, do anything for you, no matter what"—swelling in your chest, you are in trouble. If you're fantasizing about a new china pattern, drop and run for cover—from yourself!

I like to caution people that this good behavior is a veneer about a quarter of an inch deep. And your not wanting anything to be different from what you see is a danger sign. Not until some time passes do you discover that your date drinks more than you can tolerate, is bigoted, doesn't understand the meaning of "no" at the front door, or just plain isn't much fun.

Given the closeness of the gay and lesbian community, we don't make dating easy on one another. If you date someone two or three times and then decide that he isn't for you, your friends at the bar want to know why you broke up. C'mon. Do two or three dates require a divorce?

Before I give you some helpful hints, I want to mention one behavior that gay men and lesbians must develop regarding dating. STAY

PRESENT. Just because you're taking this nice man out to dinner doesn't mean you're getting married . . . or even "you know." You're only taking a nice man out to dinner. Enjoy it! Don't get all caught up in the "what ifs" of future thinking. It's nice to go out. The meal is delicious. The wine's nice and crisp. He seems okay—maybe a little too something for your taste. So what? The purpose of dating is to be dating!

As Little Kitty eventually discovered, traveling along your path is the way you're going to meet people. If you're in a sophisticated area or near a university, look up the local gay and lesbian paper and see what activities you would enjoy doing. There's always a gay and lesbian bowling league, ballroom dancing with no partner required, a shelter you could volunteer for, book clubs to join, outdoor clubs for hiking, a singles club that goes to the theater. In my town, two women put a personal ad in the paper to form a discussion group for women in their age and professional group. Their goal was to research investment opportunities. A gay man I know started a men's storytelling group where participants share their personal stories and hobbies. Another group formed to play board games, and there's a local gourmet cooking club where a monthly theme is chosen and everyone brings a dish to share. Being fixed up, or "networking" as they call it today, is also a good way to meet people you might want to date.

Many cities have gay and lesbian teacher groups, police groups, Older Lesbian Energy groups, married lesbian groups, travel groups, closeted groups, activist groups, Pride groups, hot-line groups, spiritual groups, political groups, and more. Just join and see what happens. If you leave yourself open, without anxiety or a determination other than just to learn and enjoy, nature will take care of filling the void. As a friend of mine often reminds me, nature abhors a vacuum.

By the way, I don't hold out a lot of hope for relationships that start in bars. People aren't their true selves with a couple of drinks in them. Frequently, relationships that start in bars end in bars, and all you've gained from them is a big drama.

If you're in a less cosmopolitan area, you might find it helpful to get to where there's a major college or university so you can participate in organizations or classes that will help you network. Also refer to the list of national organizations in the back of this book, and write to them for more information. If you're in a small town, you may have to be more closeted. Be cautious, but find a way to get connected in an activity that will broaden your scope of friendships.

Now, back to some of your questions. About age—I always had a dating rule I called the "where were you when Kennedy was shot?" test. My generation all know where they were when J.F.K. was assassinated. If my potential date was getting bathed in the sink by her mom when I was a junior in college, I didn't go out with her, other than to share a nice evening or make a new friend.

The older you both are, of course, the less this rule applies. If, for example, you're thirty, you might be disappointed if you are dating someone twenty and hoping for more. A young man or woman of twenty, no matter how mature, just doesn't have the life experiences of someone who is thirty. Dating may be fun for a while, but watch your heart. If, on the other hand, the ten-year span is between forty and fifty, you're developmentally closer, and more likely to share goals and interests and a willingness to explore dating in earnest.

Who pays on a date? If you ask someone out, are you obligated to pay? This reminds me of high school. Back then, of course, the boy always paid! But today this is not the case. When my teenage daughter goes out, there's an unspoken understanding of dutch treat. Sometimes the kids take turns—she treats sometimes and he treats sometimes—but basically the cost is split. If your date considers this practice "cheap," maybe this is the signal for you to limit dating that person. The who-pays-for-what dilemma is the most complicated on the first date, because people want to make a good first impression, and they may withhold their true feelings on what might be a touchy subject.

When do you tell a person you're dating the personal things about yourself? This is tricky, but I'm of the old "honesty is the best policy" school. Tell them early in the relationship, maybe by the second or third date. If you don't tell the truth about yourself, someone else is bound to, and then your personal information is out of your control. Wouldn't you rather know from the start that someone has HIV or is in an alcohol recovery group? If you're afraid of being rejected because of your personal issues, aren't you better off knowing this in the early stages than when you feel more invested?

How do you start to date again after being in a long-term relationship? First, please be sure you're even ready to date. Wait to grieve the loss of your relationship *and* the reason you're now alone. If your partner died, left you for another, was abusive, or just faded away, give yourself at least a year, see a therapist, and work out your loss before you even begin to nose out into the dating scene. When you feel better about yourself, then your therapist and your personal wisdom will help you decide if the time is right. Give yourself lots of room to look around, and don't jump into anything that isn't right for you.

Personal ads? These are usually a disaster. If you really want to use them, be careful to meet in a public place. Don't feel that you have to stay if it doesn't feel right, don't give out your phone number or other personal information, and don't be afraid to ask for references! The date should be a short coffee in a very public cafe during the busy hours. Take an object to identify you, but don't describe what you'll be wearing. That way, if you have to, you can hide whatever it is and duck out without being identified.

Finally, what is this interview process I mentioned earlier in the chapter? Your first date should be a short one. Make a list of what you absolutely won't tolerate on a date, and then don't accept those things. If someone pressures you for sex, understand that you're not obligated under any circumstances. If someone triggers some red flags for you, write them down later and see if this is a pattern on a second or third date. Don't be too quick to judge. Some of us can be real jerks on a first date, or can try so hard to make a good impression that we do the exact opposite. If what you experience is a pattern you find difficult, become friends and move on.

Make a list of what you want to gain from a date: a good time, no pressure, good humor, enjoyable conversation, whatever. Keep those goals in mind, and don't break into the song "Love me or leave me and let me be lonely."

CHAPTER SEVEN

Boundaries

Good Fences Make Good Neighbors (and Good Lovers and Friends)

Do you recall the expression "Dogs come when you call; cats take a message and get back to you"? If you're a pet person, I'm sure you're aware of the total love that pours out of a dog's eyes. I never met a cat, on the other hand, that wasn't willing to show me her tail on the way out of the room. Most dogs have very close boundaries. They want to sleep pressed against their owner's side, or at least in the same room. Cats, however, have rigid boundaries, and do what they want when they want. I'm sure there's an inherent reason for dogs and cats to have different boundary operations. But what about us humans—and, specifically, us as gays and lesbians?

Many of us tend to go to extremes in setting boundaries. Some of us seem to have boundaries as close as our noses. It's not that hard to understand how important it is to have balanced boundaries if you think back to the game of Patty Cake, which you played when you were little. First you clap your hand and then the hand of your partner. If your partner doesn't hold his hand firm, you might end up losing your balance or accidentally hitting him in the nose. If you keep your hand too stiff in front of you, your partner may end up hurting his hand when he is patting back.

Now fast-forward this game into your adulthood. You may be one of those people who think they have to spill their thoughts and feelings to everyone in their life. Somehow you didn't learn to say, "That's private information," or "I'm really not free to talk about that." You feel guilty, or worry that you may insult someone by withholding information. You think you may lose a friend. You may feel that others are more valuable than you, and that you should do whatever they ask. Your boundaries aren't firm enough.

By contrast, many of us set rigid boundaries that are designed to protect us at any cost. You may recall too vividly what it's like to have been rejected, abandoned, or betrayed by a lover, friend, or parent. After these painful examples of openness followed by betrayal, it's easy to retreat deeply within yourself and hide your feelings, dreams, or longings—from others as well as from yourself. You feel unsafe. You can't trust. Your boundaries are so stiff that people around you get hurt when they try to reach out to you. Soon even friends don't want to play with you anymore.

If your boundaries are too rigid, it may be hard for you to let go and have fun. Your feelings may be overwhelming to you, so you subconsciously keep them from surfacing. If your boundaries are too flexible, you may not realize that you're entitled to your own thoughts and feelings. In either case, you may not know how to set limits. Perhaps you never gave yourself the chance to stay with your feelings long enough to learn that you can control them. You may chase your feelings away, and not allow yourself the intimacy that thrives in healthy relationships. There may be constant tension in your relationship. There may be a big power struggle going on as you draw back even further from experiencing pain, enjoyment, or love.

The possibilities for different types of boundaries seem endless, don't they? If you don't know how to manage your boundaries, you may be too flexible and then too rigid for no apparent reason. For example, you may be too rigid with your kids, and have weak boundaries with your friends. If you have issues with food, you may be too flexible when you're eating, giving yourself all kinds of permission to be unhealthy. Then you may be too inflexible in confronting an issue that needs to be resolved with your lover.

When Your Boundaries Need Strengthening

Having *weak* boundaries is a way in which you surrender who you are for the sake of "the relationship." This surrender of self is a key symptom of codependency. How did you get this way?

One theory suggests that if the adults in your childhood exposed you to worries and problems that were inappropriate for children, you felt responsible for the problems yet inadequate to fix them. Now, as an adult, your boundaries may be too flexible. This may show up in your being too vulnerable to your partner's moods. Do you try to mind-read every gesture your partner makes because you think you're responsible for her feelings? Some theorists say that you may be trying to fix what you couldn't as a child.

How did you get involved with trying to fix your parents' problems when you were young? Triangulation. Human geometry! Let's say your parents are having a problem. Rather than keeping it between themselves, one of them turns to you and says, "Did you know your dad is having an affair?" or "Do you know your mother hates sex?" Several things can happen in these kinds of families. The child becomes overly attached to the mother to protect her from her husband. The child develops a phobia or illness that distracts the parents from their problems so that they stay together for the child's sake. The child becomes a victim of sexual abuse. The parent expects the child to take care of him or her emotionally.

When you take in too much of your partner's negative energy without considering your own feelings, you may come to feel inadequate and responsible for something you can't fix, just as when you were a child. For example, let's say your partner has a jealous fit of rage over your occasional conversations with your ex-lover, and she doesn't take responsibility for her jealous behavior.

You have some choices here. You can never talk to your ex again. You can avoid the ex from now on, but always feel that you need to know where she is just in case your partner thinks you had a conversation. You can lie. Or you can express how you feel about being mistrusted after so many years of devotion. Realize that you can't fix your partner's childhood issues of abandonment, and that together you can improve the situation for both of you. Mostly, your partner needs to address her issues with trust; your only obligation is support. You can't fix her problem. "Fixing" is old behavior you're leaving behind.

If you're not sure why you feel uncomfortable in your relationship, you may be having a hard time with your boundaries and accepting your feelings. There may be a tendency to become enmeshed with your lover till it's hard to tell where you end and he or she begins. Remember Patty Cake?

How do you know if you fall into this category? Here are some statements I frequently hear from clients:

1. I have a hard time saying no.
2. I always seem to get involved with people who hurt me.
3. I rarely ask for what I want or need.
4. I feel ashamed a lot of the time.
5. I neglect myself for the sake of others.
6. I don't know how or what I feel.
7. My moods or feelings change to match those of other people around me.
8. I feel empty inside, as if something is missing.
9. I'm embarrassed when someone I'm with behaves poorly in public.
10. I put more into relationships than I get back.
11. I stay too long in relationships that hurt me.
12. I have a high tolerance for inappropriate behavior from my lover.

Can you identify yourself in any of these statements? Here are some examples of having weak boundaries: "Where do you want to go on vacation?" "Wherever you want to." Or, "I feel hurt when you say that." "No, you don't." Or, "How was your weekend?" "We loved it." These are all statements that indicate poor boundaries in relationships. I'll bet you have some examples of your own to add. Are there times when who you are or how you feel doesn't seem to count? Are there conversations when you may as well not even be there? Are you tired of feeling that way? What can you do about it?

Begin by increasing your self-awareness. Get that notebook out again, and, for one week, jot down every time your opinion, value, or preference differs from those of the person you're with. Learn to notice how you feel when you have a difference, and make a note of how you respond. Don't change anything you do! Just observe. Review and discuss your notes with someone you trust who won't try to talk you out of your feelings.

The following week, take some stabs at being heard. Read a book about communication skills, so you can learn to express your feelings. You can practice by listening to the news or to an annoying talk show on radio or television. When you disagree with something, practice stating your own view. Don't be afraid to give the media an earful of your opinion.

Disagree with a friend when you notice that your views are different. Don't be tentative or back away by saying something like, "This is really hard for me to say, but I see things differently." Be aware of *why* it's hard to disagree. Are you afraid of losing your friend? Is your heart beating hard in your chest? Take a deep breath and try anyway. Write about your feelings at that moment and what the results are.

Start paying attention to your needs and how you react to having them. If you need affection, do you ask for it? Or do you shop, eat, or drink instead? Give yourself a plus every time you take care of your needs and a minus when you don't. Spend twenty-four hours meeting your physical and emotional needs. If you find that you're tired during the day, devise a way to give yourself a break. If you're not having fun, make fun plans and follow through. If you need to talk, call a friend who cares about you. Above all, see if there are any roadblocks to taking care of yourself and make a note of them. Talk to a friend about what you're doing.

Having good boundaries requires attention and awareness. The more you take care of yourself and your own needs, the less likely you'll be to get into relationships that require you to sacrifice what's important to you for the sake of "love." You'll find that you don't want to be in a relationship where you're constantly worrying about what you're saying or what he or she is thinking. You'll keep yourself safe, and trust in your ability to take care of yourself. Most important, you'll want to share your life with someone who's equally capable of being authentic with you.

When Your Boundaries Need Relaxing

Do people say they can't "read" you, or that you're hard to get to know? Do you feel that you have to control your feelings of pain, love, anger, or fun because you don't know where they'll lead you? Is it hard to belly-laugh, or cry, or feel the passion of human experience? Do you feel like an observer of life rather than a participant? These are some of the symptoms of having rigid boundaries.

More than likely you were raised by parents who wore suits of armor and were emotionally detached or critical. You may have felt isolated, with little or no support for your ideas. New ideas were unacceptable, and you developed a narrow view that didn't allow for differences. Your thinking became very black-or-white.

Distant boundaries mean you probably didn't get enough affection or bonding with your parents. As an adult you may experience an intimate relationship as smothering. If your lover shows interest in what you're doing or where you're going, you may think he or she is keeping tabs on you or prying. You may have difficulty being touched and find that you shrink away from affection. You may have difficulty expressing your feelings or even realizing that you're having them. Communication may be very difficult.

The expression "lighten up" was invented for those with rigid boundaries. People with rigid boundaries sometimes have a more difficult time recognizing that they have a problem than someone with boundaries that are too flexible. If you find yourself living behind an immovable wall, it's time to change into something more flexible. You have to give love to receive it—and for this to happen, those boundaries have to give a little.

An interesting quirk of human nature is that those with rigid boundaries are frequently attracted to those who are too flexible. What a combination! Another way to look at it is that one person in the relationship is overfunctioning and the other is underfunctioning. Of course, the person who is underfunctioning is perfectly happy the way things are, while the overfunctioning person is wearing to a frazzle. They're both continuing their old behavior and avoiding real intimacy, and they don't even know it until the relationship falls apart.

Developing Healthy Boundaries

It's never too late to build healthy boundaries, even if you're already in a relationship. Having healthy boundaries says you want respect while respecting others. Healthy boundaries protect you but don't keep you distant. They come from an awareness of your inner world, and free you to be truly intimate without living inside your partner's skin *or* keeping her a world away. Understanding your boundaries too late in a relationship may cause you to suddenly have new boundaries with a vengeance! But good boundaries are not weapons, and learning to calibrate them allows you to be both strong and responsive without overcompensating in either direction.

To have the boundaries that *you* need, it's time to go shopping at the mental health warehouse for a mix that suits you! Look for flexible boundaries and definite limits. Preserve your values and priorities, but be able to communicate them to people who are important to you. Be clear about your individuality, and at the same time be open to new ideas and experiences. Remember, if a boundary is too rigid and distant, you can't communicate with the world. If a boundary is too flexible, you lose your identity.

You'll begin to feel instantly better when your boundaries are clearer to you. For a while you may feel fuzzy, as if you have no definition; but that feeling will go away with time and practice.

Be sure to tell people who are close to you that you're doing this work. Sometimes people can become angry when you start to change your boundaries, because you're also changing the rules of your relationship with them. This is why it's so important to communicate what you're trying to do. But as long as your relationship is healthy and open, you'll both grow through your efforts.

Gays and lesbians have some special boundary issues, and these come once again from our socialization. If a lesbian couple begins to resemble my favorite therapy prop, a snake with one body and two heads, I begin to worry. If you're a lesbian couple who asks for a table for one as a joke, then you know what I'm talking about. *Enmeshment,* or poorly defined boundaries, however, is not intimacy. Intimacy requires two individuals who have firm values and respect for themselves as well as their partner.

On the other hand, gay men may find they need a passport to find their partner's inner self! Men are not conditioned to the female role of disclosing feelings or taking care of the emotional aspects of a relationship. When there are two walls between two people, there has to be a willingness to move toward each other with love.

Gender role training plays a big part in our lives. Check into your socialization patterns and see what you'd like to borrow from each other's gender training. Confront yourself and reorganize your boundaries until they're balanced, safe, and healthy.

CHAPTER EIGHT

"I Am You and You Are Me and We Are Three and We Are All Together" (About Codependency)

"Codependency"... it's got to be everyone's favorite pop psychology word, second only to "dysfunctional." My teenage son was watching me gather my thoughts for this chapter, and he quipped, "Mom, I don't want to be codependent, if that's okay with you." In one short sentence he just about summed up everything I want to tell you about this topic.

Originally, codependency was a "woman's problem," such as when she gave up every part of herself to rescue her chemically dependent spouse. The term came from Al-Anon, a self-help group that emerged in the early sixties and is modeled on the twelve-step program of Alcoholics Anonymous. At first, Al-Anon was geared toward helping wives be supportive of their chemically dependent husbands. Since the seventies, however, codependency groups such as Al-Anon have been rightfully directed toward teaching people how to take care of themselves and fix their own problems, separate and apart from their partners. Your partner's recovery is a function of his or her choice. This can be a hard lesson for codependents because it means suddenly having to redirect your behavior inward toward yourself instead of outward toward "fixing" your partner.

Most of the larger cities have gay Al-Anon meetings or codependency groups, and many have other gay or lesbian codependency groups as well. If this is not the case and you go to regular Al-Anon meetings, you might want to take along a gay or lesbian friend to help you reflect on the special issues that straight folks might not recognize. Actually, you might prefer going to regular Al-Anon meetings anyway, because the gay community is so small you may not want to bump into someone you'd rather not see in this setting. This is one of those times when it's okay to be gay and anonymous!

Fortunately, codependency is no longer considered to be an issue "for women only," since there are plenty of men who are codependent. It's also no longer just about being the partner of someone who is chemically addicted; rather, it affects men and women who come from dysfunctional or abusive families as well.

Where does codependency come from? Often it's learned as part of your family's collective personality. For example, you may have been socialized to be the caretaker in your family, and now find it difficult to drop that role in an adult relationship. Continuing to caretake, when you really don't need to, may make you a codependent adult. Sometimes you learn codependent behavior from your parents' role-modeling. If your dad, for example, grew up in an alcoholic family, he may act very controlling or protective toward your mom. You may behave the same way as your dad in your relationships because that's the only role model you have. Addiction doesn't have to be an issue in your life, but if it was for your dad, then you observed his behavior. That's how a family personality of codependency may have been passed on. Your awareness of where your behavior comes from can be really helpful to you. Take a few minutes right now to reflect on your family history. Consider what you learned from your parents' interactions with each other, and think of what you do that's the same.

Were you prevented from developing healthy instincts as a child, and now lack the confidence to say "no more" when you really want to? Does your lover have a problem with alcohol, but you stay with him way beyond what your heart may be telling you to do?

You may have been sexually, physically, or emotionally abused when you were growing up, causing you to lose your childhood completely. You may not have been allowed to express your feelings as a child, and continue to step back from being in touch with them as an adult. You may regularly allow others' feelings to take priority over your own.

A significant codependency problem for a gay and lesbian couple comes from your family not respecting the boundaries of your committed relationship and your allowing that to happen. For example, you may find yourself, as the single daughter, being the primary caretaker of a sick mother because your fifteen-year lesbian relationship is not valued as a "real" marriage. Your siblings are just "too busy" with their spouses and kids. You, without agreement, find yourself the delegated caregiver. Codependency in this case is you putting your own life aside; displacing your love relationship; not expressing your feelings honestly to your siblings; being fearful of rocking the family boat; feeling driven by guilt; saying yes when you want to say no; and getting angry because of finding yourself in an involuntary caretaking position.

Remember, codependency issues are not just about how you are in your love relationships, but about how you respond to your family as well. It's important to observe how easily you may be taken advantage of, and how quickly you jump just to feel accepted. You may have guilty feelings about being gay or lesbian that cause you to believe you're the only one to take care of family problems because you don't otherwise fit into society's picture. Do you think that your family will love you more because you're taking care of them or relieving them of their responsibilities? Will that make being gay easier for *them?* What does this do to you? Are you afraid of being called selfish if you express your needs? Who do you worry most about?

Caution!! Most of us have at least some codependency issues. *Helping* to take care of Mom is different from doing it all by yourself, and it doesn't make you codependent—or mean that you're crazy, were abused, or need therapy. It just means that you're human. As one of my clinical psychology professors stated, "We all live in some of these diagnoses at some time during our lives. It's when the behavior gets out of our control and we can't get back to ourselves that it becomes a problem."

There's no specific number of traits that indicate when someone is codependent. In her book *Codependent No More,* Melody Beattie lists over one hundred characteristics of codependency. She explains it as "a dependency on people—on their moods, behaviors, sickness or well-being, and their love. It is a paradoxical dependence. Codependents appear to be depended upon, but they are dependent. They look strong but feel helpless. They appear controlling but, in reality, are controlled themselves. . . . If concern has turned into obsession; if compassion has turned into caretaking; if you are taking care of other people and not taking care of yourself—you may be dealing with codependency."[9]

There are many definitions of codependency, and they range from calling it an addictive, compulsive disease that increases, to calling it a condition that, according to Robert Subby, "develops as a result of an individual's prolonged exposure to and practice of a set of oppressive rules—rules which prevent the open expression of feeling as well as the direct discussion of personal and interpersonal problems."[10]

To all the definitions of codependency I'd like to add that our society supports codependent behavior by our music, through advertising, and through sexism, religions, schools, and any other institution that forms us to accept control rather than to develop, acknowledge, and express our deepest feelings and instincts.

Pia Melody, in her book *Facing Codependence,* lists five primary areas of difficulty for the codependent.[11] I'd like to expand on these.

1. Difficulty Experiencing Appropriate Levels of Self-Esteem

What is self-esteem? It seems to be one of those nebulous concepts that people say they want but don't know how to get. Healthy self-esteem, however, comes from within you, and is an *internal* experience. You can't get it by talking but by *doing.* When you have good self-esteem, your sense of self stays intact even when you make a mistake or are confronted by someone's anger or betrayal. When you have good self-esteem, you don't have feelings of worthlessness when someone seems to have or know more than you. On the other hand, you're not arrogant and don't feel superior, and you don't view other people as less than you because of their faults or differences. *Internal esteem* comes from the sense of pride you gain from doing something you thought you never could, such as courageously taking responsibility for and trying to correct your behavior, or helping others who are less fortunate.

Self-esteem does not come from acquiring things. This doesn't mean that having a nice car or a good job or excelling in an activity shouldn't be something you enjoy—but when you base your self-worth on what others think of you or what you have, then you've centered on *external* or "other" esteem. You've probably already discovered that you can lose your external source of esteem in a heartbeat. That's to be expected. *External* sources of self-esteem are undependable and fragile at best.

You may have poor self-esteem just because you're gay or lesbian. If society thinks you aren't good enough to go into the army, to be a teacher, or to parent children, how do you think of yourself? This is external esteem, or the measuring of yourself against what religion, society, school, and family say you "should" be. As a gay or lesbian, you have to get beyond thinking like everyone else. Your self-acceptance will help you to behave in a way that's true to you, and you will not act out of guilt or remorse you feel because of your sexuality. Understanding that you're fine being gay or lesbian will help you to keep from behaving with apologies for who you are, and you will not be inclined toward codependency.

2. Difficulty Setting Functional Boundaries

The issue of setting boundaries needs an entire chapter of its own, and it has one elsewhere in this book. Briefly, though, a boundary is where we end and another person begins. It's an invisible line that helps us set reasonable and healthy limits. When we know how far we're willing to go and how far we'll let others go with us, we have good boundaries. One sign of poor boundaries is taking on someone else's feelings. If your lover doesn't like you to have friends outside your relationship, for example, and you then stop having those friends, you are taking on your partner's problem—whatever it is. You have to know yourself and what you think and feel to have good boundaries. This is easier said than done, for sure.

In the gay/lesbian community, the issue of boundaries has special implications. The desire for long-term relationships in a less than nurturing societal environment has many couples staying together much longer than is healthy for either person. Same-sex partners frequently bond in crises. Family rejection, divorce problems, or coming-out issues can cause too much dependency between same-sex partners and weaken interpersonal boundaries. Statements like "I'll be there for you no matter what (it does to me)," or "I have no one else," or "We're just the same—it's us against the world" sound like big problems just waiting to happen.

Some think that setting limits or having healthy boundaries may cause their partner to get angry and leave. For gay or lesbian adults, there is a constant awareness of the small pool of friends and lovers available for relationships. Many go too far in accepting outrageous behavior from their partner because they think they have to or they risk being alone forever.

Without boundaries, you may lose yourself in your relationships. On the other hand, with too many boundaries you won't have relationships to worry about. Boundaries should not be too rigid or too pliable. Developing healthy boundaries is your responsibility. Good boundaries will help you rescue a self esteem that may be imperiled because of your sexuality; and good self-esteem will come from discovering your boundaries and the behaviors that reflect your sense of self. Make a list of your boundaries that are too rigid or poorly defined. What can you do differently?

3. Difficulty Owning Our Own Reality

Do you sometimes wonder if what's happening to you is real? Codependents frequently have difficulty experiencing the here and now. Children who come from families in which they were ignored or abused, saw abuse, or were abandoned, learned that to express their feelings is dangerous. These children shut down and later become adults who either hide their feelings or don't know what their feelings are. An example of this is if you, as a child, witnessed your parents having a terrible fight, with yelling and hitting. When you began to cry, which is a natural instinct, you got accused of spying on them. You were told that "Everything is fine. We're not really fighting. Go to bed." You began to wonder if what you saw was real. You saw the hitting. You heard the yelling. But you were told it never happened. You doubt your reality. You doubt your feelings—except that you feel crazy.

If you don't know your feelings, can't show them, or hide them, you tend to adopt someone else's view—and that view is usually skewed because it isn't coming from you or your experience. Sometimes such a lopsided vision derives from someone who is homophobic or has internalized homophobia. It would be a shame for you not to explore your world from your own viewpoint. If you suffered abuse or abandonment as a child, this can be difficult to do.

Often people who don't know what they're feeling also don't know when they're experiencing pain; and they have poor limits on what they will tolerate from others. If you're not sure about what you're feeling, you may dissociate or seem to go away. It's difficult to stay present—but it is important to develop confidence in what you're experiencing and to be able to express yourself. Facing what happened to you as a child, getting in touch with your reality, will allow you to make choices in your adult life that are not codependent.

4. Difficulty Acknowledging and Meeting Our Own Needs and Wants

There are several ways in which you may have difficulty acknowledging and meeting your wants and needs. If you're *too dependent,* you expect other people to take care of you; and if they don't, you become angry and disappointed. You may be passive and just gratefully accept whatever you're given. By not asking for what you want, you don't have to risk not getting it.

If you're *antidependent,* you'd prefer to go without rather than ask for what you want or need. Some people would rather just hope that their lover is a mind reader, since it lets them avoid rejection or feeling like a bother. When your lover doesn't manage this impossible task, you distance yourself from the relationship and your lover doesn't know why. Some people feel that if they have to tell their lover what they need, the act of getting it is meaningless. "He should know what I need. I shouldn't have to tell him." Well, why not tell him? If your wants and needs are reasonable, expressing them to your lover is very important.

Seeming to have *no wants or needs* may mean that you're simply not aware of them, or that you get wants and needs confused. For example, you need to be cuddled but you go shopping or go on an eating binge instead as a substitute for soothing. Maybe you stay in a relationship because you think you need that person so much that they're the key to your happiness. Do you expect someone to always be there for you the way you need them to be—to make you feel safe and whole at all times?

Some clients come to me because they continually become dependent on troubled people for love but then find that person is unable to nurture or emotionally bond with them. Some settle for the *illusion* of being cared for, and stay in a relationship that's destructive. What action can you take to change this codependent pattern? Make a list of your wants and needs. Don't be afraid of making it a long list. Which ones do you take care of yourself? Which ones do you expect others to do for you? How do you tell the people you love what your wants and needs are? Do you take care of someone else's wants and needs to the detriment of your own? Answering these questions will help you become more clear about your own requirements and bring balance to yourself and to your relationships.

5. Difficulty Experiencing and Expressing Our Reality Moderately

Do you have difficulty with moderation? Are you in a good relationship but feel too insecure to detach from your lover enough to take care of yourself? You could be smothering the other person or driving her away by caretaking her to death! You may be totally miserable or totally happy, have too much or never enough. Whichever is the case, this symptom is about being too intense or extreme. "It's my way or the highway!" You may even have tantrums. This type of behavior may have developed from your family of origin if you were not heard or listened to, and you had to act out or exaggerate to get attention.

Early childhood experiences may translate into your adult self being out of control, or having unmanageable emotional episodes or extreme behavior. For example, you have the habit of drinking milk out of the carton. Your lover tells you that this annoys him and to please stop. Do you think that the best solution to doing something your lover finds so inconsiderate is to leap out of the relationship so it will never happen again? Do you begin to pack? If so, you may be having a problem moderating your feelings and actions.

Learning to moderate your extreme reactions also includes getting in touch with the shame you may feel at being "wrong." If you're less than perfect you're not "bad," and if your lover is less than perfect she's not "bad" either. The point is not to hold your feelings in so long. Be willing to talk with those you love about the impact of their words and actions on you. If you were brought up not being heard by the adults in your life, you may find it uncomfortable expressing your feelings this way. It's easier to yell or run away than to talk reasonably.

If you were abused, your feelings may be locked within you, and what you do is react rather than think. Moderating your behavior and thinking takes slowing down and doing things differently. Remember the last time you reacted in the extreme or had black-or-white thinking? Back it down and find a more reasonable way to respond to the daily process of life.

This list of core symptoms will help you assess your situation, but it isn't all-inclusive; and if you think you have a problem with codependency, you probably do. How do you get back on the right track? You can make a good start by first acknowledging the problem. You may want to get one of the books I mentioned, go to a codependency group, or talk about your thoughts with a friend. Set goals for yourself, such as examining your family-of-origin issues, taking responsibility for your actions, and accepting yourself. Don't ignore your feelings, including the angry ones. Think about things, and *respond* instead of *react* to what goes on around you. Have your own goals for caring for yourself.

Getting your balance is not an impossible task. Healing from codependency takes time and can be difficult without help and willingness on your part. Start by being aware, and do things differently. We can change those old behavior patterns. We *will* change.

CHAPTER NINE

Getting Over Your Fears

Imagine: You're walking up a mountain path. It's a beautiful day, and the higher you go the more at peace you feel. Suddenly, a stone slips from beneath your foot, and your eyes are drawn into the spiraling, steep decline.

Looking down, you become hypnotized. Your heart races, your palms are damp, and a chill sweat forms on your face. You gasp for breath. *"How did I get this high? Can I ever get down? I'm going to die."*

Imagine: You've met that certain someone at Pride, and he's coming over for dinner. You spent all day cooking and cleaning while blasting your favorite tunes. You look great. You feel great. You ARE great. Then, as you catch a glimpse of yourself in the mirror, you suddenly begin to stare. Your heart starts to pound. Your palms are damp, and a cold sweat is forming on your face. Steel bands seem to clamp around your chest as your breathing halts. *"Oh my God. What am I doing? He probably won't even show up. I wish I were straight so I wouldn't have these problems. I feel like I'm going to die."*

Same symptoms, different situations. Can you identify this feeling? If you said "fear," you're absolutely right! Not a pretty picture, is it? Fear is what drives a good percentage of our behavior—and whether it's fear of failure or fear of success, it holds us back because it's convinced us that maybe we aren't good enough or we don't deserve more.

There's the fear of abandonment, which says your lover will leave you if you express your needs or expectations. You fear change in yourself, in circumstances, or in others because you can't predict the future or what the results will be. There's the fear of your gay or lesbian sexuality, which prevents you from seeking healthy relationships. You may also fear your feelings of anger, hurt, or love. Clients frequently say, "I'm afraid to show my anger because I don't know what I'll do." It's true that some people won't let themselves cry because they're afraid they'll never stop. They're afraid of losing control. And it's fear that causes the high rate of substance abuse in the gay and lesbian community.

It seems that fear is in charge of an awful lot of your thinking, doesn't it? The good news is that you can control your fears and have more fun in your life!

To start, identify two or three things you fear. You may have a fear of heights or a fear of love. You may be thinking, "I *want* love—I'm not afraid of it!" If that's true, why aren't you in a loving relationship? If you're in a job you hate, what's keeping you from getting another one? If there's someone in your life who abuses you, what's keeping you in that relationship?

It's comfortable to stay with the old thinking that keeps you in the past, the way things were. It's also easier to try to predict the future than to move yourself forward. Living in the past or the future keeps your *todays* away. When you say to yourself, "I used to feel better," or "I always did it that way," you're looking behind, thinking about something that doesn't exist anymore. If you say, "I wish I could," or "When I feel better I will . . . ," you're projecting into a future you know nothing about. A wise person once quipped, "If you want to tell God a joke, tell him your plans." All we can really be sure about is today—right here and right now—and that's where we need to be to get over our fears.

Where does fear come from? Some psychologists believe that all fears are ultimately the function of the fear of death. This thinking can be traced to different religious philosophies. People are afraid of the unknown; and a supreme being gives people reassurance of some sort of life after death, whether through reincarnation or cosmic consciousness or a heavenly paradise filled with angels. Frequently, people worship God(s) because they're frightened about what will happen to them after they die and leave the known for the unknown. Human beings rest easier within a faith that promises them that everything is going to be okay.

Family patterns of fear are similar to religious ones. Until the age of five or six, children usually behave as if they have nothing to be afraid of. The unknown is exciting, and an adventure. Children generally don't believe that there could be anything wrong with them, and they're almost never self-conscious. I saw a two-year-old on the beach the other day who had taken off all his clothes and fallen asleep with his butt sticking up in the air. Two older women were chuckling to themselves, while the parents were totally unaware of their son's posture.

Children are curious and want to learn new things. They often feel capable of accomplishing anything. Remember those innocent days? Kind of like the Garden of Eden of your youth.

But then you got socialized! Enter the serpent. You were taught to focus on others' view of you rather than on your own self-confidence. You became less and less eager to learn and explore. You learned to feel less competent and increasingly anxious as your instincts and innate intelligence weren't supported. The adults in your life taught you to fear the same things they feared. *The assumption was that fear would keep you safe from the unknown (death),* when, in fact, fear only serves to keep you in the same old place.

Because children are naturally fearless, they often find their way into dangerous situations. However, when as a child you were told that you should know better without the benefit of being taught, you became humiliated. You stopped exploring the unknown to avoid feeling bad about yourself. A child needs someone to explain how to work with the tools of life and not be scared. You may think that the fear you learned as a child protects you, but what actually keeps you safe is your own intelligence.

If you close your eyes, I'll bet you can resurrect the words you internalized when you were little. These are the words that were supposed to keep you "safe" but instead undermined your confidence, such as "What is the matter with you?" "Is that the best you can do?" "Don't act like a sissy, act like a boy." "You can do better than that." "You don't deserve any more." "Can't you do anything?" "Girls shouldn't be so loud." And so forth. You know the drill.

If someone on the outside has programmed you to believe you're not capable, and the someone on the inside of you agrees, this converts to fear. When you're living the old messages of fear, you're living in your yesterday. And when you're projecting ahead, wondering "what's going to happen if . . . ," you're trying to predict the future. Either way, you're giving up what you have now.

Remember the dinner date example? Just as in your early childhood, at first you feel confident and satisfied. Then your old theme song starts playing— *"I've never been good at this. Will he want to be in a relationship with me? What if I don't like him? Why even bother—gay relationships never last very long, anyway."* Fear keeps you in the past and makes you project the worst for the future. The evening therefore becomes uncomfortable because you can't focus on what's in front of you. You feel blocked and want to run away. What this means is that you're resisting being present. You're resisting having a good time!

Resistance is the key to where your fear is, and to where the work is for you. Listen to the scared voices that are keeping you away from being present with yourself. Are you fretting and predicting? Are you afraid of the unknown? What's the worst thing that could happen if you have a nice evening—or if you don't? Are you using "I'm bored" or "I don't feel like it" to rationalize avoiding a new experience? How does your fear look? What is your habit of avoidance? How do you maintain your fear? Starting with a small fear, try to find the answers to these questions. Go slowly to desensitize yourself. Identify the part of yourself that's afraid. Make peace with your fearful feeling. Stay with the discomfort—be present! Write down your sensations, your thoughts and emotions about the experience. Be mindful, and pay attention to what you're doing as you are doing it. There are no rights or wrongs—you're just *experiencing.*

One last, crucial point has to do with your gay or lesbian sexuality. Chances are you were taught by family and society that same-sex sexual feelings are wrong. You tried to act straight when you were a teen. You may have married, or become deeply religious, homophobic, or addicted to drugs or alcohol to keep from accepting your sexuality. *Resistance to your gay or lesbian feelings is the key to your fear of being present with yourself.* When you stop resisting who you are, your life will open up. You'll learn to love yourself for who you are today.

CHAPTER TEN

I Am Who I Am

Are You the "L" Word or a "Lesbian"?
(About Internalized Homophobia)

What's your internalized homophobia quotient? You may not think you have that problem, so you'd better close your eyes and imagine this: You're at a Pride march with your good friends. A group of ten men goes by you, dressed either like Priscilla, Queen of the Desert, Marilyn Monroe, your grandmother, a mermaid, Barbie, or "leather brides" walking arm in arm, with veils, beards, and all. Flash to the next group queuing up for review: women on Harleys, dressed in black leather studded jackets, smoking cigars and revving their engines . . . so to speak.

What is your reaction? How do you feel? Do you and your friends nudge each other and smile, enjoying the celebration? Do you feel relaxed in your leather jacket? Are you having fun? Don't open your eyes yet! Now imagine the same scene, the same day, but this time you're with your parents and a few other members of your family. Bet you're not smiling now! Has your anxiety level gone up? How's your blood pressure? Are you worried about what your family is thinking? Do you wish you could hide your head under your wing like a little bird?

Even the most "out" persons go a little weak-kneed at having to face their same-sex orientation in some situation at some time. Test your internalized homophobia quotient with this fabulous questionnaire. Mark your answers, using a scale of 1 to 10, where: 1 = Totally Horrified at the Thought; 5 = Neutral Nelly; and 10 = Out, Proud, and Over It. Each question is worth ten points. Good luck!

_____ 1. I love going to Provincetown or other gay/lesbian meccas for a summer vacation so I can hold my sweetie's hand (as opposed to going in the dead of winter when I won't have to be around too many "gay looking/acting" people).

_____ 2. My children don't have to have a parent of each sex or only straight teachers to be well adjusted.

_____ 3. I love greeting nongay friends with a hug and a kiss because I'm secure enough to know that they understand I'm not making sexual advances.

_____ 4. I'm not attracted to potential lovers who are nongay or are in other relationships. I've been there, done that; it doesn't work and I deserve better.

_____ 5. I no longer gag on the words "lesbian," "homosexual," and "gay." As a matter of fact, I have no problem referring to myself as "a queer bull dyke from hell," even though I'm a guy.

_____ 6. I stopped laughing at "fag" or "dyke" jokes along with everyone else at work. I may not be out there, but I don't have to degrade myself either.

_____ 7. I don't care if I'm around "obvious" or "flamboyant" gays and lesbians. I'm okay enough with myself not to be uncomfortable with those who express themselves differently than I do.

_____ 8. I don't try to change how I look to pass as nongay. I just know how to make my looks appropriate for different occasions.

_____ 9. I'm learning how to have or have succeeded in sustaining a love relationship beyond a couple of turbulent years.

_____ 10. I no longer think that gay men and lesbians are better than nongays. Although we have differences, there are many ways in which we are alike.

Add up your score. If "Neutral Nelly" is your bottom and your score is between 50 and 100, then you're in a good comfort zone in dealing with your internalized homophobia. On the other hand, if Neutral Nelly is your top and your score is between 0 and 50, you may have some reevaluating to do about how comfortable you are in the world as a gay man or a lesbian.

Let's face facts. Just because you're a gay man or a lesbian, you are a victimized minority in our homophobic culture. You live in an environment that is hateful toward your sexual orientation. As human beings we can't help but absorb society's hostile and negative characterizations. Otherwise, why are there certain situations where you feel exposed, ashamed, and vulnerable?

Homophobia is a prejudice, or an irrational fear based on untruths. Homosexuals are supposedly condemned in the Bible, we recruit young children to our lifestyle, we are unnatural, and we have a "gay agenda" in which we're trying to get more rights than others have. These awful statements are sworn to be truths by the self-proclaimed guardians of American morality in their attempt to gain power and control. They've even managed to win a few congressional seats.

Homophobia is a form of xenophobia. (I am not referring to fear of Xena, Warrior Princess, who skips my heart a beat.) It's a prejudice that develops from fear of anyone different from yourself. And I don't have to remind you that plenty of us are different.

Here's where internalized homophobia rears its ugly little head. You may have cringed when you read the newspaper accounts about the mostly naked stilt-walking guy at Boston Pride. For weeks afterward, letters to the editor poured in to New England papers, and numerous editorials appeared, filled with outrage from both gays and nongays. Then there were the reports about the lesbians who were topless while gazing out their hotel windows at the Pride march in Washington. "Shameless," the commentators said. "Disgusting." What is your reaction to this bottomless or topless public behavior?

There are many heated discussions in the gay and lesbian community about flaunting our sexual orientation in public. Those who act flamboyantly are looked down upon as degrading "the cause." You may feel as if this behavior reflects on you, but it really doesn't. Everyone is responsible for his or her own behavior. If you look around at Pride parades, you're more than likely going to see crowds of regular-looking gay and lesbian folks with their dogs and baby carriages.

You may wish that other gay men and lesbians would act more like you in public. After all, what will nongays think about you when they see drag queens and dykes on bikes looking tough and making their presence known? The more we're like nongays, after all, the more they'll let us into the mainstream. The more we "behave," the better off we'll be. The less we appear to have a "gay agenda," the less "threatening" we are to nongays. Now wait a minute. If you're agreeing with any of these last few statements, "sounds like homophobia to me," as the song goes. Internalized homophobia, that is.

This is a tough issue. The media are obviously into sensationalism with their inflammatory reporting style; but even worse are the right-wing moral guardians filming the more "out there" Pride activities to make it seem as if *all* gays and lesbians are repulsive perverts with no self-control. These self-righteous and self-appointed protectors of "family values" make thousands of videotape copies of our gatherings and send them all over the country to keep the hate level high. The moral guardians want to divide us with infighting, thereby weakening our resolve to gain equal rights. When we opt into this homophobic way of thinking, we become part of the problem. We are maintaining the fuel that supports the very same homophobia that's bringing us down. Some of the acting-out, in-your-face behavior is very often a reaction to the moral guardians' indignation. "I'm here. I'm queer. Get over it!"

Frankly speaking, I'm not that comfortable with naked men on stilts, either, but not because of "gay" flaunting. I do enjoy the "theater" aspect of Pride and what people are willing to do publicly. In general, there are those of us who just aren't comfortable with any overt sexualized public behavior, including nongay behavior. So, instead of getting caught up in the extremes, walk with others like yourself at Pride. I was proud to walk in Washington Pride one year with a group from my state, which had our state bird, a big red rooster, leading the way.

As a sidebar, after years of being on the front lines defending our local abortion clinics, I know for a fact that the so-called moral guardians don't have anything on us! Talk about a public display of inappropriate behavior—throwing pink plastic baby dolls at terrified and clearly distraught women; sprinkling "holy water" in our faces; stalking women and their partners who have the right to make a very difficult decision; little old men carrying huge wooden crosses with little pink dolls hanging from the crossbar and statues of Mary swinging from their necks, while standing in front of clinic doors and swearing at you. This is truly obscene behavior at its height, and not very attractive at all. At least guys on stilts aren't denying anyone their rights. So I guess it's a matter of perspective, isn't it?

We all develop certain protective behaviors in order to survive in a homophobic culture. Sometimes it's necessary to be "rationally out" or protective, but sometimes internalized homophobia or self-hatred keeps us from fully expressing ourselves when it's safe. Think back to the questions at the beginning of this chapter. If you find yourself trying to look less obvious, or if you only seek out straight-acting/straight-looking friends and lovers, or you don't like to be seen in public with "obvious" gay men and lesbians, this is a symptom of internalized homophobia, which is called "identifying with the oppressor."

Here's an old but famous example of this defense mechanism. In the 1970s, Patty Hearst, daughter of the wealthy Hearst publishing mogul, was kidnapped and beaten by a group of fanatics called the Symbionese Liberation Army (SLA). A few weeks later, we saw news footage of Patty participating in a bank robbery staged by the SLA, sporting a machine gun and calling herself Tanya. What was going on? Did she think this was a great adventure? By subconsciously identifying and going along with her kidnappers/oppressors, Patty was able to survive. Her behavior was the result of a defense mechanism that allowed her to protect herself. When Patty was finally released, she needed many months of deprogramming from the experience in order to resume a relatively normal life.

You may think this is a pretty far-out example, but guess what—if you try to "pass" as straight . . . don't like gay resorts . . . avoid having "obviously gay" friends or lovers . . . think your kids won't be "normal" . . . or are fearful of what nongays think of you—then you are identifying with your oppressor, just like Patty Hearst. If you are *like* your oppressor, you feel safe. "He's not like those other queers. He's just like us, so I guess he's okay. The others aren't, but he is."

Do you read only gay-themed books? I know some lesbians who go so far as to read only lesbian books. How totally boring. Do you only go on gay and lesbian vacations? Olympia Cruises only take you so far. What about the rest of the world? I know gay men who won't leave the East Village in New York, or lesbians who won't leave Northampton, for that matter. Do you feel that you have little in common with nongays? Do you volunteer only for gay and lesbian benefits? Is your internalized homophobia keeping you from experiencing the world? Do you give only gay or lesbian businesses your trade without looking elsewhere to others who may charge less and do a better job? If so, then you are rejecting nongays the way many of them reject you.

Your differences, talents, sexual orientation, looks, creative ideas, and intelligence make you who you are, and that is wonderful. So why isolate? Why let too much pride get in your way? Of course it's fun to do all of the gay stuff you can, but to exclude the rest of the world, where so much is interesting and valuable, is depriving yourself.

Is the "family values" right wing grabbing your attention and making you question the validity of your love and skills in raising sensitive and productive children? There are so many ways to be a family: single moms, single dads, adoptive, foster, and gay/lesbian. Whatever the combination, if you want your own family, don't keep yourself outside the world of kids and all the ups and downs that go with it.

If you find yourself having short-term and unfulfilling relationships, there may be a part of you that thinks this is all you can have in this "lifestyle." Also, by not being committed to anyone long-term, you can neatly avoid all the issues around bringing a lover home for the holidays. Internalized homophobia strikes again.

"How is it," you may think, "that I fall in love but it never works out?" Well, if you keep being attracted to those who are having addiction problems, are already in relationships (especially heterosexually married), or are not a good match for you in a million other ways, you may be in for a lot of Saturday nights alone. Safe, but alone. You may think, "I'm just a maiden aunt/bachelor uncle to the family, and no one knows about me. I'm safe." You may have avoided confronting your sexual orientation, intimacy problems, and emotional involvement, but you may only be fooling yourself and allowing your internalized homophobia to dictate your life.

Another important indicator of internalized homophobia is thinking that being gay or lesbian is just like being heterosexual. Granted, there are lots of similarities, but don't forget the differences. Remember, starting with your closet, that you are subject to internalized homophobia, political and family struggles about your sexuality, and living in a society that's homophobic and often unsafe. Along with gay bashing, there are more subtle displays of homophobia. For example, a gay man who was ill recently had to pull off the road into a rest area to take his medication. He was arrested for soliciting before he even got the top off his heart medication bottle. After a humiliating experience of being handcuffed in a holding cell, he pleaded guilty. If he made a fuss, he figured, it would get in the papers, his boss would find out, and he would lose his job.

Let's fix this mess. Facing our internalized homophobia is part of our development in a homophobic culture. Lighten up that heaviness and get into life. We have many nongay friends who are there for us with love and support. Don't leave them out of your life. A good thing to do is to keep a journal and record your feelings. Be careful not to beat yourself up—there are plenty of people on the other side to do that for you! Take the least threatening feeling that you have and see how you can change it.

Here's a success story. I know a lesbian who was always in short-term, disastrous relationships with lesbians who were very straight-looking. The lover she ended up with for a real long-term commitment, however, was someone she never thought she'd be attracted to. She systematically worked at getting in touch with her internalized homophobia. She found she could come out safely at work, she confronted her parents for putting her down, she became a little more politically aware, and she chose to go to Pride in her hometown, although she practiced first in another state. Broadening her range of attraction seemed like a natural next step. No longer afraid of being identified with an "obvious" lesbian, she found a deep and beautiful love.

So get out and get involved in challenging your internalized homophobia. Don't be totally horrified at the thought anymore. Be out and be proud a little more each day. Your self-esteem will grow, your world will get bigger, and your spirit will fill with peace and harmony.

CHAPTER ELEVEN

"Ch-Ch-Ch-Ch-Changes"

Do you remember when you were little and it seemed that you had no control over your life? You HAD to go to school. You HAD to move to a new city with your family. You HAD to endure your parents' fights, drinking, or divorce. You HAD to, even though you might have felt bad about what was happening to you. As a kid *you* couldn't change your circumstances. You needed the adults in your life to feed you and provide shelter and clothing. Family is all a child has, so you either complied or put up with things that in retrospect you hated. As a kid you were pretty powerless over what the adults did to and around you. Your life was all you knew, and it all seemed "normal."

In order to survive your various childhood circumstances, you adopted certain behaviors that psychologists call "adaptations." Do any of these adaptations apply to you? Some children "zone out" to shut down the craziness going on in their lives, although you may not remember very much of this. You may have been a compliant child. Some kids become clowns or overachievers, or act rebellious or irritable as ways of adapting to their families. As a young gay boy you might have been beaten up by your older brothers for being effeminate. You adapted by becoming a good fighter and good at acting out your anger. If you were a little on the butch side when you were a lesbian-to-be, you may have learned to clown around, hoping that your family would accept you because you were funny. Unfortunately, the underlying messages were that you were not unconditionally loved, and that you had to be "someone else" to be part of the family.

When you became an adult, you may have found that you had adopted the behavior of the adults who raised you and become homophobic, prejudiced, rigid, abusive, or alcoholic, or you may have trouble communicating intimately with your partner. Maybe you work hard to be the exact opposite of your family. Do you overcompensate by being "too good," hoping to get those you love to love you, only to be disappointed? Do you overfunction on your job or in relationships, hoping that being the perfect employee or partner will get you the love you always wanted? Rather than listening to your true feelings about what's going on, you're continuing to adapt your behavior in your effort to "be better" than what you had. If you have children, this behavior becomes even more apparent when you give your kids *what you want rather than what they really need.*

As an adult you may not know exactly why you want to run away when there is conflict in your life. But when you give it some thought, you realize it's probably because of what you felt or did when you were a kid. You may not recall the exact incident that makes you shut down when you hear your lover raise her voice, but chances are you're triggered by the memory of people yelling at you or each other. You may not be sure why your heart races if you perceive your lover is upset with you; but with some self-reflection you may remember being overdisciplined as a child so you would conform to your parents' expectations. Your racing heart is old business that's still part of how you operate today. Your need to "fix" everything and everyone is really the result of your unconscious attempts to fix your past hurts by re-creating them in your present.

One of the first things I learned during clinical training is that the body has 100 percent recall even if the mind doesn't let the information surface. We're programmed to respond physically to life's circumstances, at the survival level, from our experiences growing up. We react. We're triggered by a look, a tone of voice, a perceived injustice. Our body sends a signal, and, before we even think, we're doing the same old thing. The difference now is that you're an adult, and your reaction is probably no longer appropriate for this time in your life.

What does this mean for you? There's a popular greeting card that says, "No matter where you go, there you are." These words are meant to be supportive, but I see them another way—i.e., no matter who you're with, where you live, or what jobs you try, unless you make some *interior* changes, your new circumstances are likely to take on the patterns of your old ones. Unless you evaluate your part in how your life is going, you're still reacting at the body level just as you did as a child. Today's events trigger yesterday's reactions.

I slipped a word into the last paragraph that's the scariest word in this entire chapter. If you guessed it's the word "change," you're right on the mark! We've all experienced exterior change. We've moved, we've taken new jobs and new lovers. Sometimes we blame our "exterior circumstances" for our unhappiness. "If only I had a better job I would be happy." "If only my lover would pay more attention to me I would be happy." "If only I were [taller, richer, better educated, had blond hair and a talk show, etc.], I would be happy." Did you ever change jobs, apartments, and lovers, only to find yourself just as unhappy as before? Exterior changes generally aren't the answer. As a matter of fact, I'll bet you keep getting into some of the same types of unhappy situations over and over again! What does that say about you? The interior you?

You've probably heard the expression, "You know you're ready to change when the pain of staying the same is greater." When people go to therapy, they're usually at that painful place where they can no longer tolerate being the same. They know something isn't right but don't know what or why. My job here is to help you recognize your old patterns and gain enough self-confidence to step into the scary place of not knowing what to do next, and be prepared to do nothing for a while and let life evolve. The situation of not knowing what "to do" is frightening for most of us. Our bodies are pulling us in one direction while our minds pull us in another. On the other hand, when I told a young man the other day that his challenge for the next six months is to do nothing, he smiled with relief. He is so tired of adapting, trying to be the perfect son and lover yet continuing to feel an emptiness inside because he still doesn't have love the way he dreams it could be. This young man, who has had four apartments and six or seven jobs in the last three years, is ready to stop blaming his exterior life and get to his inside work!

The hardest part of being in therapy is recognizing and then staying with your feelings of sadness, frustration, shame, or anger—but after you stay with them for a while, new solutions will occur to you and new ways of dealing with those feelings and behaviors will become clear. Staying still for six months and being mindful of yourself is *not* an easy or pain-free process, and I don't want to make it sound as if making changes is a snap. Sometimes people need to take breaks in the process just to integrate and practice what they're learning about themselves. As a therapist, though, I have to say that my happiest days are when clients look at me and say, "I feel better than ever." I know then that they're feeling in charge of themselves, and liking it.

I want to give you an important hint. There are things you can change and there are things you cannot. It's crucial to know what about you is just the way it is, and to learn to cope with the facts. Every year, billions and billions of dollars are spent on self-help tapes, books, and videos. Seminars on stress management, time management, depression management, practice management, and just plain management are offered all over the place. I get four or five brochures a week on how to manage difficult people; how to manage difficult clients; how to be optimistic; or how to control my finances, win friends, fall in love, fall in love with the right person, and so forth. The bottom line is that you can't change your sexuality, your body type, or your past. The good news is that you *can* change your feelings, your moods, depression, panic and anxiety, your racing heart, your reactions, and the triggers you learned as a kid. You are more powerful than you imagined!

If you want to make some changes for yourself, start by keeping a journal and write down what you can change in your life and what you can't. Record how you react to people around you. Decide whether you're happy with your behavior and whether your reaction is something you do frequently. Is your behavior advancing your feeling good about yourself, or does it lower your self-esteem and get in the way of your relationships? Trace back to the times in your life when you responded differently to similar situations, and see if you felt better at those times. Write down what you'll do differently next time, and rehearse with someone what you want to think or do in the future. Recognize when you're in an "old reaction" situation, take a deep breath, stay with your feeling, and then respond in the new way that you planned.

As you see, you *can* change the old patterns that have kept you repeating the same cycle for years. It's not an easy process, but it is very worthwhile if you find yourself doing the same old thing and feeling trapped in getting the same old thing in return. One caution: As you begin the process of changing yourself, some people who know the "old you" may not understand or want to be around the new one; and sometimes this is for the best. By contrast, new people will emerge in your life because you'll be open to new and healthier ways to live.

Visualize a grand mobile hanging from a high ceiling by a fine thread—this is your social system of family and friends. If you "ping" just one of the delicately suspended pieces, the entire mobile begins to quiver, and many of the pieces seem to be trying hard to get back to the way things were before. You can see the challenge when you're a part of a system that resists your new behavior.

What path do you take now? Do you simply leave the parts of the system that can't support the healthier you? Do you stay the same even if you're miserable that way? Or do you take charge of yourself and make changes that are positive and worthwhile? Similarly, do you want to be with people who want to keep you the same for their own reasons, or do you want to find others who accept you in your quest for healthy change? No matter what, when you make up your mind to change your feelings or behavior, you're going to find an inner strength, new support, and peace within yourself.

Some friends or family may try to hold you back so that they won't have to change with you. For example, let's say you're the person in your social group who always does the organizing. You always get them special guest-house rates in P-town for Memorial

Day weekend. You plan parties, or organize New Year's pot-luck din-ners. You even put your own money out for tickets to events and then have to chase down your friends to get paid back. Sound famil-iar? Now, what if you decide to resign from this position? You're sick of it, and you say so, but no one else is willing to take it over. People keep calling you and asking, "What are the plans this year?" "I don't know," you answer, waiting for the ax to fall. "What's wrong with her?" they say.

At first you feel that you've let everyone down. You're met with stony silence. People want to know what your problem is. They talk about you, or call you selfish. You find yourself left out when others plan parties or events. You're aware of a subtle vindictiveness or anger on their part because you're no longer conforming to the group's expectations. These are very powerful group behaviors! People seem to be telling you that if you don't stay the same you're no longer welcome. What's really happening, though, is that by changing, you're causing others to look at themselves when they may not want to. You may also find that some of these people were never really your friends to begin with.

At first you feel sad about no longer being a part of something familiar—but often, when people first begin to take care of them-selves and stop overfunctioning within their group, there are inter-esting and important lessons to be learned. In the small gay and les-bian community, changing can be especially difficult. If you find yourself being shunned because you no longer want to drink, gossip, have group sex, listen to everyone's problems, lend money, pick people up when they're drunk, stay in an abusive relationship, or whatever, you may have to go it alone for a while. On the other hand, you may be pleasantly surprised at who surfaces by your side as a loyal friend. There are others out there who went through similar experiences, or who see the value when friends make positive changes in their lives. These new people are a wonderful part of your lesson!

CHAPTER TWELVE

"Let's Talk About Sex, Baby—
Let's Talk About You and Me"

The pressure is on. You're with your dream date and HE WANTS YOU! Your heart is pounding, the lights are low, and passion is coursing through your body. But then—oh no!—suddenly, out of nowhere, you're stung by the Doubt Bug. As you're swatting it away, you look up and see a swarm of Doubt's cousins buzzing around your head. You must know some of these little monsters: Guilt, Rejection, Shame, Internalized Homophobia, Self-Consciousness, Vulnerability, and The Forbidden. These little bloodsuckers belong to the Low Self-Esteem family, and somehow they always manage to find you when you finally get the nerve to be sexual with that special someone. After all, why should you feel too good about yourself? If this sounds familiar, you may be suffering from low sexual esteem. Do you want to become "sex positive"?

This discussion is about sexual activity, between consenting adults, that is not harmful to yourself or others. "Consenting" means that both parties agree *freely*; and "adults" is defined by the law of the state you live in. "Harmful" includes medical as well as physical and psychological harm. Not being honest about STDs or HIV status is an example of harm, and you need to take these things very seriously. This chapter, though, is just about sex and some of the psychological reasons why we have difficulties "doing it."

Low sexual esteem is a problem in general, but being gay or lesbian adds dimensions. For example, internalized homophobia, no matter how content you are with being gay, magnifies feelings of shame. Shame drains self-esteem. Why do you think it's so painful for many people to come out of the closet? The sharp focus on sex is frequently the underlying reason. So many times I've heard, "If people know I'm gay/lesbian, they'll forget who I am as a person and only think of me in terms of sex."

Here's a good example of sexualized thinking by heterosexuals about gays and lesbians. It's one of my favorite cartoons, by Andrea Natalie.[12] Awilda, a lesbian, is leaning against a bar and talking to a straight man. She says, "Really! Straight? Well, I want you to know that that's *perfectly all right* with me. You like women, sir? *Doesn't bother me a bit!* Just tell me—what is it you *do* to her? In bed, I mean. What do you and your wife *do?* . . ." The caption reads, "Awilda loved to give hets their own back."

Jane, who was just coming to terms with her lesbian sexuality, was plagued by an unsettling dream of being a tiny little woman who lived in an arcade game under a glass dome. She was naked and had to live on a revolving disk. Straight men would put money in a slot to see "the lesbian." The disk would turn around and around, exposing her to their stares and comments. The tiny woman was desperate for a place to hide.

In her dream, Jane cried and cried as she tried to crawl into a little cave. When she woke from her nightmare she was enraged, but she was also mortified at her loss of privacy and privilege. As she came out as a lesbian, Jane had to deal with people who, although they respected her professionally and as a friend and daughter, were now thinking of her in terms of her lesbian sexuality. Heterosexual curiosity about gay/lesbian sexual behavior *is* a fact of life; and Jane's acceptance of her sexuality was the hardest part of her adjustment because she felt she was being judged as "dirty" by those she cared about.

Internalized homophobia comes from living in a world that doesn't like gays and lesbians. Laws are in place that make it illegal to have oral sex. Lovers are "roommates." "Queer" jokes are told at your workplace. Custody battles are lost during divorces, and sometimes children are taken away. Your life is filled with secrets—not everyone can tolerate coming out. Society and many religions teach hate and bigotry about being gay and lesbian. These negative and destructive messages rub off on you, and they turn to self-loathing that you bring into the bedroom.

Another esteem drain is interpersonal meanness in same-sex circles. Men report to me that they're very tough on each other in the dating/sex scene. But youth and a well-toned body just aren't in every man's genetic makeup—or time in life. I hear from them that it's difficult to be a single gay man at midlife if you don't already feel good about yourself.

What is wonderful in same-sex relationships may also be a drawback or a barrier. When you're in a relationship, whatever socialization you had as a young boy or girl becomes manifested times two. If, for example, as girls you were socialized to tolerate delayed gratification instead of "going for it," you and your partner will do the same as adult women. As a result, you may find yourself going for a very long time without sex when you really want it. Girls who have been socialized to be demure and passive may translate that message to adult lesbian life as, "Ask for sex? I can't do that. What if she rejects me?" My answer to this passivity is, "Why not ask anyway? And don't reject yourself before she does."

On the other hand, boys are more likely to be socialized to be distant and not show feelings. That distancing behavior follows us into adulthood, and it may be difficult to find a sexual partner for whom you have an intimate or emotional attraction. Men often come to counseling because they have difficulty working out issues of monogamy and closeness with one person. What this boils down to is that Joan and Janet hardly have sex, while Joe and John don't know how to comfort each other.

What are some other symptoms you may note that affect your sexual esteem?

1. Being afraid to have or initiate sex
2. Fear of disappointing your sex partner
3. Finding or desiring inappropriate sex partners
4. Promiscuity

5. Comparing yourself to others or being compared to others
6. Using sex to bolster your ego
7. Feeling ashamed of your fantasies, or denying having them
8. Shame or guilt about having sex

According to many sex therapists, these negative messages come from a variety of sources:

1. Not enough affectionate touch when you were an infant or a small child
2. Early messages you learned about sex from religion or parents
3. First and usually poor sexual experiences as adolescents or young adults
4. Difficulty accepting your body
5. Your perception of sexual attractiveness
6. Your feelings of power or powerlessness
7. The way you perceive and handle rejection/acceptance
8. Shame regarding your sexuality
9. Guilt and shame over your past sexual experiences
10. Difficulty with intimacy

It's important to have fun when you have sex! You get into sexual esteem trouble if you have goals such as "we both have to have orgasms each time," or when you compare one sexual partner with another. Instead, enjoy the experience you are having. Sex isn't meant to be work but a joyful, playful part of your life.

To help yourself increase your sexual awareness of yourself, write a description of an ideal sexual partner both physically and emotionally. Write about your ideal sexual relationship. Think about what is erotic to you and what turns you off. Talk to friends about the gender socialization you had when you were kids and how it influences your behavior and sexual esteem today.

Remember, you need to take responsibility for your sexual esteem by making healthy and empowering sexual choices. Those choices should be sensual and erotic rather than esteem-robbing.

Most important, when you're going to be sexual with someone, respect your gut reaction and be sure there's no esteem-damaging conflict going on. You are in charge of your own behavior. Be kind to yourself.

Once you're in a relationship with someone, your sexual expression will undergo many changes over time. The first few months are the honeymoon phase. Everyone has been there: Everything is wonderful ... perfect ... the best. Then reality hits. If the sexual aspect of your relationship is only so-so, and you never talked about it, the time has come to share with your lover some very sensitive new information. Be gentle. Keep it safe. Be objective. This is not the time to bring up how great all your other sexual experiences were and how this experience doesn't measure up. If your other lovers were so great, why aren't you with them now?

When there's a lot of sexual fire in a relationship, there's frequently nothing else. Your "perfect" lover may have been a sex addict (gay male or lesbian) who controlled you or manipulated you through sex. Perhaps, after the sex died down a bit, you found you really didn't like your lover as a person.

It's not uncommon thinking that if you and your lover are the same sex that you like the same approach. Wrong! This is a setup for sexual failure and an esteem drain. Mind reading is also not a good idea. If you're expecting your lover to know what you want, then the first, second, or third time—or third month—you'll be disappointed. Sexual intimacy is a dynamic presence in a relationship that needs a chance to grow and mature as the relationship matures.

Some same-sex couples express feeling flawed if their sex life is less than ideal. In reality, unless there's some physical or psychological reason for sexual impairment, you and your partner need to learn to appreciate your differences. The passion will grow as you feel safer with each other's techniques. At first, teaching each other may not seem worthwhile. "If he doesn't get it now, he never will." If everything else in the relationship is improving, the sex probably will too. If the relationship has many other aspects that aren't working, sex may become the symptom of your relationship problems and actually mask what else needs to be worked on.

You want to have sex . . . she rarely wants to have sex. This is a couple with high-and-low-desire problems. (And, by the way, gay men have the same desire problems, so don't be fooled by my reference to "she"!) People with low desire really don't like therapy. They're "fine" the way they are. When one partner wants more sex than the other, low desire is an obvious conflict. Low-desire persons may be depressed. They may take medication that affects sexual functioning or have problems with drug or alcohol abuse. They may have a history of sexual abuse, or have had oppressive religious training. They may have received negative family messages about sex or be obsessive about contact with bodily fluids (saliva or lubrication). Such a person may suffer from internalized homophobia, or need to be in control, or feel unattractive. Perhaps he is not attracted to his partner, or is just plain stressed out.

If there is willingness and desire to adapt and expand, and your relationship is stable, low desire can improve. There might also be fears about improving a low-desire lover because it will change the context of the relationship. As one client once said to me, "What if my boyfriend improves and then I can't perform?" And that did happen for a while.

I strongly recommend that you consult a therapist who can work with you if you and your lover need help with sex. First and foremost, the atmosphere must be safe for both of you. The therapist doesn't have to be gay or lesbian, but should be someone who is affirming and who can teach about how to communicate feelings safely. There are exercises developed by Masters and Johnson and by JoAnn Loulan that are very helpful and that work to decrease performance anxiety and increase desire.[13]

Learning to ask directly for what you want from your partner will definitely add to your sexual self-esteem. Whether you just want hugs or you want to make love, it's good to know you can express your wishes clearly—and be loved enough to feel that it is safe to ask.

CHAPTER THIRTEEN

Wrapped Too Tight or Plain Worn Out

Sex Therapy

Have you been to one of those super-big bookstores lately? Goodness. They used to have two dinky shelves of books about or by gay men and lesbians. When I went last week, there were at least three full cases.

The assortment of books was interesting, too, but what especially caught my eye were two picture books and a sex manual. The picture book for men was unwrapped and well worn. Obviously anyone could see the Adonis like lovers right out there in public. The picture book for women, however, was heat-seal wrapped. A written description offered a very enticing promise of what the pictures are, *after* you spend twenty-five dollars to purchase the opportunity to turn the pages.

What other types of books can you find? Well, there are numerous "joy of sex" books. There are a couple of *Joy of Sex* books for nongays, and there is *The Joy of Gay Sex* for gay men, but no *Joy of Sex for Lesbians*. I guess lesbians don't have joy. Or sex. (Actually, a book called *The Joy of Lesbian Sex* was published in 1977, but it quickly vanished, never to be seen again. The women who wrote it were accused of being "straight," because no decent lesbian would or could know of such things, much less write about them in a book. Clearly!)

Currently there are a couple of "how to" sex books intended for lesbians, but there's no mention of joy on the cover. One is an "ABC" book that goes through the alphabet, with each letter representing another interesting sexual fact or function. I forget the name of that book because my lesbian clients won't return it; they just keep circulating it among themselves. I think it has an orange cover, in case you see it at a party somewhere.

On the same note, I recently accompanied my friend Bill to the men's magazine section at a gay/lesbian-friendly store. Bill was enjoying all the slick, glossy pictures of guys in guy poses, and he flipped casually through the many volumes, taking his time choosing one to purchase. No one hassled him. Glancing around while I waited, I quickly became annoyed. Just as in the big bookstores, the women's magazines were higher than I could reach and were heat-seal wrapped, except, that is, for a very heavy-duty S&M magazine that I was afraid to even open. "What's the message?" I thought out loud to anyone who was paying attention. "Women can look at men, but it's not okay to look at other women? Bill gets to look before he buys, but I have to buy before I can look? Do I want this 'protection'? Where is my choice?"

A few days later I went to the same store with my girlfriend Paula to buy a newspaper and possibly rent a video. She went over to the magazines and found one for women by women that was miraculously not sealed. As she was flipping through the pages (to find articles for me, of course), the same saleswoman who had gladly allowed Bill the freedom to browse *barked at Paula to buy or get out.* Well, Paula had been planning to buy, but not anymore. Was this a comfortable place to be an interested lesbian customer? The big bookstores may have conveyed the same message but with more quiet civility. And that message? "Go get it, man. Be still, woman."

I'm a pattern person. What's the pattern here, and how does it relate to the therapy that takes place in my office? Since some of my work is sex therapy, I couldn't help but ponder the obvious metaphor about lesbians being heat-seal wrapped and excluded, *and* the fact that gay men, on the other hand, seem to have to compete with the magazines' image of perfect men with unbelievably sized "parts." One side offers little or no information, and the other conveys "information" that would make the average man feel insecure.

Why are books and magazines for lesbians sealed or out of print? What does this represent? JoAnn Loulan, in her book *The Lesbian*

Erotic Dance, says, "A critical expression of our lesbian horizontal hatred has been that we have been afraid to take a stance on our sexuality, except to punish each other for doing it wrong."[14] In my office this "wrong" appears in the context of women unable to have orgasms, low sexual desire, sexual inhibition, and the relationship issue of *lesbian bed death,* where there is tacit agreement between partners not to be sexual at all.

We're all born with about the same amount of hormonal material. So what happens to nature's perfect balance that creates adult sexual imbalance and dysfunction? Where does sexual taboo come from? Who shut off the switch to your innate sexuality when you were growing up? For some men and women, the religion in which they were raised may have taught them that sex is dirty. I had a client whose Catholic education specifically included instructions never to touch herself "down there" because it's a sin. This client remembers being told at age six or seven to roll over and pray if her hands wandered between her legs. As my client got older, she learned how to orgasm by rocking her body instead of touching herself. The adult result was that, in her fifteen-year relationship, my client has yet to remove her underwear in bed. Her girlfriend doesn't see her partner's breasts unless a couple of drinks have loosened her inhibitions. Even then, the next day my client is angry with herself at her "lapse" into sexuality. This is a common example of being heat-sealed and untouchable, even after the purchase.

Not so long ago in our history, antimasturbation devices were sold to parents to prevent their children from "sinning." One of these devices was a bell attached to the child's bed that would alert the parents if "it" was happening. The parents were instructed to immediately run into their child's bedroom before "the sin" could occur and tie down the child's body so that he or she couldn't move. Other anti-sin products included ropes and straps the parents used to keep their children (at all stages, from infancy to young adulthood) pinned down. It's easy to see how this would become an adult fetish.

While such devices aren't openly used today, families can still be very powerful in passing sexual taboos on to children. Lesbian and gay sexual development is even more taboo because of the homophobia-laden messages most families foster.

Socialization is the third arena for sexual repression. It tells us that what lesbians do is dirty and disgusting—too awful to see, let alone think about. Get out the heat-wrap sealer! Don't publish that book! And it's socialization that sends gay men to the gym every day to attempt to develop genetically impossible perfect bodies. Get ready for the chase! Flex those arms, and go conquer!

Why can't women access sexual stimulation as easily as men, and without censorship? Why must men be bombarded with unattainable standards of how they should look or who they should be with? What does it mean that this stimulus is so public? As a result of society perpetuating this male sexual mythology, I constantly treat gay men who have difficulties with hypersexuality—that is, sex addictions. A gay client may be habitually seeking anonymous sex as affirmation that he is attractive and sexy. Or he may be stuck in a depression about his body and his age. Some men have performance anxiety and are unable to have erections. Some experience premature or retarded ejaculation. And yes, there are men with low sexual desire as well. Believe me, it's more common than you think.

Many gay men express the feeling that they'll never look good enough for anyone to love. After thirty they're "too old," or it's "too late." Men can be so unkind to each other, and they can set such unreasonable requirements. Some eventually even become suicidal because they're "not big enough, young enough, or beautiful enough."

In the natural course of long-term relationships, sexual relations tend to decline. This is difficult for gay men to accept because of society's emphasis on men as sexual predators. Men are socialized to be "ready" to have sexual relations at a moment's notice. They're supposed to want sex even when they're less than enthusiastic.

Women are socialized to wait to be asked by a man who is completely responsible for when and how to have sex with her. You can see the problem that lesbians may have in being the initiators in their relationships. It may become too easy for lesbians to decline in sexual activity because the emphasis is on women being passive receivers.

Remember the magazine metaphor? Women can't have it, and men must have it all.

When a couple comes to me for counseling, I always check in on their sexual relationship. What I've discovered is that if a couple is doing well but needs help adjusting to their personality differences, sex makes up only about twenty percent of their relationship concerns. If sex is their main reason for coming to counseling, about eighty percent of the relationship is consumed with the problem. The problems typically are sexual performance anxieties and low desire.

Along with religion, family, and society, homophobia is also high on the list of reasons for gay and lesbian sexual problems. Indeed, it seems that homophobia and internalized homophobia are at the root of many gay and lesbian issues, including sex. The truth is that the hate perpetuated by society unfortunately turns into gay and lesbian self-hatred. Unless internalized homophobia is addressed at every turn, it will permeate every aspect of your life. If the public is disgusted by your sexuality, this affects your sex life. If the church is disgusted by sexual pleasure, don't you think that might give you a problem? You may also find yourself avoiding sex in order to short-circuit the images your family gave you about "lezzies and fags."

Now, I know that I'll catch it on this one, but I feel that being "politically correct" (or is it politically incorrigible? collectible? intangible? correctable? attachable? whatever) is a form of internalized homophobia. "PC"—that thing that tells you how to behave, the correct way to think, and by implication that straight-acting/straight-looking is preferred, and that being butch, femme, or Nelly is bad—is *not* about liking yourself, accepting your lifestyle, or honoring your diversity. Political correctness today has become oppression personified —the direct opposite of its original intent, which was to address patriarchal heterosexism, racism, and other isms.

If we are to challenge homophobia, we must start liking ourselves. We have to appreciate our differences, stop blaming others, embrace our wounded, and be responsible for our own. Society does enough damage; we have to stop damaging ourselves.

Understand that your sexual repression problems developed when you didn't have control of your life. Close your eyes and visualize putting your own hand back on the switch and turning on your sexual healing. Challenge your internalized homophobia and your inner critic.

If you and your partner decide to go for sex therapy, the experience, though difficult at times, can be very rewarding and surprising. You may discover, for example, that you want to expand your sexual activity and your partner seems reluctant to try new positions. Through safety exercises and your partner's new willingness to try, you may suddenly find yourself freezing up at doing something different. Maybe all along you said you wanted to try new positions, but when the opportunity is presented in fact, the prospect scares you. Surprise!!

The first real sex therapy that seemed effective was developed by Masters and Johnson in 1970. The procedures they devised were both educational and behavioral. In those days, clients were pretty receptive to learning techniques and doing special homework assignments to develop increased arousal, and many were simply looking for permission to be sexual.

Sensate focus, which is nonsexual touch, was and still is the cornerstone of sex therapy. Two people learning to be safe with each other in this manner is very important. What's different today in sex therapy is that many people are resistant. They've already tried sensate focus on their own from having read books about sexual dysfunction. They don't like it and don't want it.

Oh, how times have changed! In the days of Masters and Johnson, sex therapy was new and everybody wanted to try. Now you can read about sexual techniques in the magazines while you're in the checkout line at the supermarket!

On the other hand, a good sex therapist won't be discouraged that you already know some techniques from self-help books. If what you tried didn't work, there must be other underlying reasons why your sexual life needs some modification. There might be some anger in your relationship that has to do with trust. There may be shame issues or other distresses that make sexual communication difficult. It's really pretty complex.

Once a therapist has helped you to communicate safely out of bed, you may be more willing to change some of your sexual habits as well. Being "dysfunctional" is sometimes a symptom of other issues in your relationship, such as intimacy, power, and trust. Sometimes the dysfunction is low desire, lack of attraction, inability to blend love and sexual desire, or difficulty with orgasm or erection. Whatever the symptom, what happens in bed is frequently a metaphor for what's happening out of bed. It's worth looking at.

Sexual dysfunction may be a subconscious behavior that's taking up all of your worry time and helping you avoid what may really be troubling you. For example, if you were taught to hate your sexual orientation, you may use sexual dysfunction as a subconscious excuse not to deal with your internalized homophobia. After all, if you can't enjoy sex, maybe there is "hope" that you're not really gay or lesbian. The fact is that you are, and you know you are, but you'd rather not deal with it. So you develop a sexual dysfunction that takes up all your time and worry. In this case, sexual dysfunction is the way you resolve the negative messages about your sexual orientation.

If you have been sexually abused or raped, were purposefully given sexual misinformation, or were threatened by your parents for expressing sexual curiosity, get help from a professional. Be sure you pick someone who doesn't think your sexual orientation is the problem. These serious situations can definitely be the cause of sexual dysfunction, but they can be addressed successfully by both of you. Resolving old abuse issues doesn't have to get in the way of your present and future relationships.

What's to be done about being heat-sealed or worn out? First, examine the reasons why you may be experiencing sexual difficulties. What are the messages you absorbed from your religion, family, society, your internalized homophobia? Make a list of what the messages are and how they affect you today. Talk with a friend over coffee about his or her experiences. Admit to one of your behaviors and try to trace its origin. Then challenge the irrational belief behind that behavior. You *are* worthy of healthy sexual fulfillment.

CHAPTER FOURTEEN

"Looking for Love in All the Wrong Places"
Sex Addiction

Food, drugs, alcohol, gambling, credit cards—these are the addictions we hear about most. Then there is sexual addiction. Everyone freezes! "Oh, no! There's that sex thing again!" It's important to realize, however, that when someone is peeling away their addiction skins, sexual addiction is often the core addictive behavior left behind.

What is sexual addiction? Like any addiction, it's a negative pattern of behavior that is compulsive, unmanageable, and continual. And, like the other addictions, it's a very destructive, high-risk behavior in which the addict's entire life revolves around the addictive situation—in this case, sexual activities.

Sexual addiction has many levels of severity, from an overuse of chat lines to more victimizing behaviors such as obscene phone calls, voyeurism, and harassment. The most serious, of course, are crimes such as child molestation and rape. The "milder" levels, however, should never be taken lightly, *even* in their early stages. Addiction, by nature, is progressive; and the addict is daily moving closer to the dangerous levels in which his or her life becomes more seriously at risk.

People who are sexually addicted believe that sex is their most important need. For these people, sex becomes confused with nurturing and caring because we live in a sexualized society where sex is confused with love. Certainly, everyone wants to be cared for and nurtured; but for the addicted person, this need translates directly to sex. Sex addicts in a relationship may demand sexual contact with their lover several times a day. They may feel that their partner owes them sex as proof of love. These addicts aren't just "horny," but rather they are consumed with their need for a fix.

Addicts frequently feel unworthy and deserving of humiliation. They have a distorted view of their inner self, as well as a distorted sexuality that developed during childhood. Many addicts, as children, were emotionally or sexually abused by people close to them; and sexual abuse may have been the only "love" or attention they received. I've seen pictures of children auditioning to become models for ad agencies. These are not images of kids who look like kids. The little girls are made up to look like sexually functioning women, with full makeup and adult, almost pornographic poses. The boys are dressed and posed as "little men." This type of sexualized behavior is rewarded in many families. For some sexually abused or sexualized children, such a view of sex as love evolves with adulthood.

Many sex addicts also have the feeling of being unloved or unlovable; or they may worry that they're about to be abandoned. They're consumed with a constant search for love mixed with a dread of being alone. Sex addicts fear dependence on the one hand, yet crave connection on the other. This duality of feelings, along with social isolation, progresses with the addiction. In a kind of desperation, addicts continue to escalate their behavior in the endless quest for "love."

Another belief of sex addicts is that if they become dependent or committed in a relationship, their needs will not be met. They harbor a deep feeling of resentment because they feel they must manipulate others in order to be loved (i.e., to get sex). Moreover, because they feel unlovable and unable to depend on anyone, they often seek out that "love/sex" with a stranger.

Life without sex terrifies the sex addict. Much of the day is spent trying to find potential sex partners. Addicts fear losing control over people, or losing a source for sex. Old relationships are kept open, just in case there's a need for sexual contact later on. I knew a woman who contacted three or four of her most recent lovers every time her current relationship broke up. She was checking out her supply to see whether they showed enough interest in her to tide her over until her next attempt at fidelity. Meanwhile, the "supplies" would talk from time to time to see if the others had been contacted. (By the way, the "supplies" were all in happy and committed relationships, with no interest in ever getting involved again with the addict. The addict couldn't have cared less about their relationships.)

It's the chase, not the act, that is exciting for the addict. After all, anonymous sex generally doesn't take very long: a few minutes, or sometimes a one-night stand. But waiting in the bookstore to see what might happen next is very exciting. The gamble and the anticipation are intoxicating.

What is being acted out in this chase? The responses I hear most from sex addicts are: "the conquest"; "feeling momentarily attractive"; "feeling wanted"; "the secret life that no one knows about." For how long? "Just one more time," or "until I have the best I could ever have." And why? "I have to have it"; "the exhilaration"; "for relief"; "it keeps me from being bored, or lonely." And finally, "After all, it doesn't really count." On the surface, these responses may seem quite different, but they spring from the same negative inner feelings.

The sex addict rarely feels guilt or remorse for acting out. Some tell me they dissociate or don't "feel present" during sexual encounters. The addict has little or no understanding of the impact of his behavior on himself or others. Many men who cruise the bookstores, for example, are in long-term relationships, but they think that what's happening below the waist has nothing to do with the heart. "I love my boyfriend. He would kill me if he knew what I was doing. But as long as I'm there for him, this doesn't matter." When the addict is caught by his lover, he may finally see how much hurt he has caused. If the relationship withstands this betrayal, the addict may eventually feel remorse for his behavior.

Sometimes sex addicts come to seek help because they've been beaten up during the chase, become scared, and finally want to quit the behavior. Others want to stop because of the fear of AIDS. Some have lost their jobs after being caught and charged by police. Others come to therapy only because their boyfriend will leave them if they don't. For some there's a gradual realization that there's something harmful about their behavior, making them want help to stop. But often they can't quite take that step. It's not unusual for men to call me five or six times before they make an appointment because they aren't ready to stop acting out. "Just one more week," they say. "Then I'll get help."

Although the statistics for sexual acting out are greater for gay men, women also have sexual addiction problems. However, the emotional content is different. Women tend to be more involved in a "relationship" as a segue to having sexual encounters. Men are more able to keep sex external and therefore anonymous, with no emotional attachment required.

Male addicts will frequent adult bookstores, rest areas, or other local cruising spots, whereas lesbians do not. Gay men in relationships will also forgive each other for sexual acting out more often than lesbians will. Lesbians tend to break up with their girlfriends if one is caught having sex with others, because the heart as well as the body is involved in the chase. The "heart" is very dear in lesbian culture, and the loss of emotional intimacy is a difficult breach to overcome. Given socialization and the way people view anatomical differences, this is not surprising! (Lenny Bruce, many years ago, did a routine about how disgusted his wife was about what he did with his penis. She would yell at him, "You don't care where you put it as long as it feels good. It could be a cantaloupe, a tree, a chicken. Fine! Put it in a chicken and then ask the chicken to cook dinner for you. Go ahead. See what you get.")

Are a larger number of gay men sexually addicted? No, the percentage is no greater than for the general population. It's important to realize that some people may be too quick to label a gay man as sexually addicted without considering the cultural differences between gay and heterosexual men. Such rapid categorization may be a homophobic response. For many gay men, first sexual encounters may be anonymous. Then, following a period of anonymous sexual experimentation (a behavior often encouraged for heterosexual men), the gay man will generally settle down, just like his heterosexual counterpart. Think about the famous heterosexual "bonding" myth in which the father takes his eighteen-year-old son to a prostitute to make him a man. Why should that kind of heterosexual anonymous sex be more acceptable than gay men being with other gay men? Does going to a prostitute institutionalize the experience and make it acceptable?

Heterosexual men have many outlets for anonymous sexual behavior with women, and our culture has historically either tacitly encouraged this pursuit or looked the other way. Why should this behavior be overlooked or considered okay if you're straight but make you a sex addict if you're gay? It shouldn't.

The real question to ask is, What's the difference between sexual addiction/compulsion, sexual experimentation, and avoiding intimacy? The answer lies in the *intent* of the behavior.

If someone has a sex buddy, is he or she a sex addict? How does sex addiction play out in a monogamous relationship? If a person has obsessive thoughts about sex but doesn't act on them, is that sexual addiction? Is calling chat lines a type of addictive behavior? Does cheating on one's lover mean that one is a sex addict?

It isn't a matter of where you go to have sex but of how you approach it. If you feel compelled to have sex at the cost of intimacy; if you're constantly choosing sex over other interests or activities that address your basic need to feel good about yourself; if you feel a momentary excitement but no satisfaction afterward; or if you're using sex to ward off emotional pain, then you need to think about recovering and direct yourself to healing. You're in a high-risk behavior category, and you're putting yourself and others in jeopardy. You have to stop and deal with yourself right away. You have to examine the *intent* of your behaviors.

Some people wish they could continue their compulsive behavior until they feel better about themselves. I frequently hear, "Can't I act out once or twice a week?" As long as you're continuing to act out, you're not recovering. As with any addiction, the "supply" has to be eliminated in order for a person to recover.

There are some sex addicts who don't go outside their relationships but who use their lover to provide the sex fix on demand. Then, if they don't get cooperation, the addict may turn violent as the control issues play out. On the other hand, if the addict is acting compulsively outside the relationship, the partnership is in serious danger. Say you're anxious or upset about your lover—or anything else, for that matter. By acting out you don't have to think about what might really be bothering you. For example, sometimes in committed relationships one person starts going to highway rest stops for sexual encounters. This behavior is a symptom of other problems that aren't being addressed. Also, if the partner who is acting out doesn't use protection, both are in jeopardy of dying.

A sex addict who wants to be in a long-term relationship must first come to grips with his or her behavior and stop. New behaviors must replace old ones. Sexual addiction is frequently about the need for other, healthy ways to soothe yourself when you're having uncomfortable feelings. However, what I've seen is that the addict spends so much time thinking about and going after the ultimate sexual rush, there is little time left to join in activities where a healthy relationship may develop. Rest-stop lovers sometimes stay together, but this is rare. The sexual compulsion will most likely emerge once again when the honeymoon is over.

If you have a secret sexual compulsion and are entering a relationship, the compulsion may be abated for a while, but it's bound to resurface if not treated. All in all, sexual addiction is a behavior that keeps real intimacy away.

"I'm bored" was a reason I got from one sex addict I was working with. "When I'm acting out it's exciting and I'm not bored anymore." Dan quit all of his addictions except sex. He quit drinking and gambling. Quitting smoking was hard, but he accomplished it. Food continues to be a source of aggravation, but Dan has become more self-accepting. After some treatment, my client came to realize that his boredom was really fear in disguise. He was afraid of his anger and self-hatred that developed from being emotionally abused, and from having been sexualized and used as a sex object when he was very young. Dan had never been comforted or held when he was hurt, so he didn't have any self-soothing skills or ways to help himself feel better. If anything, he was ridiculed and hit for wanting affection. Dan eventually realized, along with many that I treat, that his addiction will be a lifelong problem that needs to be consciously dealt with but can be overcome. Today Dan feels more spiritually connected and in control of his compulsions. He feels as if his entire life is just beginning, although he is in his forties.

Recovering from sexual addiction is often compared to recovering from an eating disorder. Someone with an obsession about food has to learn to eat in a healthier fashion. Similarly, a sex addict must learn to be sexual in a healthier way. Recovering from sexual addiction means:

- understanding that there's a problem
- getting out of denial
- giving up the excitement of the chase
- getting help from a qualified counselor
- for some, a period of abstinence

For many, it also means getting into a group for support.

When you're the partner of a sex addict, you're living a life of constant betrayal. In addition, your health may be seriously at risk. You may be a person who does not have a strong core identity. You have to make changes regarding yourself and what you're willing to tolerate in the context of a relationship. You must stop putting the addict first and start taking care of yourself. Find out what you really want and need. How do you really feel? What does your gut say? Set limits! Stop disregarding your own needs and overlooking hurtful and demeaning behavior. Don't be so willing to take the blame for the unacceptable. You'll need support if you choose to stay with the addict as he or she comes to grips with the addictive behavior—but the behavior itself is a problem only the addict can choose to fix.

Even with support, recovering from sexual compulsion is difficult. The more you abstain from sex, the more your feelings are going to surface. The more your feelings surface, the more you may want to act out. When you abstain from your compulsion, you may find yourself crying and feeling depressed. *This is normal for someone who is attempting to control a full-blown addiction of any kind.* The pain that drives you to act out is still there and must be addressed. The hardest part is coming out of denial. If you even think you have a problem and that you're making a mess out of your life, face yourself, get help, and you will get past it.

Therapy is a very important tool to help you get control over sexual addiction. The therapist should be someone who understands sex addictions and the gay/lesbian lifestyle. You must be willing to go through the steps of healing from this debilitating addictive behavior, but you do not have to do this alone. There are resources available to help you, and many of them are listed in the back of this book. It's very important to get support from SLAA (Sex and Love Addicts Anonymous)[15] or other groups to help you through this time.

CHAPTER FIFTEEN

"I Can't Live If Living Is Without You"
Love/Relationship Addiction

"I can't live without her." *It feels like that now, but you will.* "I could never love anyone like this again." *Good thing, too.* "I don't understand what I could have done." *Let's try to sort this out.* "The first three months were so perfect." *Perfect?!??*

If someone were to ask me what problems I see most frequently as a therapist, I'd have to say "relationships." Either we're in one, or just out of one, or trying to live without one, or looking for one, or "depressed in spite of" one. In the last chapter I talked about sex addiction and its impact on gay and lesbian relationships. Now let's look at two other addictions that cause people confusion, agony, and heartache, depriving them of an opportunity for real intimacy. These are romance and relationship addictions, also collectively known as love addiction.

First, there's the romance addict. The buzz or fix for this type of addiction is the perfect romantic experience—a candlelight dinner, cards, gifts, and flowers . . . as opposed to sex, alcohol, gambling, or food addictions.

Don't the romance of flowers and those breathtaking interludes under the stars sound harmless enough? Isn't this a great way to start a new relationship? Maybe!—but a relationship may not be what you're getting. *A romance addict is a pro at illusion.* When you're vulnerable (or if you're a relationship junkie) you may find yourself acting in someone else's fantasy. If you've had this experience, you know that you're only going to be there for a short and heartbreaking time.

The behavior of romance addicts is superficial. They don't really want to get to know you. They just want to look good *with* you. Did you ever have a fantasy about that tall, dark stranger with big blue eyes coming into your life? When that person is a romance addict, they remain a stranger, and two months later when they're gone, you sit wondering what you did wrong.

That person who gets you to feel instant love from the first time you "looked into those beautiful blue eyes" may be breaking your heart next week when you see her at the bar, giving that same mooning look you thought was just for you to someone else.

While you're in the romance addict's fantasy, things may seem harmless on the surface. *Beware.* As the addiction progresses (and all addictions do), romance addicts begin to have multiple affairs while still trying to fit you into their fantasy—and when you don't fit anymore, you may find yourself in a humiliating or even violent situation. As the need for the romance fix increases, addicts frequently have affairs that can put your life or their life in danger.

This escalated behavior has very little to do with sex. Actually, after the first couple of weeks, you may find that your sexual contact with your lover decreases as he or she begins to move away from you toward that next perfect love. Many romance addicts report that they don't even like sex very much.

There's certainly no intimacy with the romance addict. As with all addictions, the addict's primary relationship is with the fix or rush. In the case of a romance addict, the fix is "love" and all the excitement of the conquest.

Frequently, romance addicts have affairs only with "unattainable" people, such as those who are already in committed relationships. The fix here is the excitement or the intoxication of new love, the thrill of that mind-altering situation, the danger, and the chase. There's very little concern for harm done to the other people involved.

Romance addicts have the same poor self-esteem as other types of addicts. They see themselves as having little value; and being in a romantic situation is an escape from what they view as a hostile world. For just a little while, their new connection seems to supply what they need in order to feel better. Unfortunately, as with all fixes, the rush lasts for only a short time. Then the addict quickly begins to look for his or her next fix, leaving you crushed and miserable. (It's not fun being someone else's surplus, is it?)

Often the romance addict comes from a home that puts on a good front or creates a good impression. However, inside such a family there is likely to be chaos and abuse. The kids may all be perfectly dressed for church, and the parents are the perfect couple, but the children, who are constantly being told how perfect they are, frequently find that they can't fulfill that illusion for themselves or their family. When a child from this type of family grows up and finds that he or she can't get love and approval just by impressing people, anger and feelings of worthlessness begin to build. The child grows into an adult who is trying to assuage that anger and repair that self-image by finding the "perfect love" to prove they are "okay."

Romance addicts set up artificial situations because they don't know how to be authentic. They orchestrate, manipulate, and con to keep the illusion of perfection alive, and to stay on that edge of excitement. Have you ever been a victim of a romance addict? Are you one? Being gay or lesbian makes you very susceptible to romance addiction because of your deep need for the acceptance and love that may not be forthcoming from important people in your life.

Unfortunately, our society encourages love addiction by reinforcing our feelings of not being good enough. Look around at the advertising you experience daily. Plastic surgery will make you more beautiful, and if you're more beautiful you'll have more love. Diets will make you more perfect-looking—for that perfect romance. Alcohol will make you feel better and look cool—for the one you love. A plethora of drugs are overprescribed to make you better behaved and more compliant. The media empire of feel-good products undercuts our innate wisdom and the power we have to *feel good as we are* and *on our own*.

Now, just because you like romance in your relationship does not mean that you're a romance addict. Addictive behavior is about intention. Therefore, it's not the concept of romance itself but rather the desperate behavior and constant search for the unattainable that places the out-of-control romantic into the addict category.

Relationship addiction, the second love addiction, meshes perfectly with addiction to romance. Anne Wilson Schaef, in her book *Escape from Intimacy*, asks, "What do sexual addiction, romance addiction and relationship addiction have in common? Sexual addicts 'come on,' romance addicts 'move on,' and relationship addicts 'hang on.'"[16]

There are two types of relationship addictions to choose from! Do you fit either of these descriptions? The first type of addict, called the Type 1 relationship addict, is addicted to the concept of having *any* relationship. The second, or Type 2 relationship addict, is addicted to another person. This is the "hang-on" person I see the most often for therapy in the lesbigay lifestyle.

Type 1 addicts want any kind of relationship they can have. For instance, I had a roommate in college who wore high heels, short shorts, and stockings in the winter just because a guy she had barely started to date wanted her to. When the shorts weren't short enough, he humiliated and then dumped her.

This woman had spent three agonizing weeks trying to be someone else's dream girl. She couldn't figure out what she had done wrong, and she blamed herself for not wanting to meet his mother dressed so absurdly. Besides being a jerk, this guy was a romance addict. My roommate, who had struggled to do anything to fulfill this man's fantasy, was a Type 1 relationship addict. She was desperate to be in a relationship with anyone, even if it meant self-abasement. (She was also on her way to some serious codependency!)

Type 1 relationship addicts have little real concern for the other person in the relationship. The fix is the relationship itself, along with the fantasy and the obsession that go along with the concept. When I see clients slide from one person to another without a break, I have to question the authenticity of those relationships. These clients may be in a cycle of pseudo-relationships where, in a very short time, they find they can't stand their new love and want to move on to someone "better."

Some clients and colleagues have heard me refer to this rapid change of heart as "The Lesbian Slide." This is the bar dance in which, every year on May 15 at 8:45 P.M., you can go to the club and look at the couples dancing and holding hands. Then close your eyes and look again. All of the couples will have changed partners, and you will have again missed your window of opportunity to find someone of your own. You must have experienced how hard it is for you to stay out of a relationship when you so desperately want to feel love. But is love really possible in this scenario?

Your assignment is to listen to the songs and look at the movies, TV shows, and ads that proclaim that we aren't good enough as we are, and that we have to be "in love" or somehow attached no matter what. Then find some that support real intimacy between people and encourage us to love ourselves as a prerequisite to loving another. If you can't find any, write one! Then take a long, close look at the differences.

In the next chapter, we'll talk about being addicted to another person.

CHAPTER SIXTEEN

You Will Survive! You Will Survive Your Relationship Addiction!!

The room was rocking. The dance floor was bouncing. The dancers were stomping their feet while shouting the words to a popular seventies song—an anthem in which the protagonist discovers that there *is* life after her lover leaves her, that she has strength and life is good. I witnessed this spontaneous "I Will Survive" festival at DeVille's, a local women's bar, last spring. For one extraordinary moment, the entire club population participated in this cleansing ritual. Women were shouting the words in each other's faces. Others were dancing or exchanging knowing looks. The members of the tribe were ridding themselves of the final horrors of getting out of awful and destructive relationships.

I recently related this experience to a straight woman, and she said, interestingly, that the same thing happens in straight clubs as well. For some reason, women are again the primary participants.

The unfortunate fact is that this anthem is usually sung too long after "I can't live without you." Until you want to survive, you may find that being addicted to a person is as debilitating and destructive as addiction to drugs or alcohol. If you really want to have the life and spirit sucked out of you, then "hold on" to the person who doesn't reciprocate your love. "Hold on" until you feel as if you're in a wasteland of loneliness or a battleground of abuse. "Hold on" to being completely out of touch with yourself. Then, when you can't "hold on" anymore, get help!

In the preceding chapter you read about Type 1 relationship addiction, where the "fix" is the relationship. Type 2 is about being addicted to a person. Although there may be feelings of love and commitment in an addictive relationship, sometimes we limit our freedom to choose another person. How do we limit our choosing?

- First, if you're addicted to a person, you have a compulsive drive that keeps you in the relationship even when you know it's not good for you. You seem to have buried your gut instincts that are screaming for you to get out.
- Second, you feel panic at the very thought of breaking up. How many times have you gone back, saying, "Oh, I love him. I have to give him a second chance." And a third, and a fourth. How many more chances have you given without any real evidence that things would be different this time?
- Third, if you're addicted you have real withdrawal symptoms after the breakup. There is craving, longing, crying, physical pain, sleeplessness, and serious suffering. These symptoms frequently drive you right back to your lover, just for relief from the pain of withdrawal.
- Finally, when you're finally able to break up and get out of your addictive relationship, you go through a grieving period followed by great elation. A nonaddictive relationship that breaks up is followed not by relief, but by a deep and lingering sadness. This sense of relief is a sure sign that the relationship you just got out of was not good for you.

Of course, being glad you're out of it doesn't mean that you won't miss the excitement of being with someone. That's natural, too. However, you were born to be healthy and happy. When you're free from the compulsion and you finally feel better, you'll wipe your brow and smile! I've seen that smile many, many times, and I'm proud of my clients who stick with themselves and succeed in growing beyond their relationship addiction.

This information is important! If your pattern is:

- feeling compelled to be with a certain someone against your better judgment

- panic and dread at the thought of breaking up
- painful withdrawal symptoms followed by relief and exhilaration

—it may be time for you to take another look at what you're doing to yourself.

So, what is going on with you? A Freudian therapist would explore your attachment relationship with your parents (translate "mother") and how your nurturing needs weren't met as an infant. Attachment hunger is very powerful. Those needy feelings come from a time in your life, up to the age of eighteen months, when you didn't have words for your feelings. The memories of attachment are in your body chemistry, and as we've said, the body has 100 percent memory. As an adult you express your attachment hunger when you talk about loving someone with "every fiber of your body." You feel that your physical reactions must be telling you some truth about the person you've chosen; but if you can't put your finger on what that truth is, you may be looking at the beginning of a compulsion. You may even think this attachment hunger is "love"; but think again.

A Rational-Emotive therapist would tell you that this initial compulsive feeling comes from a mistaken understanding of love. You *can* control your attachment feelings and not engage on a baby level or use irrational thinking when considering relationships that could be harmful to you.

Be on the alert so that you don't let your body feelings overpower your judgment. When you're in an attachment hunger mode, you may find yourself in a pseudo-relationship that has little to do with who you are today. Calm your heart, be clear, and make balanced decisions that aren't based on old panic, fear, or neediness.

What are some of the red flags that indicate pseudo-relationships? Do you:

1. Attach immediately and intensely to another?
2. Have instant "intimacy"?
3. Attach to another in a dependent way or foster dependency?
4. Get immediately high on love so that it interferes with your routine?
5. Define your life in terms of someone else's existence?

6. Have continual instant physical attraction to anyone who gives you an "opportunity"?
7. Ignore your unshared values, dreams, and fears?
8. Look intimately involved but stay hidden?
9. Interpret intensity as love?
10. Stay in a relationship past feeling sane?
11. Feel immediately "comfortable" with the new person?
12. Feel as if you've known this person all your life?

If you see yourself in this list and want to change your pattern of addictive relationships, there is hope. Changing your pattern is not without discomfort, and it takes time—but when you realize how unhappy you are, the changes you make will be empowering.

Now that you're aware of the problem, what next? This is a good time to get into your feelings and experience yourself in the here and now. Being present will help you get back to who you are, not who you were ages ago. You'll make peace with your attachment hunger and make better choices based on the adult you are.

Keeping a journal, particularly about your relationships and your feelings, is very important. You'll begin to identify your patterns, and you'll be able to monitor your contacts with the person of your addiction. Keep track of your feelings as you change your interaction with him or her. Maintaining a record of how you feel will help you keep from going back to all that pain. For now, accept that the pain has to be remembered and recorded.

You'll probably be able to identify other similar relationships in your life. What was the emotional and sexual content of the relationships? Was the sexual part the most difficult aspect to break from? This is often true of relationships that are too intense.

Some help from friends at this time would be great. Try to visualize the Greek hero Ulysses. He desperately wanted to hear the lovely Sirens' song without having to throw his ship upon the rocks to be with them, so he had his shipmates tie him to the mast. Your friends can tie you by helping you become interested in new activities and supporting you through your withdrawal. As you resist the temptation of unhealthy relationships, your addiction will diminish. You're on a healthier course to a happier life.

One caution about friendships in the gay and lesbian community: often there is a mind-set that ex-lovers need to be friends. This is not always true or necessary. Make sure your friends are supportive, and not undermining your need to be separated from your "fix." You need to declare your boundaries with your friends. Tell people that you don't want to know who "she" is with or what "he" is saying about you. (Of course you do want to know, but this "knowing" can be pretty upsetting when you're trying to move ahead. So skip it.)

Eventually a friendship with your ex may be possible—or maybe not. Either way, you have to be in charge, without interference from "friends." Declaring boundaries will have to become a part of the new you.

As you're breaking away from your addiction, it is extremely important to abstain from all romance and concentrate on your own healing and personal development. Take time to get to know yourself. Develop friendships; volunteer on the Pride committee; take classes; improve your diet; meditate. Explore what a healthy relationship is, and consciously seek that path.

CHAPTER SEVENTEEN

"Circle in the Sand"
The Path to Nowhere

I'll bet that you and your lover keep having the same argument over and over. I'll also bet that no matter who you've been in a relationship with, the pattern of anger and arguments keeps repeating. If you're recycling your anger and argument pattern, it's time to stop and re-evaluate.

John and Steve have been together for a long time—almost forty years. When I asked them if they argue, they said they discovered in the first few years together that they always got angry and argued about the same things: sex and money. After a while they noticed that John's complaint was always "never enough sex," and Steve always complained "never enough money." What they found was that each of them could only go so far in changing, and that if they wanted to stay together they would each have to adjust. They also figured out that the anger and arguing had to stop. John and Steve knew each other so well that they didn't even have to voice their arguments anymore. When one just said the word "sex," they both knew the discussion and the solution, so why bother with all the hyper-emotion and anger? Anger, they realized, was corroding their relationship.

Relationships have a life of their own; and a healthy relationship is about two people recognizing their differences and having the capacity, love, and desire to see things through. Abuse, of course, does not count—no one has to stay in an abusive relationship or one where addictions are involved. Huge differences don't count either. There has to be a good match of values and goals, a willingness to communicate, acceptance, and a commitment that allows for intimacy and love. Unless you feed your relationship it will wither, become toxic, and die.

Too often in the gay and lesbian community, I see people match up too quickly just because it feels good to be attached. When the bonding period subsides and the differences become clearer, the couple finds that they can't stand each other, or are arguing all the time. Sometimes it's too late to do anything about the arguing, and the couple breaks up. The relationships that work are the ones in which the couples take their time before moving in or becoming committed. When a couple has a lot invested in a relationship, they will want to figure out a better way to be together—but that's another story!

When everything is right, don't those first few months together feel wonderful? Make a list of what was working between you from the time you met and fell in love until your first uncomfortable disagreements. Here are some hints:

- You felt close.
- You talked about everything.
- You did things together.
- There seemed to be a lot of sharing.
- You talked about your feelings, hurts, goals, and expectations.
- You had fun.
- You looked at each other.
- You held each other.
- Annoying little things didn't seem to matter.

In fact, when there is just a little irritation, a little hint usually takes care of it. Cathy and Jean have been together for four months. Jean isn't as neat as Cathy and leaves her bureau open each morning with things hanging out. This irritates Cathy, who finally says something like, "I shut your bureau drawer and put your stuff away this morning." Jean gets the hint, she apologizes, and they talk about their differences in neatness. The two feel close again and on top of the world because they have "communicated." It was easy. Neither of them was defensive.

Time goes on, and Jean closes her bureau drawer but leaves things all over their home—a shoe here, a coffee cup there, tissues that missed the trash. She's not dirty, just disorganized. Kind of in her own zone. Cathy hints and hints. After all, when things were new between them, a little hint worked. A little mind reading went a long way, and changes were made. Now Cathy is getting really annoyed at always having to pick up after her girlfriend. Not only that, Jean does other irritating things that are also not changing to Cathy's satisfaction.

Since Jean isn't tuned in to Cathy's hints, she doesn't have a clue that her girlfriend is angry. Other irritations accumulate, and a distance grows between them. The sex isn't as good, they aren't holding hands, and there seems to be a lot of frustration. After a few little arguments, Cathy and Jean begin to feel mismatched. Because being together is so uncomfortable, they start doing things apart until one day a huge emotional argument erupts. They're screaming at each other over everything. They feel trapped.

Screaming matches are negative and draining experiences where people say horrible things to each other, angrily defend their positions, and still feel put down and guilty. They're a useless waste of energy and toxic to relationships. Still, many couples have these screaming matches all the time. They feel it's a good way to "get their feelings out" and "vent their anger."

But is it venting anger, or is it a temper tantrum? Did your parents scream at each other? Do you use your "cultural heritage" as an excuse, saying that screaming is the way your ethnic group communicates, so you can't help it? How happy were the people in your life who plowed over each other just to make a point? How did it feel growing up? Were you afraid? When did you learn to scream back? Or do you want to run away when someone is having a temper tantrum?

Anger is an important emotional tool; but screaming at someone is not about anger. Actually, the early theory about anger or "letting off steam" goes back to the 1800s, when hydraulics and Freud got to-

gether. Simply put, Freud believed that when we have internal conflicts we have a blockage of our energy, which then causes neurotic
behavior. Freud believed that instead of repressing our conflicts we
should undergo a catharsis, or relieving of our subconscious, such as
when a hydraulic engine lets off a head of steam.

Freud would be horrified today to see how some therapists have
clients practice this "relieving" with aggressive, hostile, and confrontational acting out. The pillow-smashing, screaming reenactments that
some call "relieving the tension" or "experiencing your anger" are
destructive and actually generate more rage.

Many studies have shown that angry behavior gives birth to even
angrier behavior that escalates into abuse. Where there is poor control, anger frequently cycles into violence in relationships. Angry, hostile
behavior is a rehearsal for a still higher level of angry behavior in the
future. What clients learn from a good therapist is that they can take
responsibility, control their angry behavior, and actually choose how
they're going to *respond* to a difficult situation, rather than *react* and
ruin everything good in their lives.

Besides causing heart attacks, poor digestion, and a shortened life
span, anger results in the loss of friends and lovers. Isn't it a pain when
your friend's new lover always has a scowl? Isn't it a downer to be
around someone who barks at you for every little thing? Aren't you
relieved to be out of that old relationship where your lover would
blow up at you out of nowhere? If you're a chronically angry person,
do you wonder why the people who work for you seem frightened
when you enter the room? Do you feel less and less effective after
each angry episode? What do you consider a perfect partner? Can
anyone reasonably live up to your expectations? Is it difficult for you
to find those "perfect" relationships? Are you unsure how to relieve
the tension and stress so you don't explode when someone fails to
meet your standards?

Let's get back to our couple. What went wrong between Cathy
and Jean that turned their love into hostility and distance? Remember the "hint" that was ignored? That's the place where things started
to go wrong. Jean didn't get Cathy's hints. As time went on, Cathy

became angry and hurt that things seemed to be different. After all, she thought, a "good" lover knows what to do without having to be asked; and having to ask means that receiving isn't as good. A "perfect lover" just knows.

Cathy buried her feelings of hurt and disappointment but also continued to let her annoyance grow deeper and deeper. Jean didn't have a clue what was going wrong. She knew that the early feelings of closeness, sharing, and talking about everything seemed to be diminishing. She was depressed, anxious, and confused. The couple started to do things separately as a way to manage their frustration until finally they had a big, angry argument.

The odd thing about arguments is that they closely mimic the early bonding stage of relationships. Each person is listening closely to what the other is saying so they can respond. They're looking at each other. They're sharing feelings and expectations. The behavior is intense, highly emotional, even passionate. When two people care for each other, they find ways to connect; but connection through anger and arguments doesn't nurture a relationship—it destroys it. Closeness and intensity resulting from arguments is a negative.

After Cathy and Jean's big argument, they decided to solve the "problem," but I'm not sure they knew what the problem was. They tried to be extra kind toward each other and spent a lot of time communicating. They went back to being a loving couple, but something was lost. Some of the trust from the early days was still shaky. Cathy and Jean were connected again, but did they do the work they needed to do to stop making circles in the sand?

Clearly, something different has to happen for loving couples to break the cycle of anger and arguing before it's too late. If you and your lover are still at the early "hinting" stage, this is a good place for you to start. If, on the other hand, you're in a long-term relationship, it's not too late to start examining your argument cycle. First talk about the mind-reading expectations and what part hinting plays in your relationship. What do you want your lover to mind read? Is this a reasonable expectation? What does he or she want you to guess about him or her? Do you get upset if your lover doesn't "get" it?

Where did you learn mind reading in your family of origin? Were you expected to do things for others without being asked, or to know how they were feeling without being told? What happened if you didn't? How did your family argue?

Talk about your relationship now that you know it can be vulnerable. What are the goals of your relationship? What is your dream of a "perfect relationship"? Is it to bring your lives together with love? Your way, that is? What does being in a relationship mean to each of you? What scares you about it? Is it difficult for you to ask for what you want or need from someone? Do you become annoyed if you have to ask your lover for what you want? Is your lover less than perfect? How about you?

Talk about intimacy. Do you resort to anger and arguing when your relationship is getting too close for you? What is intimacy to each of you? How can you be intimate and still be individuals? Talk about your arguing cycle and how you each contribute to it. Let each of you come up with three things you're going to do differently, and keep a journal for when you catch yourself doing the same old thing. Write down what you've changed and how that felt. How did your changed behavior make a difference? It's good if you feel a little uncomfortable trying on new behaviors—your discomfort just means you're not doing the same old thing. The old behavior didn't work anyway!

After a week, sit down and go over what was better. Talk about what still needs to change. Try it again. Get a good book on communication skills. Learn how to listen and express yourself more clearly. See a therapist to help you communicate better in a safe environment. Don't be abusive or nasty. Use your sense of humor. Find appropriate ways to relieve your stress, such as joining a gym, or getting back into some old hobbies. Go for walks, take a refreshing bath, take yoga or dance lessons.

Both of you have to take responsibility for what happens in your relationship. You have a choice: you can act with anger, blame, groans, or eye-rolling if things get off track, or you can sit back and problem-solve. Get into the process of being in a relationship that can work over time. Get back into the fun of life. About 2500 years ago, the Greek philosopher Zeno observed that we have two ears and one mouth so that we can listen more and talk less. His conclusion is just as valid today.

Think about this the next time you're ready to tear your lover apart with angry words. Same-sex relationships are tough enough to negotiate without all the baggage we bring that sets us up for failure. Realize that you won't have immediate satisfaction all the time. Don't give up on each other just because you're not a "legally married" heterosexual couple with children to consider. Try to work on being together *with* all the flaws. Then, if after you've tried everything and you still break up, at least it won't be because of anger and arguing. It will be because of real differences that just couldn't be worked out.

Yes, it's true that not every relationship will work, and not every good relationship will last. But anger is a vicious circle that sets a pattern of hurt for the present *and* the future. You both deserve the happiness you can bring each other. Isn't it worth a try?

CHAPTER EIGHTEEN

The "Second Closet"

Gay and Lesbian Partner Abuse

When your partner pushes you, do you push back? Are you being hit or slapped by your partner? Does your partner destroy your property? Do you feel scared or crazy? Does your partner tell you that you make her or him act violently? Does your partner threaten you with suicide or act in a self-harming way, such as driving recklessly? Do you find yourself making excuses for your partner's behavior? Do you work very hard at making sure others will see you as a perfect couple? Does your partner control your money? Do you find yourself isolated from your friends and family? Do you believe that you are at fault for your partner's abuse toward you? Are you afraid to say what's on your mind because of the violent or threatening consequences? Are you ashamed to tell a friend about the abuse? If you answer yes to any of these questions, you are most likely involved in a dangerous and abusive relationship. If you feel trapped, you must find your way to safety.

The topic of domestic violence in the gay and lesbian community is unpopular, but the problem is substantial. Gay or lesbian battering is rarely addressed in therapy, nor is there a lot of publicly accessible information. There are only a very few books or articles on the subject, but these are hard to find and usually need to be special-ordered.[17] There are shelters for abused women, but the shelter population does not reflect the number of lesbians in battering situations. New York City has a shelter for lesbians who are battered, but this is the rare exception. There is no shelter for men in danger, gay or straight.

Unfortunately, gay men are the least acknowledged victims in the area of partner abuse. In all, the problem of gay and lesbian battering is sorrowfully minimized.

There is no system to hold gay and lesbian batterers accountable for their behavior. Because most laws don't recognize homosexual relationships, victims have no legal recourse. Even in nondiscrimination states, judges have "asked the girls to just make up" when one pressed charges. This would hardly be the case for a heterosexual woman who had just been beaten by her husband! Other states have laws that explicitly exclude same-sex relationships from statutes governing domestic violence.

In order to break the wall of silence that shields gay and lesbian domestic violence, we need to understand:

- the nature of the violent behavior
- why the abuse is kept secret
- the differences between homosexual and heterosexual domestic violence

Gay and lesbian domestic violence is a fact of life. A recent study by Kelly and Warshafsky showed that 47 percent of their gay and lesbian subjects use physical aggression and some hitting.[18] Of those, 3 percent use extreme violence, including guns and knives. The only significant difference between men and women is that gay men tend to be more physically aggressive than lesbians.

Domestic and relationship violence takes many forms. In gay and lesbian relationships as well as in heterosexual relationships, the most common form is pushing and shoving, followed by hitting with fists and smacking with open hands. If your partner is throwing things at or around you, or throwing punches or objects at the wall next to you, this is violence. Physical restraint or refusing to let you leave the room is also a form of violence. Stabbing and shooting are rare occurrences—but the fact that these occur at all is very disturbing.

The most common abuse is psychological, especially verbal threats followed by demeaning verbal assaults in front of family or friends; interrupting eating or sleeping habits; damaging or destroying property; forcing a partner to sever ties with family and friends; threatening suicide; and last, abusing pets. Chronic physical or emotional battering is also common. Occasionally, violence can be situational—that is, a one-time occurrence during a crisis. Many explanations are given for gay and lesbian partner abuse, including alcohol, drugs, childhood sexual/physical abuse, jealousy, violence in the family of origin, homophobia, and internalized homophobia—but these "reasons" would be better termed "poor excuses."

The book *Naming the Violence,* edited by K. Lobel, calls homosexual domestic violence "the second closet"—and that's a powerful image.[19] Why the secrecy about gay and lesbian battering? Many feel that the community is silent in order to avoid giving the heterosexist/homophobic society more weapons to use. Another factor is what might be called lesbian invisibility. Women in general are not taken seriously by our legal system—and two women, where there is battering, are taken even less seriously.

Another reason for the complicit silence from women in particular is the premise that the lesbian community strives for a utopian existence, a safe place for women where men cannot violate them. To acknowledge that there are women who abuse women is to admit to a crack in the wall of safety. The fear of admitting to feeling unsafe with another woman keeps many battered lesbians ashamed and in denial.

It's precisely because many lesbians find partner abuse unbelievable that such abuse continues to thrive. The abusers are in the clubs today, fishing for new relationships in which they'll keep on abusing, largely because the abused ex-lovers have kept their secret. In other cases, the secret is revealed but not believed until it's too late for the next victim. In turn, a real problem for gay men is mental health professionals who don't believe that men can be victims of abuse at all. After all, a man "should" be able to stand up for himself, right? Not necessarily.

A common misconception is that, because same-sex couples are about the same in size, strength, and power, one partner is incapable of inflicting any serious harm on the other. This point of view certainly trivializes the problem. In reality, what is called "mutual battering" in gay and lesbian relationships is usually the victim defending against the abuser—and this minimizing causes the victim to be unfairly labeled a "batterer," effectively injuring the victim a second time.

The victim may then become confused by the label, and actually come to feel like a batterer rather than a person acting in self-defense. Because victims often feel responsible for the abuse, labeling the situation "mutual battering" makes it even more difficult for them to break free of the perpetrator. Victims in "mutual battering" situations tend to avoid seeking help because they feel guilty for fighting back. The mutual battering concept is both heterosexist and gender-biased, and denies that gay men can be victims or that lesbians can be perpetrators.

Some victims, in both gay and straight relationships, may even initiate the cycle of violence in order to "get it over with." In this way, the victim at least feels in control of the situation. On the other hand, batterers often see themselves as victims of their battered partner, and therefore justify their initial abusive behavior. "She asked for it," or "He wouldn't stop yelling at me so I had to hit him," are frequent excuses for violence. The end result, when no one speaks up, is perpetuation of the cycle of violence.

The smallness of most gay and lesbian communities makes it very difficult for someone in an abusive relationship to tell about it. After all, your abuser may now be in a relationship with your ex-lover, and they're at the club every Saturday night. Frequently, a former victim complains bitterly that others don't understand why he or she won't at least be friends with the "ex." How hard it is to explain that your lover punched or raped you, when he or she is sitting right there fooling everyone! You might even see your abuser on the television news speaking at a rally about how horrible abuse is, and everyone who knows she is an abuser is all misty-eyed with her speech and in deep denial about holding her accountable. (Such things really happen.)

Further complicating this issue is the unspoken behavior code within the lesbian community that encourages ex-lovers to become friends as soon as possible. Mutual friends might say, "It wasn't so bad.

She didn't hit you that much. And you hit back. How could you press charges against your ex-lover? Why don't you talk to her and be friends? Why are you holding a grudge? You're the mean one. What does this have to say about your ability to be intimate?" A heterosexual woman is much less likely to be subjected to peer pressure to make up with her abusive husband. In fact, a heterosexual woman often has friends who are poised and ready to get her out of the house as soon as she needs help.

Even legal pressures are used against battered lesbians. I've heard lawyers, for example, trying to get the women into mediation in lieu of pressing charges, even in cases where guns were involved! In the case of a heterosexual batterer, the perpetrator would have been jailed instantly; or if not, news reporters would have blasted the legal system for mishandling the case. The heterosexual victim is never asked to sit in the same room with the batterer to "talk it over." What is there to talk about?

Violence is just as prevalent in gay and lesbian relationships as it is in heterosexual relationships, but there are some important differences that need to be dealt with specifically by counselors who are knowledgeable in this issue. Some therapists may not understand that "mutual abuse" is often a smoke screen, and may reinforce the notion that both partners are at fault. Of course, this notion is both false and a homophobic response. *The only person responsible for the abuse is the abuser.*

Some therapists may feel they have a personal stake in helping a victim work things out with the abuser because they have strong feelings about making gay and lesbian relationships succeed. These therapists must keep in mind that the victim, not the couple, is the client seeking help. The victim's welfare must never be undermined by anyone who has another agenda.

Finally, there are therapists who advocate couples therapy for same-sex couples where there is abuse. This doesn't work for heterosexual couples, and it doesn't work for gay and lesbian couples, either. Individual counseling needs to take place before the couple is seen. The abuse must be under control, or no couples counseling is possible.

Why should a batterer in a same-sex relationship be considered any less manipulative, or more able to control his or her violent behavior, than a heterosexual batterer? Batterers need treatment.

It's difficult and painful to admit same-sex battering if it is happening to you. At this very moment, you or a friend may be in trouble and feel too unsafe, scared, or ashamed to tell. Maybe you're remembering a relationship in which you were abused or even raped. Until batterers are held accountable for their behavior, the entire community is compromised. The dream of an egalitarian gay/lesbian lifestyle will remain just that unless this violence is acknowledged and addressed. And until the batterers are identified and their behavior addressed. They'll continue to move from relationship to relationship, abusing their partners.

Some of you think you can "fix" your abusive relationship. You need to know right now that you can't. The abuse isn't about you; it's about your partner. Some of you find it hard to leave your relationship because you've done such a good job hiding the truth that you don't think anyone would believe you. Don't let that hold you back! If you're in an abusive relationship, find a counselor who will believe you. Get help, and above all, get out today. If you're a batterer, take responsibility and get into counseling immediately.

CHAPTER NINETEEN

"Midlife at the Oasis" (and Other Fun Places)

There have been pages and pages written about life's stages! For men, the "midlife" stage seems to arrive somewhere between age forty and age sixty-five—although to hear my gay male clients talk about it, midlife starts at thirty-two or thirty-three, with old age setting in around forty. One man decided at twenty that he had to stay in his repressive relationship because he was too old to find someone else. "At least I have someone!" was his comment.

Lesbians generally call the ages forty-five to around sixty-five midlife. After sixty-five we're called "aging." Lesbians seem more comfortable with the aging process, though, than gay men are; and lesbians over fifty frequently feel they're in their prime. Their careers are more solid; they've resolved being in or out of relationships; friendships are flourishing; their kids have grown. After menopause, feelings of wisdom and a sense of freedom from conventional thinking also seem to flourish for many.

While there is very little published information on lesbian sex, there have been many studies on lesbian aging. Not surprisingly, aging for gay men, or for men in general, is hardly addressed at all. As one client said to me, in confessing to recently lying about his age on a date, "I'm an old queen. To the people I meet for dating, I say I'm thirty-five." He is ten years older. No one seems to want to write about "old queens." "You have to be young, blond, and stupid to get attention these days," he complained. Ouch! his comment made me wince. We've got some work to do.

There are differences between middle-aged gay men and lesbians who have been married and have children, and those who haven't. Lesbians who are now at midlife to "aging" were raised at a time when women's careers were secondary to their husbands'. As a result, midlife once-married lesbians today tend to be in more gender-traditional careers than their younger counterparts. Their earning potential may be diminished because of the years they spent raising children rather than furthering their careers.

These midlife lesbians may be more educated than some younger ones and yet earn less. The reasons may be a fear of being out, limited job choices, or fewer years put into climbing the job ladder. Younger lesbians today are more likely to pursue nontraditional careers and to be less concerned about being out on the job; therefore they're more likely to get involved in corporate policy changes regarding sexuality issues in the workplace.

The midlife gay men who have been married generally have had more freedom to travel on their jobs. In this way they had more opportunities to explore their sexuality than the closeted married lesbians who stayed at home with the kids (although I could recount some suburban wives' stories that would turn your ears red). These men may also have retained less income when they divorced because of the expense of children and the other types of responsibilities that go along with marriage.

Midlife gay men who never married have generally been free of these financial responsibilities. Many of these men were able to spend their early years both pursuing careers and exploring their sexuality. When midlife hits gay men, they often become more interested in developing stable relationships than in remaining in the bar scene. By then, however, they also feel old and unattractive compared with younger men. Tragically, many midlife gay men have lost lovers and friends to the AIDS holocaust and are very lonely and sad. I believe there is often an unaddressed depression in many of these people.

Socialization of girls seems to play a lesser role for lesbians than for heterosexual women at midlife. Nongay women at midlife are more likely to be coloring their gray hair, dieting, going for face-lifts and tummy tucks, and generally trying harder to maintain a youthful appearance. Just look at the media hype on television, in the magazines and advertising. Are midlife to aging women shown in a positive way? Very rarely. And as for fashion, who's that for? Remember *Lear*, the magazine that was produced for the midlife to aging population? Probably not—it didn't last long enough to be noticed, let alone accepted. The *Golden Girls* on television achieved some popularity in portraying the issues of aging women. The movie *Grumpy Old Men*, however, was pretty stereotypical in depicting aging men as lecherous, pontificating creatures.

Interestingly, many midlife lesbians seem to be much less concerned about developing the menopausal belly, getting gray, or dressing comfortably than nongay women—or gay men, for that matter.

When I was growing up, I remember hearing a group of gay men calling each other "auntie," or "you old auntie." I don't hear "auntie" as much nowadays. "Old queen" seems to have taken over. Socialization for boys who grow up to be gay takes an unfortunate twist when they fall prey to the youth-and-beauty stigma/hype directed at heterosexual women. What happens then is that gay men who were socialized to be "masculine" behave toward each other as they were "trained" to behave toward women. To top it all off, midlife gay men have often become very particular about who they're seen with. "Femme" men are frequently considered to be less attractive than "butch" men. "Femme" is not a valued characteristic for gay men, just as women are not as valued in our culture in general. This attitude limits even further the choices for dating and friendship, and it reinforces isolation and depression. Straight women and gay men at midlife suffer from depression more often than straight men and lesbians.

What other little tidbits are lurking at the midlife oasis? There are dozens of other assumptions and generalizations facing those of us at this "stage," and it's important to know what some of them are so you can develop a positive outlook on the inevitable. Yes, the inevitable. So—how about having some fun?

When I was younger, I used to wonder about why I was on earth and the meaning of life. Everything seemed so senseless. But these two questions began to plague me less and less as I began my own midlife years. It seems to me that our mission in life consists of helping others, leading an honest life, and having a darned good time. This is a happy balance. Midlife-to-aging anxiety can turn into a celebration when you realize at forty that you're not going to get any taller, and at fifty that, if you have male pattern baldness, it's okay to shave your head and grow a beard!

Because there was very little information about being gay or lesbian during our youth, and very few role models available, many midlife gay men and lesbians are discovering new ways to prevent the cycle of depression and regret. Actually, we're now becoming the role models for the younger generation, as if that isn't a scary thought! Because there's a certain amount of isolation and internalized homophobia among midlife gay men and lesbians, you may find this information both interesting and encouraging.

Lesbians in midlife seem to want to lighten their workload, and to have more fun and less stress. I've seen many midlife lesbians leave their bank vice president's position at age forty-five to fulfill their lifelong dream of becoming a college coach; leave their administrator's job at fifty-two to sculpt; or leave their computer engineering position at fifty-eight to buy a sailboat, live on it, and run all-women cruises in Key West.

At midlife, gay men frequently start soul-searching and resolving issues of childhood sexual abuse and other family dysfunctions. They begin to balance their relationships and their careers more equally; reconnect with their families; and often look for ways to become self-employed instead of remaining closeted or fearful of career barriers caused by their sexuality. There seems to be more willingness among these men to leave the bars and explore intimacy in their relationships.

By this time in your life, you have friends who are about the same age or whom you've known for a long time. There's a lot of comfort in those friendships, so be sure to keep those connections going. Plan trips together, even if it's just for the day. If your kids are grown, get a smaller place so you'll have less to maintain. Use your new-found time for fun. Learn a new hobby. Get a motorcycle. Get rid of stuff you never use and lighten the feel of your life. What a relief that will be! If something isn't easy, don't kill yourself trying to do it. You don't have to prove anything to your parents anymore—or to your kids, for that matter. Allow a new creativity to enter your life. Stop hanging around with people who are bummers. You don't need naysayers, soothsayers, or negative energy draining your spirit.

If you've gained weight, buy new clothes. With elastic waistbands. If you can't remember things, buy sticky pads and put notes on everything. Can't do the Electric Slide, or the other 1990s moves? Take up ballroom dancing. Having an identity crisis? Have a costume party! Make friends with and embrace those people you turned down at other times in your life. They are themselves, not a reflection of you. Don't get into limiting your social life to people who are just like you. You may be pleasantly surprised!

Go back to some of the things you liked as a child, such as model building, or do one of those great 3-D puzzles of the Kremlin. Are you good at dyke drama? Try acting in a community theater. Want to make your own sushi? Take an adult education cooking class at your local school or college. Want to do drag? Take a sewing class. Or go to college for the first time! You'll be the smartest student in the class.

Start a dine-out club with your friends, or a gourmet club where you take turns hosting theme dinners. Start a book group, an investment club, a storytelling circle, a hiking group, a gay hot line. Provide meals for the elderly or for ill gay men and lesbians in your local community.

Want to date? Get busy and make a list of twenty-five people who are appealing to you. After joking around with names of celebrities, get serious, get numbers, and get going. And I mean lesbians too. Ask your friends to hook you up with others who are single. Go out of town to meet people—you probably know everyone in your community, anyway. There's nothing wrong with dating someone a couple of hours away. Just shift your thinking a little. Stop waiting for someone to come to you. It'll never happen, unless they're reading this book and getting inspired.

Here's a midlife horror story. I knew two women in their mid-forties who liked each other. In fact, they had liked each other for three years. They went on vacations and out to movies and dinners, alone and with friends—but neither of them had ever gotten the nerve to find some way of acknowledging their feelings! They never kissed or did anything romantic. Each was waiting for a sign from the other, and neither would make the first move. Finally, someone in their group said, "Are you a couple, or what?" As far as I know, even this didn't change anything. I always felt sorry for them—they were so stuck in their female socialization of waiting to be asked and delaying gratification that they missed their chance for happiness.

Are you in a relationship but bored with sex? You don't have to leave your lover—you didn't like being single anyway, remember? Get some sex therapy if it's hard to talk with your lover about your sexual needs. Try new positions, new fantasies, new erotica. A new lover is not the solution; you'll just be bored again in a year or so. It's natural to want to change your sex life at some point. It's unnatural not to! But you can work together at it and improve things for both of you.

Stop using those expensive chat lines and dangerous bookstores to meet men. Try networking, sports, and other interesting activities that add to your life. Classes, politics, or a local Pride committee may unearth that perfect man. You know, someone who shares your interests first. I've never counseled a gay man who was really happy about engaging in anonymous sex, so why do it? Find other ways to soothe yourself if you're feeling bad. You'll feel much better meeting someone new if you're not acting out anymore. You really don't *need* to.

Honor your age. Get in touch with your spiritual side. At midlife, this part of you can really begin to bloom, heal, and bring you balance. What does midlife look like, anyway? What does any age look like? Why get caught in the commercial hype of youth and beauty? Why be flattered when someone says you don't look your age? What does that mean? You are beautiful today, just the way you are, if you'll allow yourself that experience. Staying present with yourself will create an inner harmony. Feel your resistance and move with it. You can't change what isn't there.

Midlife at the oasis is a great place to be! So eat your vegetables, be careful crossing the street, dance in the rain, and be confident that your inner wisdom will grow and won't let you down.

CHAPTER TWENTY

"When I'm Sixty-Four"
(On Aging)

"Will you still feed me when I'm sixty-four!" After all these years, the Beatles are still speaking to me. Each time I pass the shock of my own birthday, however, this song takes on a new meaning in my life. In my twenties I liked the song because it was cute—I really didn't take the time to wonder and worry about aging. I mean really *aging,* like Grandma did. But time passes. No longer cute, the song is predicting my near future—and the Beatles' as well!

Several days ago I met a gay man who has to be close to eighty-seven years old. His lifelong companion died this year, and he has no family left. I looked around his sunny apartment filled with the beautiful artifacts of his life. These are now for sale, along with his house, to help pay for the expense of a health care facility. Besides, where would he put his beautiful stained-glass light fixture? He is long retired, with no children, a small pension, and a lifetime of memories that are quickly disappearing to the antique dealers. I can't erase the image of him, with his delicate features, as he sits with quiet dignity at his kitchen table, paying bills and talking about where he is going to spend the rest of his life. I close my eyes and see him in his youth, sitting with his lover on the soft couch, listening to music and reading the Sunday papers as the early evening light pours over them, quietly reviewing the day's shopping tour of Newport. He is precious, he is gay, and he is closeted, like so many of his generation. He is *alone.*

The book *Quiet Fire: Memoirs of Older Gay Men* quoted a gentleman born in 1926 as saying, "I've been gay longer than it's been popular. I was gay when you had to wear red socks to be identified as gay. I walked into a bar in Chicago and had the place go dead on me because I wasn't dressed in the 'gay' style for that city. They thought I was vice!"[20]

The stages of aging are part of life's continuum from birth to death. With each stage we have tasks or jobs that prepare us to continue to live happy and well-adjusted lives. If we miss some of the stages or tasks, they're likely to emerge later on and smack us in the face with reality when we least expect it. For example, if you couldn't deal with your sexuality when you were a teenager, chances are that you'll have to deal with it when you're older. You suddenly become a teenager in a grown-up body. It's very confusing, to say the least, and an experience unlike any in the nongay community.

What are some of the other differences? For those living quiet and contented lives with lover in tow, studies show that growing older as a gay man or lesbian doesn't seem to cause maladjustment. Just like most people, as we grow older we tend to care less about what other people think—and as gay men and lesbians, we seem to care even a little less what they think, especially about our lifestyle. We become more confident or worry less than our nongay counterparts. There is a self-acceptance and a resilience that rises out of a lifetime of dealing with sexism, intolerance, and discrimination. An inner peacefulness flows. Life has been okay. What is, just is. Enjoy. This attitude certainly dispels the myths of aging homosexuals leading lonely, miserable lives filled with despair and remorse.

Some studies suggest that dealing with sexual orientation at a later stage can cause such a major crisis that simply aging is a breeze by comparison. This makes sense to me. Being a gay man or lesbian in the days when the heterosexual majority considered you a "deviant" or "pervert" must make the stressors and adaptations of getting older seem like a piece of cake!

As a result of sexuality issues and an oppressive, sexist society, many gay men and lesbians were married to heterosexual partners for a long time before they realized they were deeply unhappy. On the other hand, as a result of marriage, they have children and grandchildren who are a great source of joy. Those who don't have children may seem less involved with the issues of aging. They haven't had to deal with the various developmental themes involved in raising kids and watching them grow up.

Another unique advantage for older gay men and lesbians is the circle of friends they've developed over the years that's often like family. Those who were adults before Stonewall share a unique history of having lived "The Life" before it was "radical chic" and on the covers of popular magazines. If you're in this age group, you're among the foremothers and forefathers of what became the "gay community."

What really is age, anyway? While age is thought of in groups of numbers—the years of youth, middle life, etc.—a lot of what age is also depends on health. If you're healthy and between the ages of sixty-five and about eighty, you're "young old." If you're "old old," you're between the ages of about eighty and ninety. Anything after ninety can be called "really old" or "the oldest old." The changes of aging are also very gradual. Did you ever look in the mirror and feel shocked for a moment because your face doesn't match how you think or feel? Your face, along with the rest of you, has gotten older, but you've been so busy you didn't notice. This is what life continues to be like as time goes on. My uncle Ben once said that he knew he was getting old when his body could no longer do what his mind wanted it to. This annoyed him no end because he was only eighty-one at the time!

Coming out and not trying to pass as heterosexual is a big part of gay and lesbian development at any stage. When older gay men or lesbians can achieve this coming-out task to a friend, a boss, or a neighbor, they're affirming their entire life and setting themselves free from many years of internalized homophobia. Many do stay deeply closeted, older lesbians more so than older gay men. This is probably out of a habit that developed from the lifelong and pervasive invisibility of lesbians in general. However, it doesn't seem to affect an aging lesbian's high level of satisfaction with life. Older lesbians just seem to be more selective in whom they disclose their sexuality to, and are very well adjusted and comfortable keeping things just as they are.

Marcus was eighty-two years old. He had recently lost Gill, his lover of fifty-three years, and was spending some grieving time with his kid sister, who was seventy-five. Marcus had never come out to his sister, although there was a tacit understanding between them. When Gill died, Marcus wrote an obituary in which he called himself Gill's "surviving partner and long-time companion." This was an act of love and very brave on his part, because they had always been fairly closeted and had a limited number of friends their age. Marcus then told his sister he was gay, using the actual words. His sister's remark was, "I always knew that. I was just waiting for you to say something first." From then on their formerly distant relationship deepened.

Unfortunately, most studies on aging today are only about heterosexuals. Even though there is a large population of older gay men and lesbians, they're difficult to find behind the closet door. Most of the few studies available on gay and lesbian aging address only white, upper-middle-class gay men. Although there may not be a lot of statistical information, more and more older gay men and lesbians are telling their stories, which are rich and powerful.

An elderly woman speaks in *Long Time Passing: Lives of Older Lesbians:* "Just because I'm old and sick and eighty-five doesn't mean I didn't have quite the gay life. You see, I loved a lot of women and a lot of women have loved me. In fact, if I weren't sick that would still be the case....At one point I thought that gay people were no good. But now all these gay people are helping me. It's not my family that is taking care of me; it's my gay friends. I took a bath all by myself today. I'm weak but I can still bathe by myself. You want to know about old age? That's old age."[21]

Happily, because lesbians reject the heterosexual male fantasy of the ideal woman, getting older and grayer with a slightly rounder figure and a few extra wrinkles is more of a badge of honor than for their nongay counterparts.

What will happen to older gay men and lesbians? What will happen to us? Where will you go when you are eighty-five and not as strong as you are now? Do you see yourself in a heterosexual "home for the aged"? After a lifetime of struggling with homophobia, coming out, equal rights, keeping a healthy same-sex relationship, and all the other things at which we grind away in our daily lives, it's hard to imagine.

And what about legal issues? Because our relationships are not sanctioned by law, documents to protect your partner must be carefully prepared. What if you're ill and your partner isn't allowed to visit you or help with your care because the health care facility doesn't have an inclusive policy that addresses sexual orientation?

For years an organization called SAGE (Senior Action in a Gay Environment) has been active in New York City, and it is expanding across the country. I have friends who spend time cooking gourmet "meals on wheels" in church basements for the gay and lesbian housebound elderly. SAGE provides wonderful services for the aging gay and lesbian community, such as sponsoring dances and social justice activities; helping with legal advice; serving as advocates in health care facilities; and offering daily companionship and bereavement counseling. Gay and Lesbian Outreach to Elders (GLOE) also offers assistance with health care, sponsors a variety of social activities, and provides help with legal problems.

What are we doing to help the aging gay and lesbian population? So many of us have talked about that utopian old-age home just for gay men and lesbians. We've had hilarious conversations about what we want the staff to look like. We've made up campy plans about how we want to be treated, how big the closets should be, and how many hat boxes should be allowed. This building isn't among the scheduled construction projects, at least not in my state—yet. Let's make our plans concrete! There are expanding gay and lesbian communities in Florida; let's get one in every state. There are millions of gay and lesbian elders, and we're all going to get there some day. Just as we need to be planning our financial futures, we can also be investing in our future physical well-being.

The elderly are among the most vulnerable members of our society; and older gays and lesbians are at special risk. We should all take action to help our states become socially active for the elderly gay and lesbian population.

But should we fret about aging? Hardly. In the words of the great baseball pitcher Satchel Paige, "How old would you be if you didn't know how old you was?" When you get to be as old as Satchel Paige was, let me know what the answer is.

CHAPTER TWENTY-ONE

"If You Can't Be with the One You Love" (When Your Ex Is Straight)

Mixed-orientation marriages. Now there's a mouthful. Talk about a situation that's complicated, devastating, and once again reeks of socialization and gender training. When a husband comes out gay, the majority of wives I've seen in therapy have tried to stay in their mixed-orientation marriage in some fashion. Women often look for ways to preserve the bond.

Joan's husband Nick came out to her after realizing he could no longer suppress his sexuality. She was devastated by the disclosure, but she reorganized herself in order to maintain the appearance that everything was "all right." Joan even arranged her husband's "gay" social time into their regular calendar, hoping that this would help keep him attached to her. Eventually, though, Joan became the "wife of a gay man," going to his gay-oriented events while she continued to lose her own identity for the sake of keeping her marriage.

Many wives fear—and with good cause—being rejected by friends and family because of a husband's homosexuality disclosure. Joan suffered through this while her husband seemed to be having the best of both worlds. He had his wife, who protected him from having to come out to his family or friends; and he had his gay life, which let him participate in the community where he was most comfortable. Sorrowfully, this story had a tragic end for both. Five years into this semisecret arrangement, Joan nursed her husband until his death from AIDS, leaving her with little or no emotional support from either side.

In cases where the wife comes out lesbian, the marriages often seem to deteriorate more quickly. This is frequently because the lesbian wife falls in love with someone special and no longer wants to participate sexually with her husband. Sometimes the deterioration begins with a short period of three-way sex among the wife, girlfriend, and husband—but when the relationship between the women evolves into love and away from being just friendship with sex, the marriage generally dissolves.

Kayla was married with two children, and she developed a strong friendship with Denise, who was also married. Their hugs goodbye eventually took an erotic turn and the women became sexual. Denise left her husband, which she had planned on doing anyway. Kayla told her husband that she was sexual with Denise. For many months the three of them had a sexual affair or *ménage à trois;* but eventually that broke down, with Kayla's husband becoming furious when his wife clearly preferred Denise. Kayla then left both her husband and Denise to try to find herself. She eventually met Allison and left the area. Denise moved to Texas and swears she'll never be in another love relationship. Kayla's husband was awarded custody of the two kids and remarried within a year.

Now let's backtrack and see what really goes on when a man or woman comes out gay in the context of being married. Keep in mind that in 1948 Kinsey estimated that approximately 15 percent of American white married men between the ages of twenty-one and forty-five had some degree of homosexual contact during the course of their marriage.[22] This study is still considered reliable today, or even a conservative estimate. Kinsey himself believed that the number was closer to 20 percent. That translates to about 4.5 to 5 million gay or bisexual men; and, although there are no such studies for women, you can assume that at least that many lesbian or bisexual women also marry.

Think of it. This is about 10 million married men and women in the United States today who have had bisexual, gay, or lesbian relationships during their marriage. There is no study of how those marriages work out, but obviously many of them don't. Remember that a lot of children come from those marriages as well. Why do all of these marriages happen? What complications and feelings occur? What are some possible resolutions?

Most gay men and lesbians who seek out mixed-orientation marriages do not have any evil intent. If someone purposely seeks out marriage as a cover, with no intention of honoring the relationship, then it isn't being gay or lesbian that's the problem but rather a deeper problem with morality in general. Therefore very few choose heterosexual marriage as a way to hide or to provide a front for their gay or lesbian tendencies. I've seen "front" marriages happen for gay men much more often than for lesbians. But the fact of the matter is that many people, men or women, don't get in touch with their gay or lesbian feelings until they're older, are married, and have families. Some people honestly "forget" their gay or lesbian experiences through a mysterious phenomenon called "repression"—that is, burying an experience so deeply in their subconscious that they may never remember what happened. For many people, a repressed memory will "flash" to the surface years or even decades later, in response to a trigger— perhaps a familiar smell (such as a perfume) or a song or picture. Such a sudden recollection may be startling, making the person feel that the event just happened. People sometimes feel ashamed by their flashbacks or think they're going crazy because the images are so instantaneous and powerful.

Katie, married for fourteen years with three children, told me she had never been sexual with a woman until she met Diane a few months earlier. Suddenly, at age forty-three, she found herself living in two worlds and becoming more and more fragmented. One day, six months into therapy, Katie heard some music from the 1960s and had a flashback of a short, exciting affair she'd had with a woman named Caroline. For nineteen years, Katie had repressed that memory. She had repressed her sexuality because of the role she "needed" to fulfill for her parents—being a dutiful daughter, producing children, being a good wife, and supporting her husband's career. As her children began to grow up, Katie was needed less at home. She began to be more active in the world around her, as she had been as a younger woman. The memory of her brief affair and her sexuality had finally broken through her consciousness one day, when she inadvertently heard music that was popular at the time of the affair. Eventually Katie found that she couldn't take the fragmentation of her dual life, and her marriage broke up bitterly.

Tom mistakenly thought that his short sexual affairs with men were an unimportant stage he was going through that would pass when he got married. When Tom discovered that he couldn't control his sexual impulses, he justified his behavior by saying he was just "oversexed" and didn't want to burden his wife with his need for "relief." Peggy and Tom were childhood sweethearts whose families knew all along that they would be "perfect" together. Seeing no other option, although deeply unsure of his sexuality, Tom married Peggy as he continued his "unimportant" gay sexual behavior. Tom's drinking increased as a way to forget his feelings of self-hatred, and depression set in. As his time outside the household grew, so did his guilt. Peggy had always been his best friend and ally. What would become of them? What would happen to his children? His job? His family? He deeply loved Peggy, but it wasn't enough anymore.

Was Tom in denial? You bet!! Being in denial is like trying to fool yourself—justifying your less than honest behavior, but not very effectively because anyone else can see through it. Tom knew he was attracted to men before he got married. He didn't see having gay impulses as significant or problematic, and he therefore felt justified in acting out. The idea of being gay was so difficult for him to accept that Tom didn't even consider having sex with men as "real" sex. Drinking helped to deaden Tom's feelings so that he could stay married and manage to avoid hating himself. Married men such as Tom often frequent men's bookstores, train station men's rooms, parking areas, and other places that make anonymous sex easy.

So far I've explained several reasons why gay men or lesbians may marry: repression of sexuality; denial of gay or lesbian feelings or behavior; family pressure to settle down and have children; thinking that having children will make their gay feelings go away; homophobia or internalized homophobia; thinking of same-sex feelings as a stage to go through; thinking that gay or lesbian feelings are unimportant even though they're clearly apparent; and prejudice and oppression.

Just as with coming out to your parents (addressed later in this book), the process of coming out to your spouse must be done with a great deal of care and compassion. You've been dealing with your sexuality for a long time, while your spouse may not have a clue. Some people never come out to their spouse, and remain married and silent for the duration. They would rather keep their secret than endure the consequences. I feel that *it's important to respect this decision.* It's a fact for many people, and their choice to stay married and not act on their sexuality is difficult enough without having others judge their decision.

Among those who do come out to their spouses, I've seen a variety of stages and solutions that are positive and affirming. Where there is honesty and kindness, I've seen wonderful friendships evolve between straight spouses and their gay or lesbian mates. My favorite story was showcased for me some years ago at a Pride march in New England. I saw a man and woman holding hands and chatting as they marched. His T-shirt said, "I love my gay ex-wife," and hers said, "I love my straight ex-husband." These two people didn't even have children, and they still found a way to continue their very dear friendship without the horror show I frequently see in my office.

I've had clients who have decided to stay closeted and married rather than risk losing their children, jobs, family, friends, etc. Some couples in which one partner has come out to a straight spouse have reached an agreement to stay together until the children are grown. Both spouses typically agree not to pursue outside sexual interests, although they are not sexual with each other. This is a tremendous sacrifice they make for their children. But going without a loving and satisfying sexual relationship is a tremendous sacrifice for themselves as well.

Many mixed-orientation marriages do have happy endings. One woman, Liz, began to question her sexuality a few years into her marriage. When she told her husband, his response was to drop her off and pick her up at a local social club where she could meet other women. Liz explored other lesbian organizations with her husband's support until she came to realize her lesbian orientation. The divorce was amicable, and the two are still friends today.

We're so lucky that as human beings we can choose our behavior. First we have to allow ourselves to come out of denial and be honest about what's going on. This is hard in a homophobic society that honors only heterosexual marriages. If you are choosing to go through the painful experience of coming out to your spouse, how do you take care of yourself yet still be compassionate? How do you grieve your loss of heterosexual privilege and power and yet celebrate finally feeling good about your sexuality? How do you respond to your straight spouse's anger, despair, and bitterness with kindness when you can barely figure out for yourself what's happening? PLEASE GET HELP! GO FOR COUNSELING!! This is tough for many, but it is necessary.

There has been a lot of damage to your ex-spouse that you may not be aware of. If you haven't been sexual with him or her, then a lot of unnecessary self-blame is going on. Please pick an appropriate counselor who will guide you to a place of healthy disclosure and help you work through everyone's anger and get to healing.

Men who are in denial about their sexuality may accuse their spouses of being unattractive, citing that as their reason for not wanting to have sex with them. If a straight wife wants to have more sex or try new sexual techniques, her closeted husband may deal with his own lack of desire for her by being critical and judgmental rather than looking at himself as the cause. Women are often far too willing to believe they're inadequate; and the wife's self-image and sex drive go right into the "I'm no good" basket, based on a rejection that really has nothing to do with her.

The same can be true for lesbians and their straight husbands. Men, after all, are gender-trained to base a large amount of their self-esteem on sexual prowess, and being unable to satisfy their wives is therefore a major issue. Some men resort to violence when their wife turns out to be a lesbian. When a lesbian wife comes out to her husband, he sees himself as an object of mockery, real or imagined—he "couldn't keep his wife satisfied so she turned to women." Self-doubt about one's sexuality and sexual functioning, whether gay or straight, is a very delicate issue in our culture. After adjusting to disclosure, however, many straight spouses find the knowledge that their mate is gay or lesbian to be a relief. They didn't do anything wrong after all. These issues must be addressed in therapy, if possible, to promote healthy healing for all parties.

Unfortunately, a lot of damage may have already been done by the time you come out. Your spouse may feel violated, deceived, and used while you pursued your sexuality and found yourself. Understand that even though it was agony for you, it was also agony for your spouse. You moved beyond the agreement of your marriage vows. Granted, you had to; but don't expect your spouse to be happy for you—at least not right away. When we step forward in life, we leave something behind; and in this case, what we leave is something that we still should look back upon and honor.

Because gay men seem to take longer to disclose their sexuality to their wives, a lot of damage is done to a woman's self-esteem. In some cases the wife is being put at risk for getting sexually transmitted diseases while her gay husband is still trying to figure out what's going on. I've heard men who have come out complain about how their ex-wife is a witch and angry. Anger is often an important part of healing. Take responsibility for the injury that you inflicted; and understand that if you felt that someone cheated you out of your dream of a settled and happy gay life, you'd be angry and want to strike back, too. Taking responsibility will help you to move along in your new lifestyle with a better sense of yourself, and allow your ex to feel that he or she can move ahead as well.

Children and money are unfortunately used far too often as weapons for striking back at gay men. While an ex-spouse needs anger to heal, exercise extreme caution so that innocent children are not harmed. Be angry—but don't hurt your children. Sometimes gay spouses leave their children behind and never see them again. Women may become vindictive and prevent the children from seeing their gay dads. There are ex-husbands who are so bitter that they forget they helped to create a child's life, and they simply stop parenting. Who primarily suffers in these situations? The children.

No matter what, a child still needs both parents, and everything possible must happen to preserve that bond. I've heard gay men say, "She can have anything she wants so long as I don't lose my children." That attitude alone has helped many people focus, act maturely, and remain fair during a divorce.

Other healing steps for ex-spouses include getting back in touch with their own sexuality by beginning to date again and rebuild their self-esteem. Over time, many ex-spouses are able to reestablish friendships with each other. I've seen Christmas dinners include a gay ex and his lover. I've seen second wives and lesbian ex-spouses volunteer time and money for the weddings of the children in their lives. Will this happen in a year? No, that's unrealistic. We're looking at a long process, over several years. Time, healing, compassion, counseling, education about homosexuality, maturity, and taking responsibility are the key components in extending our current links to the past and the future.

While there may be a lot of support for gay men and lesbians who are coming out, there is little visible support for ex-spouses. There is more published information available for spouses of gay men than for spouses of lesbians; and there is more information for gay men coming out of marriage than for lesbians in the same circumstance. The best support you can find in your area comes from finding others in similar situations. Ex-spouses should try to find a support group or counseling group, or they can contact:

Parents, Families, and Friends of Lesbians and Gays (P-FLAG)
1012 Fourteenth Street, NW, Suite 1030, Washington, DC 20005
Phone: 202-638-4200
E-mail: pflagtl@aol.com
World Wide Web: http://www.pflag.org

It's important to understand that the spirit of being gay is not just about sex—it's also about an emotional connection. When two people truly love each other, they find that there are many ways to express that love, and many lovers find or create wonderful solutions to even the most perplexing problems.

I want to end this chapter with a story about how two people loved each other so much that sexuality was not an issue. It's a true story. Once upon a time there were a young boy and a young girl named Raymond and Renee who grew up together in a small town. They were best friends who fell in love and got married—but all of Raymond's life he felt that he should have been a woman. When they were teenagers, he and Renee used to talk for hours about their relationship, how they loved each other, and what they were going to do about his feelings of not being who he wanted to be. Eventually Raymond and Renee got married, but he still felt all wrong in his body. After counseling and much talking together, Raymond began to take female hormones—the first step toward surgery for changing his sex.

Renee and Raymond are still together. They are now a lesbian couple. Together they faced a lot of community adversity, personal agony, and societal pressure, but they are still in love. Both are productive and happy with their lives. Most of all, they set an example for all of us: that no matter what our orientation is, when two people care about each other, with honesty it *is* possible to find positive ways to stay connected to one another with respect, support, and willingness to adapt to what life has in store—even if we never heard of it before!

CHAPTER TWENTY-TWO

To Bi or Not to Bi

Is This a Question??

A friend likes to remind me, "I have never had a heterosexual feeling in my entire life." And he is proud of it! Then there are friends who tell me they've never had homosexual feelings in their entire lives, and I believe them, too. But what about all the rest of us? Is everyone else bisexual? Is someone bisexual who is coming out of a heterosexual relationship and just beginning to identify as gay or lesbian? Or if he or she is in transition from gay to straight? (Yes, that happens, too.) Is someone who has both gay and nongay sexual relationships simultaneously, bisexual? Is someone bisexual who has nongay relationships for a while, then gay relationships for a while? Some believe that the answer to *all* these questions is yes.

Here are some more questions. In a scenario in which someone who is gay or lesbian, living in a limited environment (such as an island like Nantucket), gets married because there is no gay community, is he or she bisexual? For a real stretch, I have a friend who at first appearance looks like a straight man. He resembles a Maine logger, full beard and all, but inside he feels like he's a lesbian. His lover IS a lesbian. What is he? What is she? Bisexual? Ambisexual? Flexisexual? What are you? In the words of my son, "Whose business is it, anyway?" But, then, he comes from a generation and a segment of the culture in which a great many young adults consider themselves bisexual.

Frankly, there just isn't enough information or scientific research on bisexuality to give a hard-core definition. Sexuality by itself is very difficult to research, because so much of what we know is based on what we say, what we feel, or what we've experienced. While this is very important information, categorizing based on everyone's sexual stories simply isn't scientific. Bisexuality is especially complex and just can't be pigeonholed into a neat little definition—but this is the Western world, where everyone likes to feel secure and well defined. So here are some definitions of bisexuality.

Let's start with Freud again. Simply put, Freud said that everyone is inherently bisexual, but that sexual development *through* bisexuality and into heterosexuality is the only normal path.[23] It was okay to be bisexual until puberty, at which point we supposedly outgrow our homosexual tendencies to become heterosexual, or vice versa. Of course, if you don't get to the heterosexual stage, you're considered immature and emotionally stuck at a very young age—the "age" of bisexuality. A bisexual, according to Freud, is someone who is both homosexual and heterosexual at the same time.

Bisexuality can indeed be a stopping place on the path of our innately fluid, lifelong *sexuality process* where we choose, on some level, our sexual behavior based on what is acceptable at the time. Therefore, when society is repressive, most folks subconsciously choose heterosexuality, with a few defining themselves as gay or lesbian and, to a lesser extent, bisexual. In a less repressive society there is a distinct swing (sorry) toward more bisexual behavior.

Is bisexuality halfway between homosexuality on the one side and heterosexuality on the other, with varying degrees of orientation in between? Wouldn't it feel safe if we could neatly plot sexual behavior on a bell curve? No such luck! Pinpointing a certain sexual behavior spot denies the existence of the full range of a person's sexual expression over a lifetime.

I like my clients' definitions of bisexuality far better than any I've found in books. Clients who describe themselves as bisexual tell me they're open to exclusive relationships with both men and women, with the same amount of emotional and physical intimacy in either case. Most are in exclusive relationships with one partner. I know of some, however, who are mutually exclusive with their same-sex lover and heterosexual lover at the same time, where three people form a lifelong bond! Clients say that, for them, bisexuality is about openness and relationships rather than sexual preference.

I hope to dispel the myth that someone who is bisexual just flits from one type of sexual relationship to another in a nonmonogamous and whimsical fashion. A person who can't commit to a relationship and continually sleeps around could be of any sexuality, and most likely has problems with sex addictions, relationship addictions, and intimacy issues. Continual sexual acting out is about character, not sexuality.

The oppression of bisexuals is similar to the oppression of gay men and lesbians and comes from fears and myths. Sometimes discrimination against bisexuals is seen in gay men and lesbians as well as in nongays. Bisexuality shakes us up because we like to know exactly what to expect from our environment. In this context, bisexuals are often perceived as a threat, or as predators who will lure your mates away no matter what sex they are. Are we that insecure? This is biphobia. Just like homophobia, biphobia assumes that bisexuals can "recruit" people into their sexual orientation.

The resentment of lesbians toward bisexual women is that many bisexual women will take advantage of heterosexual privilege when it is advantageous for the moment, abandoning their lesbian lover when the pressure is on to be straight. Middle-aged and older lesbians in particular feel that they've worked hard to build a women's safety net, which a bisexual woman then uses when she's with women and abandons when she's with men. There is some truth to this perception. This type of behavior, however, has to do with the character of the person and not her bisexuality.

Sexually transmitted diseases (STDs) are on the rise in the lesbian community. Women who sleep with men and then sleep with women in a promiscuous fashion can carry HIV, herpes, and other STDs. Again, ignoring safer sex precautions is not about sexuality but about individual behavior. Lesbians can transmit STDs even if they've never had sexual contact with men. It only takes one sexual contact to pass herpes, for example, and there's a lot of it going around these days.

There are a number of married men and women who call themselves bisexual but aren't. There are men, for example, who claim that they're just following their bisexual nature by having sex with men while being married to women. If someone is bisexual and makes a commitment to a heterosexual partner, then regardless of their other sexual desires, some self-control over their sexual acting out should be possible. If it's true that being bisexual means you can love someone of either sex equally, then why the urgency to act out same-sex behavior in the context of marriage? In these cases there are probably deeper issues having to do with being gay.

Here's an example of what I mean. Last week I decided to see what the Internet had to say about bisexuality. I found a couple of support groups for bisexual married men, and one for wives who are married to bisexuals. This is good, I thought. Then, to my great disappointment, there was page after page of pictures of married men advertising themselves as bisexual, cruising for gay sexual encounters. This upset me! I have clients with serious sex addictions who report to me the numbers of married men they encounter in the bookstores and rest stops. Is this bisexual behavior? Is marriage, in these cases, a cover-up for being gay but unable to come out? Sadly, much of this behavior is both addictive and deceptive, and makes those who are truly bisexual cringe.

Sexual addiction is a profound betrayal of the women and children who are part of the addicts' lives. I'm not talking about someone who is discovering he's gay and is confused, trying to deal with his sexuality and the coming-out process. There's bound to be some acting out in this situation. I'm talking about someone who is cavalier about his "bisexual" activity and gets angry with his spouse because she suspects something, or because she has no clue what's going on, or gets clingy or bitchy, or is just plain depressed.

There are also a growing number of women who are acting out with women while married. Their behavior tends to be underground, with a greater tendency toward attachment to a lover and a much higher incidence of eventually leaving the marriage than for men in the same situation.

In many cases, spouses knew of their husband's or wife's same-sex feelings or activities before they were married but "hoped for the best." Marriage seemed like a good way to stifle a gay or lesbian orientation that may be disturbing and difficult to acknowledge. If you find yourself in this struggle, you may be bisexual or you may be coming out as gay or lesbian. It would be a really good idea to talk to a therapist before you make any decisions.

There are also differences between men and women who are bisexual. Bisexual women, for example, are more accepting of their first same-sex experience. Because of the closer friendship style for women, sex for many just feels like a natural extension of that bond. The sex was about love for the woman friend rather than about defining theirs as a "lesbian" relationship.

Bisexual men, on the other hand, get pretty upset when they have their first same-sex encounter. Women aren't tied up with society's view of femininity as men are about masculinity. Having homosexual sex, for many men, is a direct threat to their gender training, which places "masculinity" as a measure of a man's self-worth. Homosexual behavior for men does not fit into society's definition of masculinity, and men are therefore more likely to be ashamed and go underground with their feelings.

Another difference between men and women who are either bisexual or unsure of their sexuality is that while there may be a greater number of married men having homosexual contact within the marriage, there seem to be a greater number of lesbians having heterosexual contact while still referring to themselves as lesbians. I guess that clears things up for now!

Bisexuality is about having sexual as well as emotional or love attraction for both sexes. There is a bisexual coming-out process just as there is coming out for gays or lesbians. Coming out bisexual is very complex and isn't typically complete until the mid-twenties. In this process, there are many things to consider. Check in with a good therapist who can help you sort it out. Don't be afraid to ask a professional whether he or she is knowledgeable in sexuality issues—especially yours! Be sure the therapist is affirming as well as helpful. If you go to support groups, be careful and take the time to assess what you're hearing. Talk about what you see and hear with your therapist. Try to find some reading material about bisexuality. There are often chapters about it in gay and lesbian self-help books.

Bisexuality! Now there's a happening topic of the late 1990s. After all, sex is one of humankind's most intriguing behaviors, and bisexuality is fascinating because of all the possibilities. Woody Allen humorously summed things up in one of his "poor me" routines when he said he thought of becoming a bisexual because it would double his possibilities for a date. I guess there's always a funny side to our struggles!

CHAPTER TWENTY-THREE

Coming Out in Your Forties, Your Fifties, and — Yes — Your Sixties!

Just when you thought your life was all set, you have an epiphany and—omigawd!—you're gay. Does it really happen like that? Somehow I think not. Actually, the coming-out experience for an older man or woman can be quite agonizing, especially if he or she is married with children. If you leave your heterosexual lifestyle, your entire life and the lives of everyone you know will be changed forever. And not happily—at least not for a while.

Richard was sixty-two years old when he told his wife that he had same-sex emotional and physical feelings he could no longer contain. He had never acted on his sexuality, although he was aware he was gay before he married. Now he was becoming seriously depressed. Richard has grown children—even grandchildren. Now what? He has been married to the same woman for thirty-three years. They're best friends. They have an entire life together.

Tearfully, Richard asked when he was going to have the life he longed for and dreamed about. His wife, however, was devastated and shocked by Richard's long-term deception. These were supposed to be their golden years of retirement and relaxation. They had always been partners, and now this! Even though Richard and his wife tried an open relationship for a short time, the experience was too difficult for both of them. They didn't know what to do.

Chad didn't wait until he was in his sixties to tell his wife about his same-sex feelings. He had hoped, secretly, that getting married would "cure" him of these urges, but when that didn't happen he eventually told his wife the truth. Together, Chad and Sandra made the decision to stay married, raise the children, and not act out sexually. This arrangement lasted for quite a few years until Sandra finished college, which she had given up to stay at home and be the "good wife." As Sandra's self-esteem grew from her new independence, she healed from her feelings of sexual inadequacy and anger. Eventually the couple divorced, but they remain close friends. They even march in Pride together.

Joan has three young children between the ages of six and eleven. She hasn't told her husband about being a lesbian, nor does she plan to act on her emotional or sexual feelings. Actually, Joan never really knew why she felt different desires growing up, so her sexuality is still very new to her. The thought of pulling her family apart just to act on her sexuality is abhorrent to Joan. She and her husband haven't been sexual for quite a while, and she's beginning to think that he suspects her of having an affair. How far that is from the truth! Joan had always dreamed about having the perfect family, but now she feels perfectly trapped.

Susan is in her forties, married with children—and, out of the blue, it seemed—she began an affair with an older woman. For a long time she didn't consider it an affair as such. "After all," she would say to me, "we weren't really having sex." I raised my eyebrow in a way that my clients have come to know very well, and she stopped in mid-sentence. Guess what? You don't need to have a penis to have sex! Susan had a couple of affairs during her coming-out period. Eventually she left her marriage and gained custody of her children.

If you're already out as gay or lesbian, you may be having a tough time understanding how some people don't realize they're gay until so much later in life. It might be difficult to comprehend why someone who knows he or she has same-sex feelings still marries and has children. And that's the point! Some people are so out of touch—scared because of religion, or oppressed by socialization and family expectations—that the possibility that they're gay or lesbian doesn't even occur to them until they reach a certain level of education, confidence, depression, or frustration.

The 1940s and 1950s were plagued by gay "witch-hunts" orchestrated by Senator Joseph McCarthy. The movie *The Children's Hour*, a black-and-white *film noir*, portrayed one woman's innocent love for another as having ruined both their lives. Yes, let's love each other and be ruined! *The Well of Loneliness*,[24] written in the 1920s by Radclyffe Hall, is a classic tragedy about a tomboy who grows up to love women. How about that uplifting title?

In times past, being gay or lesbian made you a social and political target. In most states it still does. Until 1974, the American Psychiatric Association considered you mentally ill and without hope if you were gay or lesbian. A few brave women in the 1950s started a clandestine lesbian organization called the Daughters of Bilitis, but typically you had to be in a major city to connect with such a group.

During the two decades after World War II, society emphasized family, children, and tract housing in the new suburbs. The "little woman" stayed at home and raised the children. In general, women were isolated. Men worked hard all day to support the American Dream. Girls were raised to be secondary to boys, with career choices only as nurses or teachers. "Just a little job to make pin money and to pass the time when the kids get older." Until recently, these perennially underpaid positions were considered "women's work." They certainly didn't pay enough to allow a woman to make it on her own—but then, that wasn't considered necessary or important.

I don't mean to say that it was easier for men who were married and gay, but the opportunities were different. Men's careers often took them to urban settings where they could act on their gay sexuality anonymously and stay married. In the 1940s and 1950s there were underground clubs for gay men. I had a good laugh one day when a friend of mine was talking about a club in Chicago where the signal to be identified as gay was to wear red socks. So for years he always looked for men with red socks. There was also a "pinkie ring" signal, but I was never quite sure if that was for real!

Finally there was Stonewall, the 1969 riot outside a bar in Greenwich Village, New York, where gay and lesbian patrons had been regularly harassed, beaten up, and arrested. For the first time, they fought back and rioted against the police brutalization that had been typical for most gay establishments. The Stonewall riot was the birth of Gay Pride and the Pride marches taking place all over the country today.

Now laws and the courts are the big challenges. Gay fathers and lesbian mothers don't leave their marriages with ease, either emotionally or financially. The "unfit to parent" battles for legal custody or visitation rights can be grueling. In one recent shocker, a young girl was taken away from her mom simply because the woman is a lesbian. The child was then awarded to the ex-husband *after he had been found guilty of murdering his first wife.* According to this court decision, being a lesbian is a lot worse than being a murderer, at least in the state where this case was decided.

In another, more typical case, a husband planned to "out" his ex-wife in court just to harass her and jeopardize her job, even though he had no desire to get custody of his two children. He was told by his lawyer to "shut up" lest he wind up with his children as a result. This father used his kids in a four-year courtroom vendetta against his ex-wife; and the children were so harmed by his behavior that eight years passed before they began to talk to their father again. The mother is still paying off her lawyer after having exhausted all her assets just to survive the court battle.

Some courts assume that gay fathers and lesbian mothers have no sexual control and will do anything for sex, including having sex with their own children. A well-known statistic, however, proves that 97 percent of child molesters are heterosexual men. Sadly, the many horror stories like the ones I've just mentioned can keep a middle-aged man or woman from coming out.

As usual, socialization plays a big part in configuring what happens when a married person comes out gay or lesbian. From my own practice and in the practices of others, I've observed a trend among gay men to stay married, with the support of their wives, who will go to great lengths to keep the family together. Women are socialized to see themselves in the context of "other," and will frequently do this with their gay husband until they develop more "self." After the rage and disappointment at this unexpected turn, these women often begin to grow and prepare for the independence they need to eventually move on. In the meantime, however, the children still have two parents who love them and are mindful of their situation while remaining friendly toward each other.

In therapy, after the grieving and rage subside, the couple may work out a contract where the gay husband is allowed to be sexual outside of marriage. Somehow the "being sexual" without the emotional component works for a while. Once there is an emotional bond between male lovers, the marriage is more likely to fall apart, but this may be many years away. Coming out while married is very different from coming out at eighteen!

For women coming out in marriage, the situation is also very different. Their husbands seem to have more rage, and, at least at first, to be more shattered. Socialization puts so much emphasis on male sexual performance that the idea of a man's wife preferring a woman seems ludicrous, impossible, and a real insult to the husband's masculinity. Remember Susan's husband and the court battle? Her husband used revenge, money, and spite to make himself feel "masculine" and powerful once more, and to reduce his perceived shame. Susan's own lawyer even commented that if Susan had been to bed with a "real man" she wouldn't have these feelings for women. Susan often wondered why her case went on so long and cost so much. In retrospect, though, the answer is clear.

Whether you have children or not, when you come out older there are special issues to consider. A fifty-two-year-old woman tells me she is enjoying sex for the first time. Her lover is fifty-seven and also "new." However, they don't consider themselves lesbians. The couple keeps breaking up and getting back together. They're confused, feel sinful, and don't know how to act with friends. They're suddenly afraid to be seen in public after they've been friends and traveling companions for years, and are afraid to stay at each other's homes because of what the neighbors might think. There are no social supports and a tremendous fear of being caught. They have questions about sexual techniques but won't go near the gay/lesbian section of a bookstore. This almost sounds as if I'm talking about a couple of fifteen-year-olds. From an emotional development aspect, I may as well be. And what is interesting is that many older gays and lesbians feel this way!

Older men face the struggle of the "gay lifestyle" being extremely youth- and muscle-oriented. Whereas an older single straight man is almost always a prize to the majority of single straight women, in the gay world these men are "old queens." This new way of life can be quite a depressing shock for a man who may only have had casual sexual experiences over the years.

Perhaps a reverse example would be helpful to understand the dilemma of coming out older. Pretend you're forty-four and unsure whether you're really a lesbian. You've always wanted to be straight, but your sexual experiences have always been with women and you don't know where to start. Since you probably don't have any straight friends, you go to a straight bar where there's line dancing. This seems safe enough. You know your line dancing from the lesbian bar. Say you have a few drinks and you want to leave. Then some guy offers to walk you to your car. You think, "Isn't that nice?" Suddenly he gets pushy and tries to force you to have sex.

What did you do wrong? You have no idea. You're used to leaving the women's bar with friends; or the bouncer watches out for you as she always has. If you push away a woman who makes rude advances, she'll most likely apologize. You feel physically confident in your home environment, and now you simply don't know what to do when you try to enter the straight world. You don't know the pitfalls, the lure, the community, the safety measures you must take, the signals to give or how to give them.

If you're a gay man coming out straight at forty-four, what are you going to do? Women are all over you at the bar. You feel pressured by them for sex but you don't know how to approach it. Gay men are more accustomed to an anonymous sexual environment, but with women more intimate social foreplay is required. You offer to walk a woman to her car, and make a pass, only to find your face slapped. What did you do wrong?

A forty-three-year-old client swallowed her pride and went to a college coming-out rap session weekly for a year. Her drive to be with lesbians or others coming out, though younger, was very strong. She even ended up having an affair with one of the group members. The following school year she went back to the group, but only twice. She realized she no longer fit in. She had outgrown the group and moved on to exploring the next level of development.

If you are coming out older, you have a lot to learn that you didn't get to in your youth. You have to maintain your current level of career and family development while going through a sort of second adolescence. It's very important to develop a social network. In my state there's an anonymous group for married lesbians. Many states have gay and lesbian parent support groups. You may find yourself losing some people who were your friends, and your children may lose some of theirs. Your religion may feel funny to you until you can come to terms with your spirituality. Read about gay/lesbian sexual development. Find a gay hot line. If you live near a college or university, see what gay or lesbian services are available—maybe a class where you might meet some supportive adults to help you through. The first three years are the roughest, but before you know it you'll have no regrets about finding your identity. Give yourself a chance to grieve your losses of heterosexual living and then open up your heart to the gains of being who you are. Welcome the blessings of coming out to yourself and living a more harmonious life.

CHAPTER TWENTY-FOUR

You Can't Be My First, but You Can Be My Favorite

There's nothing in the world like Women's Week in Provincetown! Commercial Street is packed with three thousand ex-girlfriends and their current lovers. Some arrive on their own and some pile into cars together for a week of comedy, music, shopping, and lots of drama. You know, "dyke drama."

Trudy and Lydia, celebrating their first year together, were sitting in a cafe situated on a balcony above street level. They were passing the afternoon cruising the women below and enjoying a flawless, clear Women's Week October day. Lydia was feeling especially romantic about their anniversary. Suddenly Trudy jumped up.

"There's Maggie! I can't believe my eyes! You know, the one who moved with me to grad school in Colorado! I was so in love with her, then she broke my heart. You remember. I told you how she broke my heart? I'm so glad she's here."

"Oh, Maggie, Maggie!!" Trudy's voice echoed into the street as she leaned over the rail of the balcony.

Looking back over her shoulder, Trudy searched Lydia's eyes with a hopeful look. "You don't mind, do you, honey? It's been years since I've seen her."

At that moment, Lydia had some very important decisions to make. She could: be jealous and storm off; make a fuss and be miserable; cry; beg Trudy not to spend time with Maggie; beat herself up about Maggie, who is younger, bigger, and more Trudy's "type"; test Trudy's love by making her choose who she wants to spend their first anniversary with; and plenty more *drama du jour* where that came from. Surely you see the potential.

Lydia was smart, however. Even though she was disappointed that their anniversary plans were obviously going to change, she smiled and was as gracious as she could be. Trudy wasn't sure what to expect, having just emerged from a relationship with the jealous drama queen from hell.

Well, the afternoon had a happy ending. The three women got along very well during cocktails, with lots of kidding around and hugs goodbye for all. Trudy was sensitive and carefully included Lydia in conversations that could have otherwise been uncomfortable. Happy and relieved that Lydia enjoyed Maggie's company, Trudy's love and respect for Lydia deepened. Lydia was also relieved, because even though she knew that Maggie was the love of Trudy's life, clearly that was in the past and Trudy had moved on.

Because Maggie was so cute, Lydia had to ask Trudy if she was still attracted, and the answer Trudy gave was wonderful. "Seeing Maggie was fun, but in spending just a short time with her today, I remembered all the reasons why we broke up." Interestingly, Lydia was herself attracted to Maggie. This is not an uncommon phenomenon. After all, since you're attracted to your lover, the chances are that she will have had lovers you'll be attracted to as well. There's a kind of sameness or familiarity that many find appealing.

There was a little dyke drama that week, but it didn't come from our friendly trio. Trudy, Lydia, and Maggie were holding and swinging hands, walking down the street with Trudy neatly tucked in the middle of her two favorites. She was beaming and surrounded with love. Then, out of nowhere, a little black sports car lurched out of a side street where the trio was about to cross. When the car screeched to a halt, who was driving but Trudy's last ex's current lover, who kind of had it in for Trudy. The trio stopped cold. It was a stand-off on Commercial Street. Trudy and her ex's lover were glaring at each other, with each signaling for the other to go first. Trudy wouldn't go first because she was sure she'd get run over. Maggie pushed up the sleeves of her leather jacket and adjusted her mirrored sunglasses, James

Dean style. Lydia held tightly to Trudy's hand. Finally everyone, including the driver, chuckled to break the tension, and the car took off with a squeal. Maggie and Lydia shook their heads at Trudy as they began holding and swinging their hands again, laughing like old friends.

When gay or lesbian couples break up, it's like losing a best friend as well as a lover. Even if you didn't get along with your partner, there is longing and despair over the loss. How is this different from nongay relationships? Because of the small community of friends and the shared struggles that are part of being a stigmatized minority, gay men and lesbians are more willing to make friends with ex-lovers. For lesbians it seems almost mandatory. Judith, for example, kept a shelf of pictures, almost like an altar, of all her ex-girlfriends. When she was sick in the hospital, her exes all got together and had their picture taken at the club for a get-well card! Judith swears their love helped her get better faster.

Mythology about exes abounds in the lesbian community—and I'm here to report that it's all true. Sitting in the therapist's chair, I've often been tempted to draw the family tree of the lesbian community where I live. I think it all goes back to Eve! Or Melissa! Keep in mind the expression "What goes around, comes around!"

Here's what I mean. Merri has a softball party to celebrate the end of the season. Bobbie invites Sally, who was introduced by Kim, who is Merri's ex-lover and the roommate of Donna, who is dating Nicole. Nicole also dated Merri's ex-lover, Ellen, who is also an ex of Kim and Donna. At one point I had to turn away clients because, one after another, women from this group began calling me for therapy. First I saw one couple who broke up. After a few months I began to see a friend of one member of the couple, who then became her lover while she was in therapy. Then I saw the ex of the ex who was still in love with my client's ex, who was the ex of both the women in the original couple that broke up. By then the original couple had become the best of friends. Now the entire crowd goes away to ski every winter. They have a ball. Really!

By the end of two years I knew the entire crowd, at least by name if not by face. I had to stop seeing anyone new in that group, now called Group A, because I knew too much about them. When word got around that I wouldn't see anyone new from Group A, future clients made it a point of telling me in their phone interview that they were only on the sidelines of Group A and not the ex of any of them. They had their own group of exes, they said, and were only friends with Group A women. "For now," I thought.

After time and healing, I've seen exes shop together, go into business together, lend each other money, and invite each other to parties or vacations with new lovers included. You don't see this phenomenon after a heterosexual divorce. Can you imagine your father going to Disneyland with his current wife and your mother? Hardly! But keep in mind that this friendly reconciliation doesn't happen overnight. (Well, sometimes it happens overnight, just to see if the breakup is really final.)

For some reason, men handle the "ex" dilemma quite differently than lesbians do. One way isn't better than the other, just different. Probably because of socialization and intimacy differences, gay men don't require exes to be friends forever to the same degree as lesbians.

Gay men also seem to need less processing time after the relationship ends. I've seen lesbian couples break up in counseling with their gay male therapist who really thought the relationship was over. A year later the couple may still be living together and talking with a lesbian therapist about how to separate down to the next level. I've also seen gay men who are still living together after a year, but to a much lesser extent. More than likely, by the end of a year, they may also both be in new relationships while still living together.

How can two people *who were totally incompatible as lovers* then become friends without some dramas in between? Sometimes they do, but often I think the drama is necessary on some level. There's no formal divorce and courtroom drama for a gay or lesbian couple to formalize the end of their relationship. There's no legal marriage to get one started. Without these guidelines, gay men and lesbians too frequently slide from one relationship to another so quickly that old wounds don't heal. The sad joke now is, "I'd like you to meet my next ex-lover." By having a little dyke drama, or a little hissy fit, at least you have time to see what a total loser your ex was and be glad to have done with him or her. The drama becomes a divorce, of sorts, but it's not very esteem-building or even necessary.

Unfortunately, some of the breakup stories I hear aren't very pretty. Getting "divorced" with respect and dignity is certainly preferable. Some couples hire mediators to help divide the belongings, to help the separating couple decide when and how to make future contact, and to have some kind of ritual for the end of the relationship that honors both people. All too frequently there is acting-out anger and rage between two people who once felt love. Low drama, the less damaging acting-out behavior, will soon be forgotten by everyone in your crowd. This kind of behavior includes dumping on an ex at a party, discussing sexual fetishes and other hot gossip, tears and sobs at a concert, long nights of grieving with friends, burning letters and cards, a screaming match in public, sleeping in a car on a chilly night, wandering around the dunes alone, getting your hair cut just like hers, sleeping with her last ex-lover, calling her family and complaining, barbed comments at the bar, or maybe something more creative, like black balloons delivered to her big dinner party. If this is the only public display that's going to happen after the breakup, then it's not the worst.

Breaking up can escalate into high drama, however, causing real long-term harm, which certainly ruins the chance of friendship. Breaking into an ex's house to steal, not returning valuables, damaging property, stalking, making physical threats, moving into his best friend's apartment after telling a lot of lies, making false suicide threats, getting drunk and having bar fights are good examples of high drama and the reasons why you probably broke up with that person to begin with. Damaging, vindictive behavior will certainly make friendship improbable later, and it also divides the community and ruins self-esteem. If, for a fleeting moment, you miss being with this person and feel you have to do something, have your friends hold you back.

Breaking up can be devastating. You're faced with having to rebuild your life alone. When this happens, it's time to refocus on what you want for yourself first and foremost. Among other things, you need to spend some time evaluating what your part of the problem was in the relationship as well as your ex's part. Figure out what was good and what worked, as well as what you don't want to repeat in the future. After the struggle of the transition period, you'll find yourself ready to be fully reinvolved with friends and enjoying life again.

It's so important to take your time before getting into a new relationship. Yes, the comfort of immediately having someone new by your side is reassuring—but remember, you are still intensely engaged in your last relationship. How could you possibly give your new lover the attention he or she deserves? By postponing and avoiding the healing pains of anger and unresolved hurts from the past, you are delaying the inevitable and sabotaging your future. If you become involved with a new lover too quickly, you may be in a rebound situation that will not last very long. If you're soothing your hurts by acting out sexually, chances are you'll just make yourself feel worse. *Grieve your loss* before you move on. Why repeat the same problems you've had in other relationships just because you're in a rush to feel better right now? Remember, your next love can't be your first, but he or she can be your favorite. And your best!

CHAPTER TWENTY-FIVE

Passing the Torch

Don't Give Up the Fight

If you are between the ages of twenty-two and thirty-four, this chapter is for you. Now that you're out in the world on your own, do you feel kind of lost sometimes? After softball, after an evening at the bar, after a day at work and a night alone, what are you thinking about? Do you feel connected to the gay and lesbian community? Is there a "community" feeling for you? Is there a gay "lifestyle" you feel good about? Are you excited about your life as a gay man or lesbian?

You are in a place between adolescence and midlife that no one seems to be addressing as a special period of gay and lesbian development. Sure, there are books on gay and lesbian relationships and on gay and lesbian recovery. There are gay and lesbian travel guides, how-to books on gay sex, and books on how to cut your hair, how to come out to your parents and the world, how to be a gay parent, and even how to become a spiritual gay person. But what about all the space and time in the middle when you're not getting your hair cut or cruising the clubs?

Many of you didn't come out in high school when all your hetero-sexual friends and classmates were getting those approving looks at the Winter Ball. You may have thought you were bisexual, which is fine, because many of you were exploring your sexuality and weren't sure. Some of you may really be bisexual, and some of you are gay or lesbian. So here you are at twenty-four, and you missed out on what is called "normal" adolescent social development. When you left home and school you may have felt relieved, although somewhat scared to be on your own. Now you have to address your sexuality as an adult. But with whom? Where? First you have to learn how to date as a gay man or lesbian, but all you know about is the bar scene and that seems bleak. There just doesn't seem to be anything happening for you these days. Life in the 1990s with no big excitement.

During the 1950s I remember feeling that nothing of any interest was happening for my generation, either. I hungered for anything beatnik and the beat generation, but by the time I was old enough to participate, those things had passed by without me. It's kind of like my kids loving the Beatles. They can love them, but they weren't there for the edge.

I was too young to fully understand the frightening McCarthy hearings, although I did watch them on our little black-and-white television. When Elvis came along I was in sixth grade. He didn't seem like such a big deal at the time; but as he wiggled his butt on the *Ed Sullivan Show,* a lot of girls at the soda shop would scream, and boys copied the Elvis haircut if their parents would let them. I remember watching *American Bandstand,* but I was too young for that generation. I wasn't really sure how I felt about close dancing with a boy, anyway. It was all so ho-hum to me.

I was very complacent in the 1950s. Very blah. Little did I know that those times were a simmering pot about to explode.

Suddenly things began to happen. The end of the 1950s brought the beginning of the civil rights movement where I lived. Women's liberation was getting some controversial recognition, the space race was in full swing, and folk singing and Joan Baez records took up all my spare time. You could almost taste the growing tension in this country. Though it was called only an "action," we were at war in Vietnam. We were protesting. We were breaking the rules that oppressed women. I felt that I was part of something special—that I was doing my part. And I felt powerful.

Before the changes brought about by the radical 1960s, gay men and lesbians had very different and difficult lives. Their community was deeply closeted. Gay men wore a special cologne or a red tie to identify each other at clubs or bars. Lesbians were characterized as man haters who nevertheless looked like men. Homosexuals were deviants or inverts, considered mentally ill by the medical profession. The older generation lived in an underworld of codes and invisibility, making it almost impossible to find other gays or lesbians to connect with. I remember seeing my high school drama teacher, a very handsome and perfectly dressed man, wearing a red silk ascot around his neck and sitting alone at a bar owned by my friend's family. I didn't know at the time what the red ascot meant, but I thought he was gay because he was older and single. Kids talked about his drinking problem at school, and I remember thinking how lonely he must be in this little suburban town where everyone knew your business. As for lesbians, cliché as it was, I had a crush on my phys. ed. teacher, Miss Dickey, who convinced me to play field hockey in college. I would have done anything for Miss Dickey. I still wonder if she knew I was in love with her dark face and butch ways! I wonder now if she had a lover.

There certainly were no role models shouting "Pride!" and marching down the streets in 1959. Social clubs were hidden on darkened streets. Gay and lesbian writers and artists couldn't get their works published. Gay teachers were unaware of or couldn't talk about gay heroes. Not a pretty picture! Lots of stereotyping and isolation.

American gay and lesbian activism had begun in the early 1950s with the formation of the gay male Mattachine Society and the lesbian Daughters of Bilitis organization. There was a newsletter called *The Ladder*, which was mailed in a plain white envelope. The members of these groups were the early pioneers who challenged the discrimination laws. The "community" was beginning to take shape, as gay men and lesbians came out of the closet in droves and grew more visible.

Today, the older generation feels as if they were part of something special. They are our living pioneers. We read their coming-out stories, look to them as role models, and admire their strength and their long-term relationships. They are my mothers and fathers. They are your grandparents. Without them you wouldn't be reading this book today. I wouldn't be writing it. We need to preserve their history and take care of them as they get older. Theirs was a history that was quietly made until the next generation of activists took over.

The next generation of gay men and lesbians were in their twenties and thirties during the Stonewall riot era that began in 1969. During that time, assumptions were getting thrown out the window right and left. There was civil rights activism, Black Power, feminist liberation, underground abortion clinics, antiwar activities, and consciousness-raising groups for women. The more conservative gay and lesbian groups gave way to the Gay Liberation Front and Gay Power. The Greek symbol *lambda,* meaning "dynamic," was adopted by the Gay Activists Alliance, which also staged public "kiss-ins" and gay street theater. Lesbians began to drift away from the gay-male-dominated groups and formed Lesbian Feminist Liberation. And there's so much more!

By the middle of the 1970s, things had calmed down a bit. The feeling of "community" and "family" grew, as folks experienced being part of something greater than themselves. The Metropolitan Community Church for gays and lesbians was founded in Los Angeles. The National Gay and Lesbian Task Force was founded in New York City, though it shortly moved to Washington, D.C., nearer to the political heart of America. The NGLTF's first outstanding achievement was to pressure the American Psychiatric Association to abolish the designation of homosexuality as a mental illness in the Diagnostic Statistical Manual. Today the NGLTF continues to educate the public and to fight and stand up for gay and lesbian rights on every front.

During the 1970s and 1980s, gay men and lesbians worked hard within mainstream American politics. In 1980, after several failed attempts, an organization called Gay Vote managed to establish an unprecedented gay and lesbian rights plank at the Democratic National Convention by electing seventy-seven delegates to that event. Melvin Boozer, a gay activist and a black man, proudly addressed the convention and eloquently spoke about the rights of gays and lesbians.

Now all that is history. You are part of the "community," with a lifestyle so rich that I can't even begin to address its depth. The community today is more diverse than ever. Sometimes this results in division and infighting among the various ethnic and sexually diverse groups, but we must be open to our differences because this is the way of the world today. If we are going to continue to fight for our rights and not lose ground, we have to remember our common bond. If we get caught up in disrespecting each other, nothing will be settled and all we've gained will be lost.

Think about it! You are at the peak of your idealism and energy. You are at the age of vision. States are passing hard-won rights and antidiscrimination bills. Hawaii is the first state fighting to legalize gay and lesbian marriages. Lesbian couples are legally adopting children where there are two mommies. Gay men are attempting to do the same, though with greater difficulty.

We've come a long way, and we have such a long way to go. We need you, the younger generation, to carry the torch. Some of us are tired and ready to do other things like smell the roses and do yoga. Many of our friends and loved ones have died of AIDS-related diseases that have wiped out incredible numbers of wonderful men, women, and children. We have a history of victories behind us. Now we must have a future of victories in front of us.

It may seem, for the moment, as if nothing is happening in your life. The 1990s may seem as blah as the 1950s did to me. However, now that you know your sexuality, an important part of your development is to begin to get involved with our history at whatever level you can. This is the time to have a prom and celebrate your coming of age.

Will you carry the torch now? There are so many things you can do ranging from small to big, from fun to serious, from local to global. Start out small, but get involved. This doesn't mean all day long every day, but do what you can. Every little bit helps. Everything we do makes us stronger. You'll have fun, meet new people with common interests, learn new things, build your self-esteem, and make it harder for the right-wing conservatives to beat us down. Then, in twenty years, you'll pass the torch down to your little gay and lesbian brothers and sisters who are now in kindergarten!

Here are some ideas:

- Join a gay/lesbian hiking club, book club, theater/movie club, gourmet dining club, singles club, travel group, investment club, sci-fi club, ballroom dancing group, computer club, bridge club, etc. If there isn't one of these where you live, start one. It just takes three or four people with a common interest to get it going.
- Subscribe to a couple of gay and lesbian magazines or newspapers to see what's happening out there. Make note of what's interesting, such as a gay bed and breakfast in Oregon or white-water rafting in Maine. Find out what's happening politically in other parts of the country and what it means for you. Are there any local or state publications that report on what's happening on a local level?
- Join gay and lesbian organizations such as the National Gay and Lesbian Task Force. They will keep you informed of national initiatives that may affect you or that you could get involved in at home. See what state or local organizations are doing.
- There are gays and lesbians in other countries who are political prisoners. Recently a lesbian from Russia tried to gain asylum in the United States, and faced an uphill battle. See if you and some of your friends can find a way to get involved with helping gays and lesbians in other countries.
- Get involved in politics in your state. Go after the sodomy laws. Get an antidiscrimination bill passed. This alone may take fifteen years of work!
- Investigate bills and policies in your state that affect gay marriage and adoptions, and see if you can help.
- Help to elect local politicians who are sympathetic. Better yet, get elected yourself!
- Go back to your old high school and start a support club for gay, lesbian, and bisexual youth.
- Organize a photography exhibit of gay and lesbian culture in your state.
- Find out who in your state and national legislatures is gay or lesbian, and work for them.
- Have smoke-free, drug-free, and alcohol-free parties. Remember the lesbian pot luck? It's been years!

- Start a newsletter. Write an article. Write a children's book. Write poetry. Write to the editor of your local paper.
- Get involved in starting a support group for the aging gay and lesbian population in your state.
- Join a speaker's bureau.
- Find out about lesbian health issues and get involved.
- Seek out gay or lesbian spiritual activities in your area.
- See if any local gay or lesbian clubs will sponsor fund-raising activities for your special cause.
- Does cable access or your local public television station have a program on diversity? How about any gay-themed shows? See if you can do one or have one brought in.
- Home-video your friends telling their stories. Make up questions and see what the responses will be. Show the video at a party.
- See if you can get together with some other gay men and lesbians of different ages and backgrounds for a picnic. Share fun, stories, and food.

Whatever you decide to do, enjoy yourself. Feel good about making the world a better place for gay men, lesbians, and everyone else by lending some support or jumping in head first! The more we are united, the better the world will be for everyone!

CHAPTER TWENTY-SIX

"Never Going to Make You Cry, Never Going to Say Goodbye"

Grieving Multiple Losses

Is it ever possible to come to terms with losing so many of our friends and lovers? Sometimes it feels as if it will never end. What makes grieving for so many of our community different from a single loss? Could it be that so many have died too soon? Could it be that we don't have time to recuperate from one loss before being confronted with another? Could it be that because of homophobia we can't outwardly express our deep pain in our daily lives, lest we lose our jobs? Could it be that the gay and lesbian/women's community is held hostage to the medical and pharmaceutical industries, which concentrate on profits rather than the real issues of HIV and breast cancer? Something doesn't feel right, does it?

There's no single model for grieving multiple losses. Not too long ago, I went to three funerals in a row. Two of my friends had died of AIDS-related illnesses and one from breast cancer. These three are part of a long list of friends who have died over the last ten years, and I knew that there were others soon to join them. The numbness was almost insurmountable. What I really needed was a way to grieve and move on that didn't make me feel as if I wasn't "doing it right," whatever that was. I needed to find a way to prepare for more loss in the future.

I just heard on the news today that in New York City in 1995, 7,000 people died of AIDS-related illnesses. The report went on to say that in 1996 "*only* 5,000" died, and this was considered "good news" because it represented a 30 percent drop in the death rate. "Only"

5,000 people died in one city in one year because of one virus—I can't yet attach a feeling to this announcement. Somehow, celebrating this "good news" doesn't come to mind.

Statistics tell us that 44,300 women died of breast cancer in the year 1996 alone. Also during 1996, new cases totaling 184,300 were diagnosed. The rate of breast cancer is rising steadily, yet the public is much less informed about this disease, probably because of the invisibility of women in general and of women's health concerns in particular. Deaths due to AIDS and breast cancer alone constitute a holocaust. Like many other people, I am personally not prepared for these losses.

Clearly, one of the most painful of life's experiences is coming to terms with the continual illness and death of friends and loved ones. Religions and cultures offer varied rituals for grieving and transcendence of grief to help us return to our lives anew. History, however, is filled with holocausts, genocides, "cleansings," and crusades that bring death in numbers far beyond the natural laws of loss. AIDS and breast cancer are part of the list of numbing catastrophes that reach outside existing answers and the comfort of rituals and prayers. The question today is not how to grieve for our elderly parents when they die, but how to grieve for the entire San Francisco Gay Men's Softball League, whose quilt panels of forty-four T-shirts are sewn together forever in memorial. How do we grieve for the young mother of an infant and a two-year-old, whose breast cancer so ravaged her body that she was dead in six months? This friend literally went from wedding to motherhood to dying in three short years. What's that about?

How do we grieve year in and year out for the perpetual, senseless, and continuous loss of our friends, lovers, family, and community? How do we grieve for so many, and so often? What are some of the problems that make grieving our multiple losses so difficult?

As in war, these illnesses encompass losing loved ones at too young an age, or out of phase with their expected life cycle. Parents, both mothers and fathers, are dying, and leaving young children. Children are dying before their parents. Young lovers are unprepared to lose a partner, nor are friends prepared to lose so many of their own generation. Grieving multiple losses leaves even the most loving survivors with a legacy of guilt and shame, making bereavement even more difficult. One of the biggest barriers, for example, is survivor's guilt, which is the perceived failure to rescue loved ones from the behavior or situation that caused their dying. There is absolutely nothing you could have done. Your mind may know that, but your heart still aches with the possibility that you could have done something, anything, to have saved your lover or your friend. As in war, if a bomb falls on your village and leaves only you standing, you can be racked with survivor's guilt. Why me, God? Why not me, God? Why them, God? Are these familiar questions?

In grieving multiple losses, one thing you should remember is, don't try to "fix" it. There are no answers that you can see right now. Maybe there will never be an answer. Just let it be, yet be aware that grieving isn't a linear process where you go from one stage to another and expect to feel better daily in a lock-step manner. Many bereaved people want to grieve "correctly," and complain that they "should feel better by now," although the "by now" may be only three or four months. When we're grieving one loss after another, we experience a ripple effect with a lot of going back and forth. One moment you may be feeling resolved over Roberta's death from cancer six months ago and the next moment enraged at Mike's recent death from AIDS-related sarcoma. This powerful mix of simultaneous emotions may feel crazy to you, but it's because they're all valid that they're so difficult to sort. A good way to handle them is to stay present and identify what's occurring before moving on.

Grieving is like standing at the ocean's edge while the waves rise and fall around you. Sometimes they rise over you. Your heart swells and ebbs like the tides, as waves of sadness, heartache, and also happy memories scatter around you like bits of shells and sea glass. There are times when the tides are high and your memories seem to flood into your heart from nowhere. At other times it seems okay to walk the beaches and dunes where ashes of those you loved have been scattered. There is an acceptance of what is, but a sadness for what was. These are natural feelings to be honored. Your feelings aren't your enemies to be chased away. We can't fight the tides of the sea, but we can begin to move back a little as life moves us forward.

One day my partner Paula walked with me around Provincetown and pointed out where all of her friends who died of AIDS-related illness had lived, worked, danced, and partied. She told me of shows they were in and how full of life and beauty they were. I knew that the tour was, in part, Paula's subconscious preparation for her dear sweet friend Larry, who was very sick and was coming to visit us over the weekend with his lover. Larry was a beautiful man, even with only a hundred pounds thinly covering his six-foot-one frame. Paula ached simultaneously with the loss to come and the losses that came before. She also shared her past losses with me so I would know what was to come. This sharing and recalling is a part of grieving many losses.

When a friend dies far away, what can you do? The last time I saw Bob, he was as handsome and funny as ever. He had shaved his head, sported a white linen suit, and looked dazzling as we danced the night away retelling stories of when we were roommates in Philadelphia during the 1960s. The next call I got about Bob was to tell me he had died. The night we danced, Bob told me that although he knew he was going to die soon, he was happy and there wasn't anything in his life he regretted. I knew he was saying goodbye to me. I engraved his name on my heart next to so many others.

Paula cried when she got the call that Larry had died at home many miles away. He had already been cremated, as he had wished, and there didn't seem to be any release for Paula from her longing to be with him in some way. They had been roommates and friends over many years. They had worked together, and had good stories, good memories, and a deep love for each other. What do you do with that?

I gathered everything I could find that Larry had ever given Paula, including a bouquet of flowers from the plants he had put around her house. Larry was Jewish, so there could be no better ritual than to say goodbye in the traditions of his own religion. In Provincetown there is a very spiritual rabbi who generously agreed to conduct a special service just for Larry by reciting the special prayer called the Mourner's Kaddish. We brought all of Larry's memories with us and set them in the garden under the flawless blue skies. Rabbi Gary donned his yarmulke, and in Hebrew he recited the prayer that calls for "peace to reign in the high heavens . . . and all the world." Larry would have loved it. Actually, Larry did love it! So did Bob, as I silently said a prayer for him as well.

From that time on, Paula felt more at peace with her loss, although she misses Larry. Sometimes she goes to the beach where his ashes are scattered among those of many of her other friends, and says how much he loved the very place where he is now at rest. There was some resolution for Larry, until we learned that his partner is also HIV positive. So continues the chain of multiple loss.

As gay men and lesbians, we have learned to wear a shield or mask to protect us from a hostile heterosexist environment. A teacher I know took care of her lover of twenty years who was dying of ovarian cancer. Jan taught school all day and never told a soul what was going on in her personal life. Given the small community where she worked, she knew her job would be in jeopardy, so she remained deeply closeted. Because Jan had to contain, control, and keep her emotions in check for so long, when her lover died she couldn't even locate a feeling. She was frozen in grief and eventually began to drink heavily. Jan was unable to pay attention to her emotions. To recover from her loss, she needed to be able to trust someone enough to find the release to go on with her life; instead, Jan used alcohol to numb her feelings and was afraid of losing control.

It's important to remember that you can't control grief. It can't be rushed. It can't be pushed away. After getting professional help, Jan was able to finally reach out to the lesbian community, where she connected with a support group for lesbians who have lost a partner to cancer. She stopped trying to understand and control, and she found a place where it was safe to drop her mask and be vulnerable. Eventually, after sobriety, Jan was able to transform her constant grief into an understanding that she will always grieve but it will not always be the central point of her life.

Many communities have given rise to support groups like the one that helped Jan. There is the Mary-Helen Mautner Project in Washington, D.C., for lesbians with cancer; Kathy's Group in Rhode Island; and Helping Our Women in Provincetown. These organizations were the direct result of a special woman dying and the impact of her suffering and loss on the women's community. Friends and others volunteer to help women who are in serious health crises in any way they can. Many AIDS-related agencies across the country also provide services for men and women with HIV.

Never going to make you cry? Of course you'll cry. Never going to say goodbye? You'll say goodbye many times. That's just the way it is. Sometimes grieving is chronic and prolonged. If the grieving process goes badly, the bereaved may be unable to let go and may become psychologically devastated. On the other hand, if grieving grows into warm memories and allows for resolution, you'll be able to handle the loss and eventually move on.

CHAPTER TWENTY-SEVEN

Love and Marriage

Love and Gay/Lesbian Marriage and Beyond
(or, I'm Getting Married in the Morning—
Whether It's Legal or Not!)

Isn't this "Marriage for All" symbol outstanding? Won't it be wonderful when it can apply to all of us—not just those who live in Hungary or Iceland, where you have the same rights as any married couple when you register your domestic partnership? Iceland? In New Zealand, Martina Navratilova donated a signed copy of her mystery novel to an auction that raised $10,000 for the Action for Gay Marriage (AGM) campaign. New Zealand? Martina? (Be still, my heart.)

Interestingly, everyone was gearing up for grass skirt weddings in Hawaii in 1998, but had to rebook for down jackets in Vermont in 2000. In 1994, the Hawaiian Supreme Court considered an argument that it couldn't justify its ban on same-sex marriages. Hopes were high in the gay community and there was an air of excitement waiting for the Hawaiian vote in 1998. Sadly, voters in the Aloha state disagreed with the court and overwhelmingly approved an amendment giving lawmakers the authority to limit marriages to heterosexual couples only. The backlash against gay marriages was enormous. By the year 2000, thirty-two states enacted laws actually *banning* same-sex marraiges—giving the Defense of Marriage

Act a firm foothold and allowing that states do not have to recognize marriages that are not same-sex couples.

Only two years after the Hawaiian devastation and aftermath, Vermont passed a law giving same-sex couples the right to form "civil unions." Civil union partners are allowed all the benefits and rights that the state gives to heterosexual marriages. Although this is not a full recognition for gay marriage and Federal programs do not change, there are more than 200 state laws that benefit married couples that can now benefit same-sex partners. Thanks to the forward-thinking voters of Vermont, April 2000 was a historical month for all of us.

Whether you think gay men or lesbians "should" get married isn't really the issue. Some members of the gay and lesbian community say, "Why should we copy the heterosexist marriage thing? It doesn't work for them, and who wants to be like them anyway? Eventually they all get divorced—we'll have gay divorces next. The whole marriage thing is stupid." But what about the *right* to marry, for those who want it? The fact of the matter is, gay men and lesbians suffer greatly from discrimination. Getting married or not "should" be a matter of *choice*—your choice, not the law's. If you want to, you should be able to walk down the aisle with your lover. You're not asking for special rights. This is not a "gay marriage" where people are looking for special privileges; it's simply two people asking for the same freedom as nongay people, which is to be able to marry the person they love. End of story. Or is it?

Enter the right-wing moralists with their homophobic diatribe about "family values," their stealth tactics, and their self-righteous indignation. I always feel badly that the word "Christian" is so often used by this group to justify their extremist policies. There are vast numbers of Christians and many church leaders who are fully supportive of the gay and lesbian community. I don't think they would agree that the word "Christian" is being used properly when it is attached to bigotry and discrimination. Unfortunately, however, the right-wing homophobes command a lot of power in our country by using scare tactics and money to buy influence. I wonder how much this group had to do with the attempted passage of the Defense of

Marriage Act (DOMA), which bans federal recognition of same-sex marriages? Or the fact that as of 2000, thirty-two states, including California, Illinois, Florida, and Hawaii have passed laws banning same-sex marraige? Politicians are only as powerful as we let them become! Take a lesson from Vermont! Know your candidates. Make sure they know you. Better yet—**run for office yourself!**

Do you know what the right-wing moralists think of us? Here are some examples:

1. "AIDS is God's way of punishing gays." Then how do you account for the fact that heterosexual women and young teens have the greatest increase in HIV/AIDS today? How come lesbians have the lowest incidence?

2. "Only Christian marriages are sacred." Who gave this group the right to say what's sacred and what isn't? Who are these morality mongers, anyway? I'm sorry—I can't even find a funny comment about that one.

3. "Gay men and lesbians molest children." Statistics gathered over the last twenty-five years prove that 97 percent of child molestation is committed by heterosexual males on young girls under the age of thirteen.

4. "Gays and lesbians convert and recruit others to their lifestyle." People are banging on the doors of the back-alley bars to be gay and lesbian? It's so much fun to go through all the pain, struggles, alienation, discrimination, hate, beatings, loss, stereotyping, homophobia, and self-hatred? Don't be absurd. We don't recruit. We just are.

5. "Gays and lesbians are trying to destroy society." I don't know about you, but I pay taxes, work two jobs, raised my children to be productive citizens, vote, buy American, use a credit card, have a loving relationship, recycle, pay my bills, and pray. How about you? What are you doing to destroy society?

There's more, but you get the picture. The bottom line is that same-sex couples don't have the same legal rights as married couples. It's a nice start that many businesses, cities, and municipalities recognize domestic partnerships, but it's not the same as a legal marriage. When you fill out various forms throughout your life, can you list your domestic partner as your "next of kin"? No—not unless you hire a lawyer and put out a lot of money and time; and even then there's no guarantee. This means family members that you may not even like, and who have rejected you and your lover, may have more rights to your estate and property than the person you've spent the best years of your life with. They'll also have rights to your minor children. You can will your property and your children's guardianship to your domestic partner, but such a provision can easily be—and often is—overturned by family. I think this is key.

Socially, gay and lesbian couples want the rights of nongay couples: we want to be recognized. We want to be free to celebrate our relationships and our love, have or adopt children, and have tax status, partner health care coverage, and all the other privileges of nongay married couples—if that's what we choose.

Since we're going through all this trouble to be legally married, what is it really like to be in a committed same-sex relationship? Actually, there are many similarities to nongay couplehood, such as communication issues, negotiating tasks, money worries, and managing all the differences and life-story baggage that come with all of us. I find it handy to divide the components of a relationships into three parts. This is simplistic, but it's always good to start with the basics.

The first and most important component of a relationship is knowing and understanding what constitutes acceptable and unacceptable behavior for each of you. This is the stuff that doesn't change. For example, there will be no physical or emotional abuse. That is law and nonnegotiable. I also suggest to clients that addictions and at-risk behavior should not be tolerated. If a lover crosses your personal boundaries in these crucial areas, you have the right to demand that he or she take responsibility for that behavior and get treatment. If that doesn't happen, this relationship may not be the one for you.

Couples sometimes negotiate their own rules of what's unacceptable. If your lover is an abuse survivor, he or she may not be able to tolerate your coming up from behind for a surprise hug. You may think such a gesture is romantic, but it sends your lover into a panic. Once you know, you don't do it again. Most unacceptable behavior is composed of very ordinary things and is based on triggers that have nothing to do with your present relationship. Examples may be eye rolling, swearing, sarcastic remarks, or mouth wiping after a kiss. If you don't tell your lover what you find difficult, you may find yourself triggered and arguing without knowing why. One couple I worked with put ethnic slurs and giving the finger into the unacceptable category. They got along much better after that.

Negotiable differences is the next category, and working on this can actually be fun. You and your lover are decorating the house. He loves country. You love modern. The answer is to compromise, not compete. Share the power instead of engaging in a power struggle. Mix up the furniture. Each of you decorate a room. Get French Provincial and both of you try something new. It's okay to have different styles; you're not compromising your integrity but rather filling your relationship with goodwill and creative solutions. Besides, you may learn to ski when it's her turn to pick the vacation, and she may learn to snorkel when it's yours.

The last category is about letting your lover be who he or she is, with you getting the same space to be who you are, as well. For example, are you a morning person or a night person? An introvert or an extrovert? Do you have high energy? Are you artistic? Are you athletic or musical or good in math? Some things about us are simply a part of who we are and cannot change. If you try to change these characteristics, chances are you'll get back to them again. If you're a night person but are traveling and need to be up early, you can do that; but when you get home, you'll probably go back to being a night person again. Personal characteristics may be influenced and modified based on willingness, but you'll really do well as a couple when you can celebrate your innate differences.

Along with your wedding or commitment may come children, yours and your lover's. You wake up one day and you're in a "blended family." Remember the Brady Bunch? That was quite the blended family. Now imagine a *Gay Brady Bunch* series on television. One week on the show, the Smith-Jones family decides to have a holiday neighborhood open house. When it seems that no one is going to show up, one of the gay fathers hears a commotion outside and rescues a neighborhood child from the mouth of a vicious dog. Suddenly the house is filled with thankful and repentant neighbors. The tears. The laughter. Mrs. Doubtfire prepares dinner for all. (This really happened in my state, except for the Mrs. Doubtfire part.)

Being in a blended family involves lots of interesting challenges, and lots of good things happen as well. One father reported that he had tears in his eyes when his "step-daughter" told him she had "two dads." I assure you this didn't happen right away but over a long period of time where love was allowed to grow. Don't fall prey to the myth of instant love: "I love you; I love your child. You love me; your child loves me." It doesn't happen that way. Be patient. The love can happen, given time and love on your part.

Try to think of a blended family as a transplant recipient. You get the new kidney but it won't work without lots of support and awareness of what's going on in your body. It takes a while to adjust to the new component and for it to adjust to you. The process may be difficult, with a lot of pain; but eventually, after time and treatment, you and the kidney are doing great. Before the transplant, a lot of time was spent laying the groundwork. You proceeded slowly and with caution. There was a lot of anxiety and talking about the different possible scenarios. You didn't just drive up and get this done in twenty-four hours. You thought about the potential rejection of the kidney, and about how you were going to take care of yourself with the new kidney in place.

With a blended family you must also proceed slowly. Don't expect the worst, but don't expect instant results, either. There's a lot of adjusting to differences. You have to decide what the kids are going to call each of you; how you're going to deal with your exes and their homophobia; how you're going to discipline each other's children; how you're going to operate as a family; what's tolerable and what isn't. I've seen kids use the difficulties between their original parents as a way of getting their way and being spoiled—effectively holding a parent emotionally hostage. "Daddy says you're a pervert. If I don't get my way, I'm going to go live with Daddy." Sometimes blended families also have to let go.

I've also seen the most wonderful gay and lesbian blended families evolve over the years! This has occurred with effort and complete emotional support, both from partners to each other and from some of the gay and lesbian parent support groups that have cropped up all over the country. There are even child support groups, gay and lesbian family picnics and events, teen groups with an open discussion format, and a new type of family therapy where a professional can help you all to grow as a unit with healthy respect and caring for one another.

From gay and lesbian marriage, and negotiating your relationship, to gay and lesbian blended families, we've come a long way just to be able to have this conversation. But don't wait to get committed or have a ceremony if that's what you want to do. And if kids become part of your equation, don't forget to take care of your partner as you both are taking care of them.

CHAPTER TWENTY-EIGHT

Drinking

What's This About?

I am alarmed by the drinking problem in the gay and lesbian community! Doesn't it seem as if you have too many gay and lesbian friends who drink excessively? Do you drink too much? Addictions occur in all walks of life, but there is a higher rate of substance abuse in the gay and lesbian lifestyle than in the general population. Although many of the studies are considered to have poor controls, the results still say consistently that the general rate for addictions is about 10 to 12 percent—*and about 28 to 30 percent for the gay community.*

This is probably not a shock. After all, where do you go to meet friends on a Saturday night? Where can you go to dance with your lover? Where can you butch it up or be a major queen—Hooters? I don't think so! On the other hand, where can you find people who have your experiences of having to survive in the straight world five days a week, and who need a place to let go? The Bar. The Club. Someplace with a name full of promises.

Okay—so the bar is where you socialize. But why do some people consistently *choose* alcohol to drink instead of soda? Alcohol gives easy relief to tension, allows you to feel less anxious, and helps you to be socially comfortable by putting you in a dissociative or less inhibited state. For some whose first gay sexual experience took place while drunk, there is a link to pleasurable memories that can seem much more appealing than the more challenging and sober efforts of real intimacy. So my question is: if you're happy with your lifestyle, what is driving you to drink?

My friends in the nontherapy world tell me that discussing internalized and externalized homophobia is no longer politically correct. Homophobia, however, whether "PC" or not, is where I believe much of the answer lies. Nonacceptance and fear of coming out belong to a homophobic society, and that directly affects the drinking problem among gay men and lesbians.

The gay child who grows up being different often needs to hide his or her "bad" or "wrong" needs and longings while putting up a false front. Hiding in denial and dissociation are natural behaviors that help you protect yourself from pain and fear.

Then there is adolescence! Do you remember those uncomfortable years? Remember when your same-sex urges seemed out of control? Who were your positive role models? Were your parents supportive and helpful when you told them that you thought you were different from what they expected? Wanting to be accepted, you probably tried to act out what you thought people wanted you to be. This is a continuation of the pressure you experienced as a young child.

To conform, you adopted behaviors that supported the denial of your feelings. You continued to dissociate from your true self, and you backed away from shaping your own needs and longings because you wanted to be acceptable to your parents and society. This is the way you survived. In sum, when you were growing up not being accepted for who you are, you learned that you are not okay but you had better act okay or you're out of here.

This is the point where suicidal thoughts or drinking frequently enter the picture. Most teens experiment with alcohol, but for gay or lesbian youth this type of "relief" also helps to fight the effects, or anesthetize the pain, of internalized homophobia and self-hatred. Since dissociation and denial are already natural to many gay and lesbian young people, intoxication just mimics the behavior you developed to help you survive in a homophobic world. This is the bridge into alcohol addiction.

Internalized homophobia and alcohol abuse together "erode the spirit," as suggested by Alcoholics Anonymous. When you combine drinking, as a brace for rejection, with internalized homophobia, what you get are low self-esteem and depression. If you suffer from internalized homophobia and alcohol abuse together, chances are you're in denial; experience fear, anxiety, and paranoia; are full of rage; have self-loathing; are isolated and lonely; feel like a victim; feel misunderstood; and are *very* confused. Unless you deal with your sexuality, it's almost impossible to deal with your substance abuse. And unless you're sober, you can't deal with your sexuality!

There have been some interesting studies that support the genetics of sexual orientation, as well as studies that support the genetics of substance abuse. Familial pattern studies done in 1982 and 1986 point to gay men as having a greater likelihood of having an alcoholic father, and suggest that the genetic markers for sexual orientation and substance abuse may be linked.[25] One flaw in these studies, however, is that while gay men and lesbians experience different family patterns, the rate of substance abuse seems to be about the same for both groups.

Although the genetic research on homosexuality and substance abuse is interesting, the predisposition toward alcoholism is most likely the same for the general population. Experiences associated with the societal factors of being gay and lesbian probably serve as the trigger (or the excuse) that activates a genetic expression or tendency toward substance abuse. This is true in many cultures that thrive on stress and turmoil.

Whether it's society or genetics, alcohol is used to decrease religious guilt; to decrease the pain of antigay violence and harassment; to make it easier to live a dual life as straight at work or home and gay in the bars; to help you deal with the fear of losing your job; to ease engaging sexually with a lover; and possibly to provide a way to avoid thinking about past sexual abuse issues. Now what?

There are a few developmental tasks you have to pass through now, which you missed while growing up in a homophobic society. As you become sober, be sure that you focus on the issues that your heterosexual counterparts don't need to address. For example:

1. Recognizing that you are gay or lesbian, and accepting that as part of who you are.

2. Coming out, if possible, in a way that's safe and that you've prepared for with a great deal of thought.
3. Confronting your internalized as well as externalized homophobia.
4. Grieving for what you perceive has been lost by your being gay or lesbian—everything from parental love to having a bridal shower.
5. Joining groups and forming relationships with other gays and lesbians to feel as if you're part of something special—because you are!

What do you need to do to get out of the statistical pool? First, go to AA meetings. Get sober, and then get into therapy to figure out how to live happily and find love and acceptance in a homophobic society—without using alcohol. I know this is easier said than done!

Is it important to have a therapist who is gay or lesbian? There are heterosexual as well as gay and lesbian therapists who are uncomfortable with their own sexuality or are homophobic. You deserve to have a competent and comfortable therapist (of whatever kind) who can help you confront your dual problem with understanding, support, and a plan for you to be sober and happy. Look for a therapist who understands the special circumstances of being gay and issues regarding chemical dependency.

For lesbians there are added struggles to be addressed in therapy, because women are more likely to have less money, are more likely to be parents, are subject to increased violence, and have to deal with prejudice against women as well as homophobia. There's an abundance of research on gay male issues, including alcoholism, but lesbian sexuality research and substance abuse issues have only more recently been addressed. Psychotherapy cannot cure alcohol abuse, but with the right therapist it will enhance your recovery.

Some therapists prey on people in recovery, and may try to get you to "change" your orientation. If your therapist thinks that being gay is your problem, then you're in the wrong place. *You should not have to fight homophobia in the health care system.* I've also heard from more than one client who went to detox and whose sexuality was never addressed.

If your therapist is challenging your denial of your drinking problem, take up the challenge and stop drinking. You'll be surprised at the wonderful results and the new joys you'll experience when you can truly accept yourself, be in an intimate relationship, and come to terms with your sexuality as a healthy and vital part of your life.

Remember—*you* are ultimately responsible for putting that drink to your lips, and *you* are in charge of stopping. I see clients who think that their drinking is funny or cute, or smile when I challenge them to stop. That kind of response simply won't help them recover. *You deserve more in your life than you can possibly get while you're addicted to alcohol.* As you develop your self-esteem by taking more positive and healthy actions, you'll also come to realize that you deserve more than a blackout, a bar fight, a hangover, a sour stomach, a lost weekend, or superficial relationships that are the direct result of your abuse of alcohol.

We have some ideas as to the reasons gay men and lesbians have a high incidence of alcoholism, but here's a more important question: What is the impact of that behavior on you and your life? A study done in San Francisco concluded that two-thirds of the participants did not practice safe sex after drinking.[26] Substance abuse increases the possibility of contracting AIDS even further, because alcohol compromises the immune system.

Alcohol can damage your body and your self-esteem. If you use alcohol with friends occasionally, you don't get drunk, and you don't drive while drinking, you are a social user. If you drink to feel comfortable with others or yourself, to have sex, to lose yourself, or to feel euphoric, because you are shy, to escape from your troubles, or to build your self-confidence, you have a problem with alcohol. The reasons why you drink determine whether you are a person who is a substance abuser.

Alcohol is a depressant and a poison that can ruin your life. It is toxic, which is why a person goes to "detox" to get sober. Every part of your body is damaged by alcohol abuse. It causes stomach upsets, ulcers, poor circulation, liver disease, muscle spasms, poor sexual functioning, and weakened kidneys resulting from poor nutrition and from having to detoxify your body. Every emotional fiber you have is wrecked by alcohol as you lose your family, friends, and employment. Why would you do this to yourself? You didn't start out in life as an alcoholic.

As you're beginning to live sober, you'll begin to have feelings and experiences with intimacy that alcohol once protected you from. You'll begin to grow from the place where you were when you started the substance abuse. At first you may feel way behind, but you will catch up as you stay sober. Keep a journal and describe how substance abuse keeps you from growing. Who in your family used a substance? What happened to them? What is your relationship with people in your family who drink? When did you start? Do you think your problem is "not so bad"? You may be in denial about your addiction.

Most often clients have more than one addiction going on. They're addicted to sex and alcohol, gambling and alcohol, food and alcohol, spending and alcohol, and sometimes all those things and more. For someone with addictions, the primary relationship is with the addiction and nothing else. People with addictions cannot be intimate with other people. They frequently isolate, withdraw, and consistently seek the illusion of feeling better through alcohol to avoid unpleasant situations or feelings. This is a natural setup for a gay or lesbian person who is constantly feeling uncomfortable and out of place in this society.

Like other addictions, alcoholism is a progressive disease that is increasingly dangerous to the user. When abusers finally recover from addiction, they have opened up the possibility of having healthy relationships with themselves and others. They can learn how to trust, love, and have their lives fulfilled with meaningful work. If you are having a problem with alcohol, please look in the mirror and make a promise to yourself to get help. Find the strength within yourself to discover how wonderful it is to be alive without the fuzzy lens of addiction.

CHAPTER TWENTY-NINE

2001

The Cyber-Sex Space Odyssey

It takes a lot to startle me or gross me out—or so I thought—but I found ground zero this week. When I was asked to do a chapter on cyber-sex, I said, Why not? After all, I do have clients who have significant addictions to chat rooms and to downloading pornography from one Web site or another. No problem. So I logged on to see what it was all about from a writer's point of view. I was instantly overwhelmed by the sheer volume of what was before my eyes.

For those of you who aren't familiar with how the Internet works, here's a *very* brief explanation of what I did. I logged on using an Internet connection program installed on my computer. With this type of program and a modem (an electronic device attached to both the telephone line and the computer), almost anyone can send and receive information to and from other computers all around the world. Basically, my telephone line and my computer work together, allowing me to search for information anywhere, about anything, anytime. There are many information resources on-line, from the entire Library of Congress to magazines ("zines") to the Gay and Lesbian Task Force and professional organizations that want to talk to members. In order to do a "search" of all of this information, you can use any of several "search engines" that are like library assistants. You ask an engine to help you find what you want, and it does just that. For example, I asked one that's designed to locate people to find an old friend of mine from high school. I gave my friend's name to the search engine and asked it to tell me if she had an E-mail address. It told me that she did, and we've been corresponding on-line ever since.

To find out something about "cyber-sex," I asked an engine to do a search using the keywords *cyber, sex, gay,* and *lesbian.* It returned a list of an astounding 41,282 matching documents, each one with a World Wide Web site address on the Internet. Granted, most of these documents weren't specifically directed toward gay men and lesbians, but there were quite a few, at least, for gay men. The Web summaries included some pretty nasty language, along with instructions for accessing yet more Web sites with sexually explicit content. "This is some big bookstore," I thought.

A "Web site," by the way, is just what it sounds like. A spider's web has a center where the spider resides, and the spider has woven little silk trails all around her to let her get in and out. When you're at a Web site on the Internet, there are trails you can follow to other Web sites just by clicking the pointer on the screen. They're all interconnected. Some of the larger sites seem to have their own hundreds of trails ad infinauseam. Individual people (or companies, organizations, etc.) establish their own Web sites, each with a specific Internet address that people can use to find them. It's like visiting someone, but on the computer. On the Web you can tour a museum, or browse an international library, or fly in a spaceship. You can attend a live concert, or watch a soap opera unfold. And yes, you can visit a smut shop, download illegal child pornography, or engage in cyber-sex.

What does this mean to gays and lesbians browsing the Net? Many of the listings in my gay and lesbian cyber-sex search were for chat rooms. When you visit a cyber-sex chat room you can talk dirty on-line as part of a large group; you can be a voyeur and just read what others are saying; or you can go into a private room with someone, where no one else can read your conversation. It's like being picked up at a bar and going to a private place. You can have any level of sexual discussion you want while on-line, including uploading pictures of yourself to be downloaded by your new "friend." Many Web sites require paid memberships for users to receive pornographic pictures or view explicit videos.

Now, I knew about cyber-sex from years ago when I first went on-line, but I never grasped the immensity of the activity until recently. This new awareness must extend to a lot of folks, because I have yet to see one book in the trade market about cyber-sex. Magazines and news-papers are full of discussions about parents' inability to control Internet access by children who are vulnerable to sexual exploitation. This exploitation can and does occur because there are predatory sexual addicts who will use any means to satisfy the craving of their disease.

Books addressing cyber-sex will probably be forthcoming; but books on the shelves now were probably written well before the impact of this situation on the gay and nongay community had been researched, if it has at all. I found one nongay dating book called *The Complete Idiot's Guide to Dating,* published in 1996, that has just a few remarks on "cyberdating."[27] This leads me to believe that, at the time of the book's publication, the cyber-sex problem hadn't yet become reality. The book promotes cyberdating to women as an inexpensive dating service where they can "tumble into cyber love." The author opines, "Computer dating may even be producing better male lovers. At last, men have to express themselves, and focus on something other than looks!" After that rather sexist comment, the book goes on to advocate the virtues of the unreal over the real, saying, "On-line minutes easily become hours, replacing troublesome, in-person love and sex with a safely-at-a-distance electronic eroticism and Netsex." Troublesome, in-person love, eh? Get real!

The ACLU filed and won an action in the Eastern District of Pennsylvania, defending the right to freedom of Internet access to information. This is one of those times that I sent a membership check to the ACLU on one day and wanted to cancel it the next! What is information and what is abuse when child pornography can be freely accessed on-line? On one side, libertarians are trying to block irresponsible use of the Internet so that youngsters can be protected against objectionable material. On the other side, the "cyberpunks" stand poised and ready to decipher all the newly developed blocking software that parents can install to prevent their children from seeing unsuitable aspects of the world.

I'm not talking about denying kids the ability to read about tragic world events or different lifestyles. An Internet company in Canada recently had the right idea when it blocked material that is illegal. What is illegal to send out into Canada? Pictures of child erotica, preteen erotica, incest, necrophilia, bestiality, teen erotica, and so on.

Schools have to address monitoring or locking out cyber-sex access as well. Many high school classrooms and libraries have computers with Internet capability. Today's students are as familiar with computer technology as I was with the old 1940s-style Royal typewriter that my Uncle Phill gave me when I went to college.

Bookstores, rest stops, train stations, downtown, the park, chat lines, and now cyber-sex—the ultimate anonymous sexual/love experience happening today. The good news is that you can't get a sexually transmitted disease from having sex via your computer (although you can make your computer very sick—many downloadable programs contain viruses that can damage your data or even bring your system to a grinding halt). The really bad news is that cyber-sex is the heroin of sex addiction. It's always there, waiting for you to crawl into the webs—webs that hold you captive like a spider's prey.

Why do I call cyber-sex "heroin"? Because cyber-sex is extremely addictive. People who never thought they had addiction problems before are surfacing with cyber-sex/love addictions. Unlike telephone chat lines or bookstores, cyber-sex combines all the aspects of anonymous sex and more. It's often visual, predatory, voyeuristic, and nonintimate yet very intimate at the same time. Cyber-sex is fantasy-filled, convenient, and available twenty-four hours a day. It offers instant gratification while it robs you of your time as the hours slip by. It can be dangerous for both gay men and lesbians (as well as nongays), and it is a very difficult habit to break.

"Make thousands and thousands of new friends," my computer flashes. It throws enticing invitations at me—or at least invitations that somebody thinks are enticing: "Every adult image you could ever want." Huh? They know what I want? "Meet Gay Men Now!" Uh, somebody obviously didn't check their demographics. "Make Eye Contact. Click Here!" Are they serious? What kind of "eye contact" is that? Is this the way your mother told you to go out and make friends? Is this what is meant by "networking"?

Quite frankly, I've had my share of adult images on the Internet. Several years ago, when my young teenage children and I decided to venture into cyberland, the scenery looked fine, at first. I was getting poetry from a friend in New Hampshire, and the kids were doing research papers and chatting on some teen line. We had one password into the Internet and would download each other's E-mail as a favor. And then . . .

After we had been away for a few days, I was the first one at the computer, hoping to hear from an old friend. "YOU HAVE MAIL," the computer announced. "I have a GIF for you" was dancing around my screen. "They must mean 'gift,'" I thought as I flipped on my printer, hoping for some new poetry. Well, I went to make a pot of coffee, and returned to see that I had printed out some disgustingly pornographic pictures. The first thing that crossed my mind as I ripped up the printout was, "What if my fourteen- and fifteen-year-old kids got the mail and were exposed to this stuff?" Or somebody else's seven- and eight-year-old kids? I canceled the on-line service that same day, and we stayed off-line for a year until I found a different service provider.

I guess you should beware of geeks baring GIFs!! Apparently GIFs (short for graphics interchange format) started out innocently enough as an on-line business tool. Now a GIF can also be downloadable pornographic pictures—unsolicited. I have a friend whose business requires her to have a Web site, and she's on-line all over the world as part of her work. Every week she receives at least a couple dozen pornographic GIFs. As with most junk E-mail, there is no way to avoid receiving GIFs that you don't want.

Gay men and lesbians look for different results from the cyber-sex chat lines. Gay men seem to dominate sex chat, while lesbians are looking for love. I knew a lesbian couple that had been together for seven years. Sasha loved to engage in chat lines, where she met Lorraine, who was from her hometown in another state. Unbeknownst to her partner, Jolie, Sasha would come home early from work every day to get on-line with Lorraine. Actually, she was on-line every chance she got, convinced that she was deeply in love with her computer companion. Without revealing her feelings about Lorraine, Sasha convinced Jolie to let Lorraine visit for her two-week vacation. When Jolie came home from work one day, everything in the house was gone, including her partner. The note said little except that Sasha and Lorraine were in love and would not be returning. Jolie never heard from either of them again, and to this day she has no idea where they are.

Edward loved gay male pornography. He downloaded twenty to thirty pictures per day for his collection. His phone bill started to escalate to hundreds of dollars a month, but he couldn't seem to stop. Finally, when his rent was overdue by months and he'd lost his lease and his home, Edward faced a crisis—but rather than give up his phone line, Edward resigned himself to losing everything, and now he has no place to hook up for his addiction.

Selina was on the computer sex chat lines so much that she and her girlfriend didn't have sex with each other for over a year. In couples counseling it was decided that Selina had to stop her sex chats with the same person, who is also in a relationship. The two couples then decided, through E-mail, to plan a vacation together. It was bad enough that the couple in therapy was in trouble, but now the four of them were going to spend time together "on vacation." Fortunately, the meeting went poorly, the computer went into the closet, and the couple is back in therapy getting themselves "in line" instead of "on-line."

All this adds up to the fact that the old axiom is true: there is much more to sex than just genital contact. Cyber-sex has proven what psychologists have known all along—that erotica is more about what's between your ears than what's between your legs. If you find that you're spending too much time on-line, shut down your computer and try it the old-fashioned way, *with* your partner. If you don't have a partner, it may be time to sharpen up your dating skills and start getting connected to the human community again. If you find yourself going through withdrawal, you may want to check in with your local counselor. Remember, the grass may *look* greener on the other side of the netscape, but that lovely green color is just the technical output of a bunch of computer code. Real life is great—sign back on to that and check it out.

CHAPTER THIRTY

Coming Out to Your Parents
The Do's and Don'ts

Your mouth is dry. Your heart is thumping wildly in your chest. You're short of breath and beads of perspiration are forming across your upper lip. Your voice is shaky and you can't sleep at night. Is it a new lover? Twelve weeks of sobriety and going to a big party? Wrong! It's that time of year again when you're thinking of coming out to your parents. Your therapist warned you not to come out during the holidays. Now those highly stressful days are over; and even though there's a holiday every month of the year, Flag Day and Arbor Day don't count.

You're tired of de-dyking your apartment and calling your lover of five years your "roommate" when your family visits. The inside joke about the fake cinder-block "bed" with the matching spread and pillows where your "roommate sleeps" is wearing thin. Your gay closet is getting smaller and smaller. You feel like a liar. Do you find yourself exasperated when your family asks, "When are you going to get married?" Do you find yourself avoiding family functions that you used to enjoy? When you're at Aunt Bertha's wake, do you find yourself looking for that cousin who moved to San Francisco?

Take a deep breath. It is time to STOP and THINK. Coming out to your parents could be one of the most difficult experiences of your life, but it's only one of the many steps of coming out completely. The first and most extended step in the coming-out process is called "signification." This means coming out to *yourself* as gay or lesbian. Signification is when you put together experiences, thoughts, and feelings and come to realize your sexual orientation. For some people this may take a long time, including many years of heterosexual marriage and children. For others, their sexual orientation has never been in doubt. These differences are part of a sexual continuum.

The second step, after signification, is identifying yourself to someone who isn't gay, such as a friend or sister. The best bet is to pick someone safe, who can help you later on with people who are going to be less than thrilled with your good news! Your ally can also help you decide whether coming out to certain people is a bad idea. You are going to need support, so pick someone special. This person can be a close relative, such as your sister, or a good friend who knows all the players you have to deal with.

The third step for many is going public, or being proactive by joining a gay/lesbian group, vacationing in P-town, or wearing little lavender triangles. This is the time for self-exploration. Getting out there will help you feel connected and less alone. If you live in an area that doesn't have gay and lesbian activities, save up and take a gay vacation. Having positive gay and lesbian experiences will help you gain the confidence you need for coming out later.

For many of you who are coming out older, or after being married, this is a very important step. Many report feeling out of place. Some say they feel as if they're sixteen inside and are shocked when they look in the mirror. Take a deep breath and take your time. You may be feeling sorry for yourself that you didn't know about being gay or lesbian sooner. It's really okay. You are in the right place at the right time for you. That's all that counts.

Finally, realize that coming out is a lifelong process, and that the world will look different from now on. You have a new sense of yourself. It takes time to get accustomed to the new lens you're now using to view old information. Part of the new view involves grappling with the loss of heterosexual privileges, such as being publicly affectionate, or the power you experienced by having a partner of the opposite sex. Magazines look different. You may look for novels that aren't about heterosexual couples. Television ads aren't addressing the new you. Talking at work about what you did over the weekend may not be so easy because someone might ask, "Where is this Secret Lavender Haunt Bar you keep mentioning, anyway?" Perhaps you're afraid someone will want to know who the "we" is, and you're faced with the situation of not feeling that it's safe to come out. Dealing with internalized homophobia, as well as homophobia in the greater world, is a new fact in your life, and you'll be surprised how much it will affect you.

Understand that, beyond the initial step of signification, the other coming-out steps can be skipped, or at least delayed until you're ready. Not everyone has to be proactive, and it certainly is not necessary to be public about your sexuality.

Take heed. For many of you, coming out to your parents is not an option. It's important for you not to feel that you must. It's not always necessary, or even desirable, to tell your parents that you're gay or lesbian. Some parents accept their children's lifestyle but would be upset if the "L" word or the "G" word were mentioned in their house. Other parents would have such a negative reaction that the family relationship would be permanently damaged or ended.

Think about your motivations for coming out. Do you feel guilty? Do you feel as if you're being dishonest to the two people who raised you? Guilt is *not* a good reason to come out to your parents. If guilt is your motivation, you need to take the time to deal with your feelings. Figure out what the real significance and impact of coming out will be, and assess your ability to cope with the fallout.

If your motivation is to improve already poor family relationships, you're kidding yourself. If you have problems communicating with your parents, coming out to them will not improve the situation. Evaluate yourself and your family's skills and deficits in the area of communication before you decide on your approach. This will help you prepare for both a best- and worst-case scenario. Remember, new family harmony is simply not the natural consequence of coming out. However, when there's an already existing basis of goodwill among family members, it will probably be restored after the initial reaction.

Initially, you were subject to all kinds of archaic, antigay brainwashing by your religion, society, and your friends. So were your parents! They will need time to catch up with you in the coming-out process.

Parents frequently blame themselves or each other for your sexuality. They have to figure out how they're going to handle questions about you just as you did. Your parents may need some time to feel sad that they may not have grandchildren from you, if that is your choice. Again, as time moves on, many of you will become more accepted as your parents see that you're still the same person they've always loved. Of course, in some cases, that isn't what happens.

Parents are uncomfortable in thinking about their child as sexual, just as it's difficult for you to think of them that way. Unfortunately, however, many heterosexuals think of being gay or lesbian only in sexual terms. "What do they do in bed?" rather than "What do they do for a living?" is often the first line of thought. You know that sex is only one factor in your life, but it will take others a while to catch up to the idea that you're a whole and complex person who isn't driven entirely by hormones. When your parents eventually get past the "sex" hurdle and see you acting the same as usual, those sexual triggers will dissipate.

Of course, even if things go well, that doesn't mean there won't be problems later if you bring your partner home for Christmas. Or, will you *and* your partner be included in the family portrait at your sister's wedding? If the basis for communication is good to begin with, the process of life issues will be challenging but rewarding.

The organization Parents and Friends of Lesbians and Gays (PFLAG), when surveyed, stated that gay or lesbian children should be prepared for parents to be "shocked, hurt and angry."[28] There may be angry words, but you must be patient even if you are turned away. Try to keep communication open after the initial shock has worn off. In other words, you may be called upon to act like an adult while your parents act like children. Parents need time—perhaps a few months—to absorb all that's involved with your new information.

If you've thoroughly considered and chosen to come out to your parents, find a friend or family member who knows your parents and practice desensitization. For example, let your friend pretend to be your parents, and you be you. Be dramatic, but be ready to stop if the role playing is upsetting to you. Do this a few times so that you can rehearse your responses and be prepared for the screaming or the barrage of questions that may be directed toward you—or the silence—if and when the time comes. Enlist the support of your ally. Tell friends what you are doing so they can be there for you and provide a safety net of support if things don't go well, or help you process how you're feeling.

Tell your parents in a calm and rational way. Be prepared for the feelings they may express, including anger, guilt, resentment and pain. Above all, be prepared to answer questions. Take steps to have on hand books or pamphlets about being gay or lesbian, such as the book *Loving Someone Gay* or *Now That You Know.*[29] When things have calmed down, consider contacting PFLAG, and give your parents their number with an offer to go to a meeting with them.

Ideally, if you're thinking of coming out, it would be good to do so while in therapy. Your therapist can help you deal with the impact of your reactions, vulnerabilities, and feelings. You can practice being assertive in a safe environment. You also have the option of bringing your parents to a therapy session later on, to help with questions and understanding.

If your parents react poorly to your coming out, and continue to do so, there may come a time when you recognize that reaching out and being tolerant of their negative response is doing you more harm than good. Sometimes parents think it is their right to feel attacked or hurt by their child's sexuality—or any breach of conformity, for that matter. If this is the case with your parents, they may expect you to be contrite and repentant, or to put up with their emotional outbursts. Some of you may find it difficult enough adjusting to the lifestyle without having to put up with this type of hostility from your parents.

If your parents do react poorly, you may need to back away from them and their negative behavior for a while. Seek a response inside yourself that is healthy, not self-denigrating. Most of all, do not be apologetic. You may want to interact with your folks less until they can control their negative reactions and be rational.

Tragically, I have seen some parents permanently reject their children after they have come out. By contrast, some parents overcompensate. One family I encountered vaguely suspected that their twenty-eight-year-old daughter was a lesbian because, although she was very pretty, she was still "unattached" (not dating or engaged). In their mind she "should" have been married unless something else was going on. When this young woman came out to her family, her parents seemed wonderful. They called all their friends and family with the news. They took her to P-town for their vacation. They joined all the appropriate organizations and read all the right books. In other words, they now had a gay daughter—with a vengeance! The family was completely enmeshed. This young woman was going to be the best lesbian with the best family ever—even if it killed all of them! The unfortunate result was that the parents were so "wonderful" that the young woman found herself totally unable to act on her sexuality. Coming out for this young lady turned out to be very difficult. She was afraid to disappoint her wonderful family in any way.

If all goes well, you will find yourself being accepted, and find your family giving you the positive response you dreamed of. If *you* have negative feelings about your sexuality, however, you may not believe or trust their reaction. You may be projecting your internalized homophobia onto your family. "After all," you may subconsciously think, "if I'm ashamed of my sexuality, then other people must feel the same way." Get someone to help you do a reality check. You may need help to deal with your self-acceptance and any internalized homophobia.

All in all, I suggest a serious approach to coming out to your parents. I believe that people need to consider all of the implications. Don't cave in to peer pressure to come out. Your friends don't live in your experience; and although they may want what they think is best for you, it's your personal decision and no one else's. If you feel you can come out to your parents, prepare yourself emotionally and have support. Be careful not to set yourself up for disappointment. Then take a deep breath and go for it!

Now for a true story. Holly's parents know she is a lesbian. She brings her girlfriend home from time to time, and everyone is pretty much okay, except for one thing: they never say the "L" word. For a long time, neither could Holly, but she got over it. Holly's father, being a military man, would occasionally lecture Holly about her "ah, unfortunate situation." Holly loves her parents and accepts their limitations as best she can.

One day Holly's car broke down while she was visiting her family. She drove her mother's car a couple of hours back to her own house while her father got the car fixed. Over the weekend, Holly's father had a big military meeting and asked to stay with Holly. He drove Holly's car for two hours, and when he arrived in full military dress, with all the stripes on his arms and medals on his chest, he abruptly proclaimed, "I scraped off your Clinton/Gore sticker before I went onto the base, Holly. I sure couldn't be seen with that on the car."

Sure enough, the political sticker was gone, but shining up at Holly was her gay flag on one side of her bumper and a big pink triangle on the other! Holly couldn't stop laughing. "But Dad, you left my gay flag and triangle on the car. What do you think the guys on the base thought when they saw that, ahem, 'situation'?" Holly's father paled. "Is that what those mean? No wonder those guys were looking at me like that!" After a minute of dead silence, they both laughed. It was a perfect case of "Don't ask, don't tell."

This is also a case of how a typical family might be. Not a lot of talk or understanding; the same amount of love; and a live-and-let-live atmosphere that allows them to stay connected without confrontation. Holly wishes for more, of course. But times like this with her father make things okay for her.

CHAPTER THIRTY-ONE

The Birds and the Birds; the Bees and the Bees

Coming Out to Your Children

You've come out to your spouse, your parents, and friends. So what are you waiting for? It's time to come out to your children, before someone else does it for you in a not-so-nice way. Before your children become influenced by homophobia. Before they suspect on their own and think something's wrong because no one is talking directly and openly to them. Before you go crazy from having to be closeted in your own home. Before your children think you're hiding something you're ashamed of.

Mary hadn't yet come out to her eleven-year-old daughter or twelve-year-old son. She was planning on doing it after she got custody. But because Mary had come out in her forties, she was like a kid, busy discovering all kinds of new expressions about being a lesbian. She was getting into the phenomenon of "womyn's music." She went from the Beatles and disco to Chris Williamson, k.d. lang, and the Two Nice Girls. One evening when Mary was flipping through some CDs, her daughter looked over her shoulder and observed, "Mom, why do these women kind of all look the same? Really, Mom. They look like some of your friends. Are they your friends who made the CDs? Why do they all have the same haircut?"

Mary flipped—her daughter was right. The four basic lesbian hairdos is a topic for another book—but what would you say to your daughter if you were Mary?

It's important to remember, when you come out to your children, that you're not confessing something you did that's bad or wrong.

You're informing your children of the truth about you in an appropriate, simple manner. You're letting them know that there's nothing different about your relationship with them or your love for them. You're still their loving parent, no matter what! If you get dramatic, cry hysterically, or make being gay or lesbian any more than a natural part of life, they'll become alarmed and feel unsafe. It's your responsibility to set the tone for this conversation.

Be aware of children's developmental stages so you can use appropriate explanations in your discussion with them. With children up to the age of three or four, just go about your natural living and so will they! There are some great children's books today about gay families. You know, the ones they try to keep out of the libraries, such as *Heather Has Two Mommies*.[30] Keeping those books around as well as other appropriate material will start your children thinking everything is okay from the beginning. This will give you a good basis for more serious conversations as they get older.

Young children really don't know or care about sexuality, anyway. They're more concerned with themselves and being loved. Divorce is more of an issue for children because it means that both of the people they love most won't be there, although there may be some relief from their parents' fighting.

A major concern I hear from gay and lesbian parents of young children is that children can be less than discreet in what they say or who they say it to. Joe was mortified when his four-year-old son had his little friends over to play and announced proudly, "This is my dad. He's gay." This is a tough one. On the one hand you want to be an example of openness with your children and not keep lifestyle secrets from them. On the other hand, you don't want to ask them not to "tell" anyone, because that defeats the purpose of having an open and healthy relationship. If you live in the country or a right-wing community, or find yourself surrounded by ultraconservative religious groups and neighbors, you may want to think about moving. If you can't do that, you'll have to teach your children about "situational ethics." This means telling your children who they can talk to about your being gay or lesbian. While this option isn't great, it's better than the alternative, which could prove to be a disaster. Besides, you already teach your children good manners. Situations require some judgment calls, and your sexuality is on that list! At least for this time, for the child's sake.

Teaching about situational ethics can be a great opportunity to start making your child aware of discrimination and prejudice. One of the positive outcomes of being a gay or lesbian parent is that you have an opportunity to raise your child to be sensitive to the differences among people. Your children will grow up to be more accepting of diversity and how to adapt to the changing world, because it is their world to come.

Children between age six and preadolescence are usually pretty flexible and resilient. Keep in mind that because children develop gradually, you will have more complex conversations with them over time. It's as if they are coming out as a child of a gay man or lesbian. Always remember that you didn't come out in a minute, either. It's very important, after you disclose, that you observe your child's interactions in the family and with his or her friends. Be open to questions, because as time goes on there will be more to teach. There may even be a time when you get some negative reactions as your child begins to learn about homophobia from peers and society at large.

Remember Mary? Mary finally came out to her children when her daughter was twelve and her son was thirteen. The divorce from hell, which took four years, was final. After a particularly perfect day somewhat arranged by Mary, she sat with her kids in the living room, as they often did just to chat. After Mary disclosed her lesbian orientation, her son said, "I knew it all along. I don't like the word 'lesbian' very much. Can we still go for Chinese food tonight like you promised?" Her daughter was a different story. Amy sat there for a while and finally burst out, "Oh no! Things like this only happen in Hollywood! What does this mean?" What she meant was, "What does this mean to me?" Both are normal reactions! What Mary didn't expect, though, was how relieved she felt after she told her kids. "I never realized how exhausting it was for me not to tell them the truth. I feel so much better to be out of this lie."

It took Amy a while to absorb the information about her mom, but she was well on her way when she came home from school the next day and said in her own dramatic, twelve-year-old fashion, "My life will never be the same. Today when the girls at my lunch table were laughing and using the word 'gay,' I didn't think it was funny anymore. They were laughing about you. Even though they didn't know it, I did." Mary used that opportunity to help her daughter process her feelings and to talk a little about what having a lesbian mother means.

According to everything I've seen and read, coming out to adolescents is the most troublesome. Much of that is the nature of adolescence to begin with. Teenagers don't want to be different from *anyone* else in their peer group, and you have now made them different. When they're busy contending with their own hormonal development, teens don't want to hear or think about you as a sexual person; don't want to meet your lover; don't want to worry about their own sexual preference; don't want to keep secrets; and don't want to be embarrassed in front of their friends. This is also normal, and much of it will pass in time.

Be prepared for negative reactions. They may not happen right away, but still be ready. Your kids may not talk to you for a while. They may want to move out. They may say some pretty hurtful things or call you names. Practice with friends or a therapist how to handle a worst-case scenario so you aren't too rattled if your child really goes off at you with anger or hostility.

This is the time to focus on your child's feelings rather than having an angry reaction back. Arguing with your child about his or her feelings is a useless exercise. When you're hurt and angry, the last thing you want is someone trying to talk you out of your feelings; and it's the same for your child. This doesn't mean you should tolerate abuse, but try to go with the reaction instead of resisting. Come from an understanding and positive place. In most cases that I've seen, as long as the parent was steady and positive, the children have come around. If this doesn't happen, though, be sure you have someone to talk to. There are gay parents' groups in many towns; there are books;

there are Internet support groups; there is counseling and talking to friends. Many communities even have groups where the children of gay men and lesbians can meet.

Your child is bound to have questions, if not now then later. Be sure to leave the door open, but keep your answers simple and appropriate. Too much detail is not necessary. Tell some of your friends when you're going to talk to your kids so they can help you handle your anxiety. Give your children the name of someone they can talk to anytime, such as a supportive friend, aunt, or uncle.

Here are some questions people commonly ask about coming out to their children. See if these are the same for you:

1. *Will I be influencing my child's sexuality at one age more than another?*
   You cannot influence your child's sexuality any more than your straight parents influenced yours. Think about it. You grew up in a heterosexist, homophobic society, felt shame because of your sexuality, tormented yourself about leaving your marriage, and entered a lifestyle that is difficult, yet nothing anyone could say or do to you could make you change your sexual orientation. A homophobic society plants hateful seeds that produce prejudice and unfounded fear. A homophobic society says that gays and lesbians recruit young people, even our own children, into a homosexual lifestyle. This kind of thinking is why we lose our children in custody suits, hide our sexuality, and buy into agreeing that being gay means you're immoral. Be careful not to give in to the scare tactics of those who oppress you!

2. *Is it ever too soon to tell my child?*
   The sooner you can tell your children, the better. Some people wait until after court in order to protect their children from having to lie or be witnesses in a bitter divorce. But keep in mind that there's no good or bad time to tell. At each stage of a child's life there are questions and issues. The younger the better, in terms of normalizing the child's experience growing up with you. At each stage of your child's development you can expect new questions.

3. When can my partner move in with me and my kids?

I have a particular point of view on this that may differ from the way many gay men and lesbians operate. Mine is not a popular position, but it's one that must be considered seriously when it comes to affecting the life of a child. It goes like this: Children first. You had them; and whether you like it or not, they are your primary concern for a very long time. This may mean putting aside living with your partner until you are truly committed; have had many discussions about the roles you will both take; go to couples counseling; talk to other gay and lesbian couples that have children; read everything you can about blended families as well as step-parenting; *and* wait at least two years into the relationship to see how it's going.

I am not saying that you have to ask your child's permission to have a live-in partner, but that a great deal of research and forethought *must* go into your living arrangements. If your partner cannot wait and respect your position that your children come first, then this may not be the relationship for you. By the way, I'm of the same opinion regarding heterosexual relationships. I don't believe in impulsive cohabiting just because you're in love. I believe in long-term, committed relationships that are a marriage equivalent for gay men and lesbians. You have to be a role model for your children and provide the best environment you can, which may mean putting off your own gratification for a while.

Relationships—gay, straight, or whatever—are difficult enough; and children add to the complications through no choice of their own. Our relationships must be stable enough to withstand the bumpy ride, and that takes time to develop. There has to be an agreement not to run off at the first sign of difficulty or discomfort. Communication has to be extra good between the two of you. Many couples with children are doing great with their kids, so of course it is possible! Proceed with love. The more support there is for you and your partner in the outside world, the better your family will do.

4. *There is no difference between being a straight, gay, or lesbian parent, is there?*

You bet there is, so don't go fooling yourself! Actually, it's pretty homophobic to think that there aren't any differences, because there are special problems that have to do with being gay or lesbian in an oppressive, heterosexist culture (let alone being a gay or lesbian head of household). The bottom line is that most of the differences between gay/lesbian parenting and nongay parenting have to do with homophobia. What's different is that if you are a gay or lesbian parent in a committed relationship, do you bring your partner home for the holidays along with your children? Will your children, whom your partner lives with and cares about as your mate, be included in his or her family celebrations? If you're in a committed relationship, are you still considered a single parent at school or work? Doesn't that make you feel invisible? Do you find yourself monitoring your coffee-table books or conversations about going out to certain clubs or movies with gay or lesbian themes so your kids' friends don't "get" it? Have any of your children lost friends when they or a parent has figured out what's going on in your life? When you're a gay or lesbian parent you have to be cautious in a different kind of way, out of respect for your children—at least until they're young adults.

Here's a good one! I knew a fourteen-year-old girl who was flustered and upset. Her mother is a lesbian and "it's all her fault, I'm so confused."

"Over what?" I ask.

She goes on to say, "Well, it used to be so easy. I was going to grow up, go to college, work, get married, and have kids. Now I'm all confused. I've met women who have kids without men. And men who are raising their children with other men. I've met women with their partners adopting children from other countries. I've seen women living together raising all of their children, working and still going to school. I've seen married women with women girlfriends and the husbands take care of the kids. I met this woman who looks like a man, pushing a baby carriage. I know some gay men who are raising the daughters of one of them because his wife is a lesbian and wanted to move but didn't want to take the kids out of school. All of these choices! And these people are all so nice. What am I going to do? It's not all set like I thought before." I doubt if a heterosexual single parent hears this conversation very often. I've heard it a lot from children whose parents are out. And guess what! This conversation is normal! This teenager learned that there is more than one way to be in this world, and that it's okay.

5. *Is parenting different for gay men than for lesbians?*
Yes and no. First of all, there are many more lesbians than gay men who have custody of their children. Comparatively speaking, there is also much more research about lesbians than gay men as parents, for whom there is practically nothing written. Of course this research wasn't done because we live in such an enlightened culture where information on lesbian parenting will help advance our thinking. Rather, psychiatric tests of lesbian parents trying to get custody were ordered by judges to assess the mental and emotional functioning capabilities of lesbians as compared to heterosexual single mothers. I'm assuming that they were trying to prove something homophobic; but because no "functional" difference was found between nongay mothers and lesbians, benevolent lawyers use the information to help win custody cases. I should say "sometimes" win custody cases, because the truth is that if a judge doesn't like lesbians, it doesn't much matter what the research says. This degrading exercise may be used by lawyers to help their lesbian clients, but at what cost?

Since the information is generally available, I'll tell you what some of it says. When judges were trying to show that lesbians might be too masculine, are not really interested in raising children, or act inappropriately with their children (all of a sudden?), no differences were found as compared to nongay divorced women. Bless those stereotypes that keep those judges busy!

Since more and more gay men are becoming parents, I can only guess that their psychiatric testing is just around the corner. One interesting study comparing gay men to lesbian parents did show that lesbians are less likely to gender-type their children's toys. In other words, lesbian moms are more likely to let their daughters play with trucks and allow their boys to cry. Gay men are more inclined to keep the status quo. Another difference is that gay men make more money than lesbians; but men in general make more money than women, so that is not surprising.

There are millions and millions of children who have gay and lesbian parents. You are not alone, although you may feel that way from time to time. You are also in a unique position to raise your children for the twenty-first century. Our children will be the ones to change the laws and eliminate societal homophobia. If it's possible, push that baby carriage at Pride. Be as visible as you can without jeopardizing your family. One lesbian mom, Joanne, recently became single again, sadly, after an eight-year relationship. She and her partner had attended a local Methodist church for many years, and now Joanne went with her daughter to help out with some of the church events. At a social gathering this brave mom decided to take a stab at being visible. Joanne spoke about how much she missed her mate Estelle since they broke up, and no one batted an eye. Finally one elderly woman said, "Well now, dear, maybe you can meet a nice . . . uh . . . new mate."

Make a plan. Tell your children. Then maybe you can come out to your church next!

CHAPTER THIRTY-TWO

Therapy Demystified

So you want to go for therapy. You browse through names in the phone book in a state of panic. You ask your friends who they see. You're told that five years ago your ex-lover went out with the ex-lover of a therapist you really wanted to see but who won't see you because of professional boundaries. You have a flat twenty visits covered by your insurance company. Okay now, where and how do you start?

It's a good question. First, what kind of therapist do you want? Therapists run the gamut, from what I call "uh-huh" therapy to very dynamic interaction. Each therapist has a different personal style as well as a favorite area of study or expertise.

Psychotherapy has come a long way since the late 1800s. Sigmund Freud's early development of psychoanalysis was one of the first formal approaches to understanding and treating "mental illness." Classical psychoanalysis involves many years of treatment, and frequently requires daily meetings where the "patient" lies on a couch and attempts to access his or her subconscious mind through free association. As the subconscious is brought to consciousness, the patient gains control of his or her life and is considered cured. Of course, this is a very simplistic explanation of an extremely complicated philosophy and process. Also, notice that this approach uses the terms "mental illness" and "patient" rather than the more modern (and positive) "mental health" and "client."

Analytic psychotherapy, founded by Carl Jung, is oriented toward symbolic meanings (archetypes), dreams, and explanations that are hard to express in familiar words. Jungian psychology has evolved since the early 1900s and is considered most helpful to people who have been fairly well adjusted for the first part of their life but have become dissatisfied as they get older. Through analytic psychotherapy you find meaning and wholeness as life proceeds.

Alfred Adler, the founder of individual psychology, believed that life is a challenge and that we can choose how we behave in the context of our environment. He believed that we defeat ourselves and then feel inferior because of those defeats. Since we are ultimately responsible for our behavior and our mistakes, with willingness we can overcome those mistakes. Adler was considered holistic because of his belief that, when considering the individual, the mind and body cannot be separated.

The 1950s brought the development of client-centered therapy, pioneered by Carl Rogers. Clinicians of Rogerian therapy were trained to wait for the patient to say or do something before responding. It was assumed that you, the patient, should determine what happens in a therapy session (although you probably have no idea what that should be—kind of like the unknowing leading the unwitting for $75 an hour). Client-centered Rogerian therapists are considered "manipulative" if they do anything other than reflect back your words, giving "unconditional positive regard" and serving as a passive listener.

Beginning in the early 1950s, other schools of therapy emerged. Gradually, the therapist became an active participant and started to share responsibility, along with you, for the therapy session. Therapy developed a "mental health" outlook and stopped being about "mental illness," although until 1972 you were still considered mentally ill if you were gay or lesbian.

Good therapy is about working with a trained professional who will help you get the perspective you need, show empathy for your circumstances, and help you move on to feeling better than you can ever remember. Today, good therapy isn't just about reflecting, but also about learning life skills, communication, dealing with anger and hurts that get in your way, and most important, developing the ability to recognize and change old patterns of behavior that no longer work for you.

To benefit from your therapy experience, you want to be sure your therapist is a good match for you and has the skill to use different styles to make the treatment most beneficial to you at the moment. How do you select a therapist? First, interview, interview, interview! Shop around. Decide who you are most comfortable with—a man or a woman, older or younger, etc.—and who makes you feel respected and listened to. Find out if they are covered under your insurance. And if your therapist touches you other than with a handshake, walk out the door.

Here are some summaries of theories and styles to give you an idea of what you might want when you go for your initial interview.

1. *Cognitive behavioral therapy,* which evolved in the late 1960s, emphasizes that you have the ability to free yourself from symptoms such as depression or panic and to learn effective ways of dealing with problems with the help of your therapist. The early roots of this type of therapy can be traced to the 1920s. Classical psychoanalysis still dominated at that time, with its focus on repressing anxiety rather than reeducating the client to develop coping skills. Cognitive behavioral therapy revolves around educating yourself about yourself and your world. You're taught to observe your thoughts, emotions, and behavior and to see their relationship. Things don't just happen *to* you—at least not all the time. You're taught to take responsibility for yourself by doing "homework," which may include gathering data about yourself and forming new perspectives and interpretations. Cognitive behavioral therapy can teach you to relieve your depression symptoms, encourage your insights, and help you stabilize your behavior. You learn to avoid returning to old patterns of behavior that didn't work.

2. *Rational emotive therapy* (RET) is a style of cognitive behavioral therapy developed in the early 1960s by Albert Ellis. RET directly challenges you to examine your belief system to eliminate self-

defeating behavior and irrational beliefs. It encourages you to understand that you have greater control over your destiny than you had previously thought. Although it's not strong on insight, RET can be a very helpful tool in getting you to that critical point. There are lots of good and helpful homework assignments that go along with RET.

3. *Gestalt therapy* differs strongly from cognitive therapy. The main approach of Gestalt therapy is to confront the here and now by experiential role playing and confrontational exercises emphasizing the direct expression of feelings. Sometimes, however, Gestalt therapy can be misused or mechanical if confrontation is all the therapy is about. Many therapists will make use of Gestalt types of interactions or techniques to help you focus on your feelings in the present. For example, role playing your anxiety about coming out to your parents can be very beneficial.

4. *Narrative therapy* is a newer approach that attempts to be "gentle and poignant" at the same time. In this type of therapy you tell your story to the therapist, who asks many questions and writes down every word you say. Between sessions the therapist writes letters to you that are about you, and assists in developing analogies that help you interpret your behavior. The belief is that the stories we construct about ourselves are maps of the way we experience the world. When we tell our stories and they are understood through analogies guided by the therapist, we can then develop newer stories with new meaning and a more desirable outcome. In short, the therapist helps you find unique outcomes for old patterns, as narration helps you externalize your problems—that is, you come to realize that *you* are not the problem, the problem is the problem. This method of externalizing the problem is typical of most cognitive behavioral therapy. Although there aren't yet many narrative therapists around, the movement is growing.

5. *Hypnotherapy* is a powerful tool with many positive outcomes. Unfortunately, its effectiveness has been underrated because of its frequent misuses as entertainment or in sensationalized lost-memory "recoveries." Hypnosis can help you overcome many problems,

but it may not always help you to gain insight. A good relationship with your therapist in a safe environment is essential for good results. Hypnotherapy can be a great way to reduce stress, stop smoking, and learn relaxation techniques. Guided imagery and different types of hypnosis can also help you find inner peace and access your personal power. If you're considering hypnotherapy, my advice is to first research the therapist and the style of hypnotherapy he or she practices. It's my opinion that, when combined with other therapy tools, the skilled use of hypnotherapy can be very helpful.

It's important that therapists stay current with recent developments in the field. In fact, most licensing boards mandate that therapists meet a certain number of continuing education requirements in order to have their licenses renewed. Workshops and classes keep therapists on the cutting edge of new techniques. For example, *brief therapy* and *solution-focused therapy* have recently come to the forefront. Brief therapy is a way of thinking through a problem by developing and sometimes inventing solutions; challenging assumptions; seeing how you maintain your problems; and asking the question, If what I'm doing is not working, what can I do differently? Solution-focused therapy allows you to leave therapy for a while and then come back as needed to pursue other issues.

While in brief therapy you might find yourself learning how to "reframe" a problem; "shift" your thinking; listen to metaphors; remember how you solved your problem in the past; expect positive outcomes; make resistance work; get compliments from the therapist; focus as a team on your symptoms and the problem; and do paradoxical tasks.

What is a paradox, as it relates to therapy? Here's an example. A client of mine was obsessed with watching her ex-lover's driveway to see who was visiting; and since her ex-lover lived next door, every time my client heard a noise she ran to her window. She was losing sleep and felt ashamed of herself. For homework, I told my client I wanted her to look out that window even more. She couldn't look out the window during breakfast because there wasn't enough time to get ready for work; and since she was at work during lunch, she obviously couldn't look out her window then, either. So she had to eat her dinner in front of the window and stare at the driveway every night for at least two hours. Well, after about a week my client was sick of looking out the window, and she dropped the behavior, barely remembering why she did it to begin with. She stated that she couldn't stand her ex-lover anyway, and was tired of wasting her time. From that point on, we were able to focus on obsessive thinking as a pattern she could control.

Relational therapy is a very complex, intense, and important model that has been under close study at the Stone Center in Wellesley, Massachusetts, over the last twenty years. This model suggests that we grow as a result of our relationships—relationships with friends, with our lover, even with our therapist. It states that in a relationship we have a greater sense of vitality. We feel more able to act as we get a more accurate picture of ourselves in relation to others. We feel more connected to life and those around us as we evolve a deeper connection with others.

Relational therapy was developed by women therapists, and especially by the psychiatrist Jean Baker Miller. Miller felt that the male/medical model of psychology not only failed to address women's innate needs and abilities for intimacy and connection but also looked at these behaviors as pathological and problematic. She is far from alone in thinking that women's voice too often goes unheard in the therapeutic community. Relational therapy should be a part of every therapist's training. This approach works very well with gay men because of the intense desire to be intimate that has been thwarted by male socialization. The skills involved in connecting with a lover, gay or lesbian, can be enhanced with a relational approach.

It's also important to mention *family systems therapy,* because we all come from families of one kind or another. How we were and are in these families has the strongest impact on how we are today. This model is not about blaming but rather about understanding that much of the way we see the world and our ability to change comes from where we've been. Family systems therapy helps you add direction to finding solutions and making changes in areas of your life where you've been stuck doing the same old thing.

Of course, the choices don't stop with those I've listed. There are many other kinds of therapy. You may also want to see a spiritual counselor or a meditation counselor. You have a choice of whether to seek a gay or lesbian therapist, though there's some debate on the merits of that. Theoretically, therapists are supposed to be nonjudgmental and accepting regardless of sexual orientation; in reality, this is often not the case, no matter whether the therapist is gay or nongay. There are certain areas of the gay and lesbian lifestyle that a nongay therapist may not understand, such as the club scene, the limited number of people in the community, internalized homophobia, unique features of same-sex relationships, coming out, fear of exposure at work, or the absolute necessity to migrate to Provincetown or other gay and lesbian meccas as often as possible! Some clients have told me they prefer having a gay or lesbian therapist because they're tired of teaching or explaining things to nongay practitioners. On the other hand, I've seen nongay therapists who are highly skilled in working with their gay and lesbian clientele. It's your call. Don't be afraid to interview prospective therapists.

While we're on the topic of your mental wellness, let's get into managed care for a moment. I have a colleague who prefers to call it "mangled care." Other colleagues think that "managed care" is an oxymoron. The fact of the matter, though, is that your employment benefits are probably limited and have to be used wisely. If you use them to go to an "uh-huh" therapist or a classical psychoanalyst, your allotment of six, twelve, or twenty visits will quickly vanish before you feel any benefit from your treatment. Health care has become a "for profit" business where you are encouraged, or even required, to go to the lowest-cost provider rather than seek the best clinician.

Be sure to check your mental health benefits and ask good questions—especially if your health plan is about to change. Under many types of plans, you may have to be referred by a certain physician or agency, or you may be required to see someone "in the network" who was not your first choice. This can become tricky if you specifically want to see a gay or lesbian therapist. Within many provider networks, therapists may say that homosexuality is their specialty but not disclose to the referring network whether they are gay or lesbian. You may then find yourself having to pay cash and go elsewhere for your therapy.

Many managed care organizations require preauthorization before you can see a therapist. This means you must call the managing company of your health plan and talk to a case worker. The problem with this is that a client is unlikely to call and tell some stranger that they're having coming-out issues and want to talk to someone gay or lesbian. Most just say they're depressed. This can result in a lot of misdirected referrals that cost everyone time and money, and often make the client's depression worse.

I was pleased to see that a managed care network I recently joined recognizes domestic partnerships. Now I can actually counsel gay and lesbian couples as routine. On the other hand, another fast-growing network recently opened and closed applications for therapists so quickly that I never even had an opportunity to apply.

It's a tricky deal for you and for me. There are books out on one-visit cures and the "miracle question" that are the ultimate in "brief therapy." There are clients who only need to be seen a few times. In most cases, however, if there are issues of trauma, abuse, sexuality, multiple addictions, or depression, a one-time visit, no matter how fabulous, is probably not the answer for you.

Well, that's mental health in a very small nutshell (so to speak). You may not be able to pass the certification boards from this brief chapter, but I hope it will help to demystify therapy for you and let you see that asking for help doesn't mean you're incapable of solving your problems. Remember, you are worthwhile, and there is no reason why you shouldn't feel better about yourself. If your back was out of alignment, you wouldn't hesitate to see a chiropractor—so why not give your emotional self the same opportunity to achieve wellness? A therapist is part of *your* team; and sometimes, having that outside perspective is all you need to get on with your life in a happier way.

CHAPTER THIRTY-THREE

God Bless You

Religion Revisited

Are you a sinner who is going to burn in hell because you are gay or lesbian? Are you sick of listening to heterosexist or just plain sexist stories based on someone's interpretation of the Bible? Tired of Leviticus? Tired of Sodom and Gomorrah? Do you long for simpler days when you learned that God was love? When you look inside yourself, do you see a spiritual vacuum? You don't have to be a gay man or a lesbian to have these feelings, but there is a large amount of hatred being spewed at homosexuals by many religious groups, and it's directly damaging and hostile to the gay and lesbian community.

The good news is that you don't have to be a hostage to your religion. A simple answer to this very complicated and difficult situation is to go with God on your spiritual quest to find a positive and affirming religious affiliation. You can leave behind a religion that puts you down; you can be gay or lesbian and still have God. A gay friend of mine put it very well when he described his own spiritual journey. Instead of being told how to be with God from the outside in, he left his structured religion to find how to be with God from the inside out.

Hugh was raised by his charismatic Catholic mother and father to be a good practicing Catholic. He went to parochial schools all the way through college and continued to attend church regularly until he was thirty-seven years old. When his father died, Hugh took his mother to six o'clock mass every night. A rather shy man, Hugh had a couple of close friends who included him in their family parties in the hope of fixing him up with various single cousins, but it never clicked for him. A growing pressure began to fill Hugh's heart as he prayed each week in church and each night before bed. He prayed to God to help him feel love instead of pain, but no matter how much Hugh prayed, he continued to feel worse, until one day he broke down and wept out of loneliness and despair. There *was* love growing inside him, but it was unacceptable because it was love for his friend Andy. God had played a dirty trick on Hugh, or so he thought; and from that moment Hugh was filled with anger and a sense of betrayal because his prayers went unanswered.

For two years Hugh railed at God until he finally left the church and never went back. Although Hugh is not in a relationship or acting on his sexuality, he at least realizes he is gay and is beginning to accept this fact. Not having grieved the loss of his relationship with God, Hugh refuses to talk about being spiritual. He feels that part of his life is dead, and that God abandoned him by not answering his painful prayers. What Hugh has yet to realize is that his prayers *have* been answered. He does feel love. It's just that the love he feels isn't accepted by his church—and it's the church, not God, that condemns Hugh. When Hugh realizes that he can feel a spiritual connection with God outside the church and have his love at the same time, the pain in his heart will ease and he will move forward into a happier life.

You don't have to stay in the kind of religious situation that Hugh was experiencing. You don't have to leave your religious practice, either. You can stay within your own faith by shifting some of your expectations, or you can find an alternative way to be with God. There are many choices.

1. You can join a gay/lesbian church such as the Fellowships of Metropolitan Community Churches (MCC), which was founded in Los Angeles by Reverend Troy Perry in the late 1960s. Many MCC services can be found in urban centers around the country and even around the world. These services are very affirming to many gay men and lesbians who feel let down by mainstream religion.

2. If you live in a small town or have a close association with your church or temple, you may want to stay in the fellowship but remain closeted. Many people feel they benefit from their church or temple affiliation despite the limitations and compromises they have to make. You may wish things were different and experience discomfort at some of the sermons, but you may be willing to overlook this as an institutional flaw rather than a personal affront.

3. Many people are coming out within the churches or synagogues they've always attended, and are finding the experience to be better than they expected. Just like coming out to your family and friends, coming out at church may take some time. If you're comfortable with who you are and can be patient, you may be pleasantly surprised. Just as in your family, there will be those who are supportive and those who aren't. Just be yourself.

Here's a very memorable example. When Adelle came out in her forties, she felt as if her entire world had just fallen apart. Everywhere she went in her small city, she perceived hostility and danger. She even stopped taking her children to her synagogue because she was intimidated by her ex-husband's family, who never missed an event. At Yom Kippur services, Adelle felt as if everyone was staring at her. She had bought very expensive clothes for herself and her children so that when people looked at her family they could hold their heads up—but throughout the entire service, Adelle's head pounded with tension.

The second year, Adelle had an easier time. She really liked the rabbi and enjoyed the music of the Yom Kippur service. By year three, when Adelle was more involved in the lesbian community, going to the holiday services was a snap. She even wore the same expensive outfit from three years before.

The fourth year, the rabbi started his Yom Kippur speech with, "Today I am going to talk about something very unpopular." Adelle assumed he was going to speak about events in the Middle East, where there had recently been some terrible tragedies.

"I'm going to talk to you about your gay and lesbian children, neighbors, and friends," he continued, "and how they deserve your love and support." Just as in the early days of her coming out, Adelle froze, convinced that the entire congregation of fifteen hundred people was staring right at her. She glanced sideways at her children, who were looking back. Tears were streaming down her face. By the end of the service Adelle was locked in her seat, unable to get herself to move. Then, from across the sanctuary, Adelle saw an elderly friend approach, and she rose from her seat as the friend held out her arms to hug her. Adelle didn't know where her wealth of emotion came from, but tears of relief, or joy, or freedom lifted her spirit, as once again she knew she was connected to her spiritual source of peace.

4. Over the years, many gay and lesbian subgroups have evolved within mainstream religions. There are gay and lesbian synagogues, Dignity for Catholics, Affirmation for Methodists, and Integrity for Episcopalians. It's very empowering for members of these faith groups to practice their own religion in a gay and lesbian environment.

5. Unfortunately, many congregations are led by ministers, priests, or rabbis who allow their own homophobia to dictate the attitude of their congregations. If this is the case, try another church or synagogue where the religious leadership is more accepting of your lifestyle. I know of Catholic churches where there are gay-friendly priests, and synagogues where gays and lesbians are welcomed as members. This will allow you to stay within your religious tradition but in a setting that's openly diverse and accepting. It's a nice situation for those who prefer to be in a mixed gay and nongay fellowship of their faith.

6. If you want to change religions, there are many that are very accepting of gay men and lesbians who have had bitter experiences with a homophobic "religious" institution. The United Church of Christ welcomes gay, lesbian, and bisexual membership. It was the first denomination to ordain an openly gay clergyman, in 1972. Friends, or Quakers, neither approve nor disapprove of any sexuality as long as the standards of their religion are upheld. These standards include the protection of civil rights for all and a certain level

of activism toward abolishing discrimination against anyone. The Unitarian Universalist Church began offering blessing ceremonies for gay and lesbian couples in the mid-1980s. Episcopal mainstream churches are also quite liberal and provide a comfortable alternative for those who want to leave the Roman Catholic Church.

7. Some gay men and lesbians choose not to attend a formal church but have very deep spiritual connections with God or Goddess or Wiccan rituals that are intensely private or shared only with small groups. I know a gay man who rises every morning and reads the Bible or something spiritual, then exercises while he thinks about what he has read. Some cities have spiritual or meditation counselors who will help you find a peaceful relationship with your spirituality. There are counseling services in some areas for gay and lesbian Catholics who are suffering from the conflict between their sexual orientation and the religion they love. There seems to be a movement by some Catholic theologians toward affirming gay men and lesbians. So far I have heard good reports from clients whom I have referred to priests and nuns who are also mental health counselors and spiritual advisors for gay men and lesbians.

8. Many gay men and lesbians have been attracted to the teachings of Buddha because the Buddhist faith is so private yet can be practiced side by side in meditation with others. There is a sense of community, privacy, and, for many, a great spiritual uplifting through yoga, chanting, and meditation.

In the Western world, it's difficult for anyone to go through life without being affected by the Judeo-Christian traditions and the sex-negative position of many religions. Gay men and lesbians, however, get an extra dose of sex-negative dogma, which claims that homosexuality is unnatural and a sin. Everyone suffers from such homophobic interpretations of the Bible. Because of the male domination reflected in the Old and New Testaments, gay men are specifically under siege, while lesbianism is generally viewed as a lesser threat.

A little biblical history will go a long way toward helping you understand where the religious right wing gets some of its ammu-

nition. Keep in mind that right-wing conservative religious interpretation is completely out of context and has little to do with the
world today. Early in the history of the Israelites, because of disease
and the difficulties of survival, rules governing procreation (along
with other very strict rules governing such matters as diet and dress)
were considered necessary. It was believed that sperm was the same
as human life to be placed inside women for incubation purposes.
This is the point where the Old Testament book of Leviticus gets
quoted over and over again by religious right-wing groups as proof
of the Bible's condemnation of homosexuality: "Thou shalt not lie
down with mankind, as with womankind: it is an abomination"
(Leviticus 18:22).

But it was also considered a sin against God to eat rare meat, wear
clothing of mixed fibers, use two different kinds of draft animals har-
nessed together, or plant two types of seeds in the same field. Women
were completely subservient to men, and the only sexual position
condoned was "missionary."

These laws helped the early people of Israel distinguish theirs from
the other religions of the region, which had their own rules of survival. I wonder what the laws would have said about polyester? There
is no mention of same sex behavior in the Ten Commandments, and
the subject of homosexuality was not discussed by the prophets, whereas
rape, prostitution, promiscuous behavior, and adultery are clearly condemned.

Then there's the Sodom and Gomorrah saga of flames and de-
struction in Genesis 20. You know, the story in which Lot offers his
two virgin daughters to an angry mob of men in order to protect his
two male houseguests from those who would "know" them. The religious right-wing conservatives like to quote the passages describing
this rather questionable morality as proof of God's condemnation of
homosexuality.

How this story legitimizes a condemnation of homosexuality con-
founds me! One could as easily conclude from the story that God
requires fathers to give away the sexual favors of their children—a
true perversion indeed.

According to many scholars, God was angry with the men of Sodom because they were unkind to strangers and travelers as well as selfish with their wealth by refusing to help the poor or unfortunate (Ezekiel 16:44–52). In the early days of the nomadic peoples of the Middle East, the hospitality of strangers to weary travelers was extremely important.

Today the words of the Old and New Testaments are constantly being twisted by right-wing conservatives and others to further their agendas. They use religion, a very complex and personal phenomenon, as a control mechanism to advance their own personal greed and power. In condemning gay men and lesbians, such people point their fingers at others to divert attention away from their own unsavory behavior.

So what is the truth? The Bible has been examined, interpreted, and written about so many times over the centuries that we can scarcely know what it really means. What can a layperson really say at this point without being completely superficial? There are many historical reasons why the Bible is so often used to condemn one group of individuals after another. Fear, homophobia, envy, permission to do violence, ego, dominance, and other human traits are things we must all be aware of so that we don't fall into the trap of dehumanizing ourselves.

There are many ways to stay connected with religion and find comfort in a sense of something greater, regardless of your sexual orientation. Look for the spiritual practice that will support you and allow you to have a happy and good life. Your spirituality is up to you to find, and you can come to rest in a peaceful space filled with light.

The message of faith is about love, good deeds, and humility. I can't think of a modern religion that doesn't choose to advance those ideals.

CHAPTER THIRTY-FOUR

The Yard Sale

"If You Want It, Here It Is—Come and Get It"

Every spring my neighborhood is rampant with yard sales. There is even a traditional way to conduct a yard sale. First, advertise in the local paper. Then put up signs within a twenty-block radius, making sure to hit all the main thoroughfares. On the day of the sale, be outside with your stuff by 7 A.M., ready for the "collectors" who will resell your precious throwaways at the flea market for three times their value. As the day moves along, neighbors may come out and ask if they can set up a table with their stuff, which you graciously allow, knowing the favor will be returned when it's time for their yard sale.

Your friends all come around to see what you're getting rid of, so be careful not to put out any old gifts, especially with a "50 cents or best offer" tag! At the end of the day, put up a sign that says "For Free," which hopefully will take care of getting rid of the rest of the items. In my neighborhood, if you have leftovers after a yard sale, just leave them out overnight. By the next day, everything will be gone as if by magic. One time, when I was new to the neighborhood yard sale traditions, I made the mistake of leaving an expensive garden cart holding my garbage bags in front of my house overnight, instead of the usual green can. The next day the garbage *and* the cart were gone!

Usually, on the night of a big sale, I take my profits, my children, and my partner Paula out for a dinner of their choice. It's always a good dinner, too.

All year long I cull my house of things I'll never use again and put them in the garage for the big sale. By the time spring comes, I may have reclaimed some of the items, but I try hard not to hold on to things. My children always want me to save what they say they "must have" for when they go off on their own. Well, my attic is stuffed to the rafters for them. Someday, I fantasize, when I leave this house I'm going to take three things and leave the rest for them to claim. Then, when they're done taking what they want, I'm going to put a big sign on my front door that says "For Free," and let it all go. Even the Smurf collection!

Now that you're out of the closet, what about the rest of *your* house? Are you ready for that big emotional yard sale? Get your tags and markers ready, and let's evaluate what you're going to keep and what you're going to get rid of. What's broken, and what's useful? What never worked right? What makes you sad? What did you get from someone that you don't want anymore? What do you have that you don't even realize is bothering you to keep around?

It's time to unload this stuff and reorganize! Make room for what you can really use! Think about your new emotional self. Make some lists and start looking for role models, books, and programs that will help you define the new you. Would you even think of redecorating your house without checking out some magazines for ideas? Well, this is the most important remodeling job you'll ever have! See what others—people you admire—have done so you won't make as many mistakes.

Our gay and lesbian house has plenty of room, but sometimes we get cluttered—bogged down with too much stuff and things that don't fit. Our family is extremely diverse, cutting across all races, ages, nationalities, income groups, and religions. We have room for lots of different people, including bisexuals and transgendered men and women, who have so much to offer. We have to sell off our judgmental tendencies, prejudices, and fears right away! These items are of no value to us.

Sometimes, like all families, we clash and disagree about how our home should look and feel. The Log Cabin Republican gay men and lesbians are conservative, work hard to fit into the heterosexual mainstream, and don't want to appear "too gay." Our drag queens, on the other side of the house, cause all kinds of family arguments because at Pride they're "too extreme" and out there.

Our music even seems to clash at times. While "So Many Men, So Little Time" is booming in the basement where the guys are dancing, the "womyn" upstairs are harmonizing to "We Are Family." Okay, I know this is a stereotype, but there is some truth to our differences!

Absolutely, there are differences. We are everywhere and do many things. We live in a nongay as well as a gay world. Even though we're different as individuals, the bottom line is that, as family, we also have to stick together on many broader levels. We are not the enemy. Internalized homophobia is the enemy, and it doesn't belong in our house. Why the self-hatred? Is it useful? This makes a perfect item to unload, along with our addictions and abusive relationships. Actually, in this case, a bonfire might be more in order! You bring the marshmallows, I'll bring the vegan hot dogs . . .

What's the next step? Ever notice how it feels when you get rid of an ugly chair or picture? Chances are you don't really miss it. You may miss not having an object where the chair or picture was, but not that one! Pretty soon you either forget what was there or put something that you really love in its place. The key word is *love*. Why settle for less? When you care about yourself, you tend to surround yourself with people that you love and that love you back. It's much better to be in a bare room with only a few really special items than to own a lot of junk that you hate and that makes you uncomfortable!

The next step after getting out of the closet, investigating your house, and unloading the junk is to open up the windows and air the place out! Let a fresh breeze cleanse the rooms. Burn ceremonial incense or Indian sage and sweet grass smudge sticks to cast out the evils of oppression and replace them with goodness and light. Open your doors and put up that rainbow flag! (Or at least a small triangle.) Paint up the place so it looks like new, and a little at a time get some new stuff that you love being around.

How do you know what's good for you to keep and what you have to get rid of? Think about how you buy new clothes. First you see the item you think you like, and then you try it on—*before you buy.*

The item might fit and look good until you check the price tag. Then, if it costs too much, and it's going to take away from what you need for food and shelter, hopefully you put it back.

It's the same with behavior. If what you're doing in your life feels good but seems to take away from your integrity, your self-esteem, or your survival, you may be in jeopardy. This is a heavy price tag. Chances are that if you continue, you'll regret the purchase, end up keeping it in your closet, and not buy anything else for a long time because you're broke.

Redecorating your house can be fun and an adventure. You don't even have to do it alone! But don't just take my word for it. Get out there and find your style. I'd love to have you in my neighborhood to help us all brighten things up.

Notes

1. F. J. Kallman, "Comparative-Twins Study on Genetic Aspects of Male Homosexuals," *Journal of Nervous and Mental Disease* 115 (1952): 283–98.

2. J. M. Bailey and R. C. Pillard, "A Genetic Study of Male Sexual Orientation," *Archives of General Psychiatry* 48 (1991): 1089–96.

3. M. Hirschfeld, "Homosexuality," in *Encyclopedia Sexualis*, edited by I. Bloch and M. Hirschfeld (New York: Dingwall-Rock, 1936), 321–34.

4. Sigmund Freud, "A Letter from Freud, 1935," *American Journal of Psychiatry* 197 (1961): 786–87.

5. Elie Wiesel, "Morality and Psychotherapy," keynote address at the seventeenth annual Family Therapy Network Symposium, Washington, D.C., March 1994.

6. Rik Isensee, *Growing Up Gay in a Dysfunctional Family: A Guide for Gay Men Reclaiming Their Lives* (New York: Simon & Schuster, 1991), 31–32.

7. Anne Wilson Schaef, *Escape from Intimacy* (San Francisco: HarperSanFrancisco, 1989), 136.

8. Sharon Wolf, *Guerrilla Dating Tactics: Strategies, Tips, and Secrets for Finding Romance* (New York: Plume, 1994).

9. Melody Beattie, *Codependent No More: How to Stop Controlling Others and Start Caring for Yourself* (San Francisco: Harper/Hazelton, 1987), 53.

10. Robert Subby, "Inside the Chemically Dependent Marriage: Denial and Manipulation," in *Co-Dependency: An Emerging Issue* (Pompano Beach, Fla.: Health Communications Inc., 1984), 35–56.

11. Pia Melody, *Facing Codependence* (San Francisco: Harper/Hazelton, 1989), 32.

12. Andrea Natalie, *Stone Wall Riots* (cartoon) (East Guttenberg, N.J.: Andrea Natalie, 1990), 15.

13. See W. Masters and Virginia Johnson, *Human Sexual Inadequacy* (Boston: Little, Brown, 1970), and JoAnn Loulan, *Lesbian Sex* (San Francisco: Spinsters Ink, 1984).

14. JoAnn Loulan, *The Lesbian Erotic Dance: Butch, Femme, Androgyny, and Other Rhythms* (San Francisco: Spinsters Ink/Aunt Lute, 1990), 41.

15. SLAA, *Sex and Love Addicts Anonymous* (Boston: The Augustine Fellowship Press, 1986).

16. Anne Wilson Schaef, *Escape from Intimacy* (San Francisco: HarperSanFrancisco, 1989), 10.

17. My search turned up only two books that specifically address lesbian battering, both of which I had to special-order. I found one book for gay men, also available by special order: D. Island and P. Letellier, *Men Who Beat the Men That Love Them: Battered Gay Men and Domestic Violence* (New York: Harrington Park Press, 1991). There is a book of collected professional articles available: Claire M. and Charles H. Miley-Renzetti, eds., *Violence in Gay and Lesbian Domestic Partnerships* (New York: Harrington Park Press, 1996), as well as growing projects on education intervention such as the New York City Gay and Lesbian Anti-Violence Project. A Web site called "Lesbians Hurting Lesbians" is available through the Internet.

18. E. E. Kelly and L. Warshafsky, "Partner Abuse in Gay Male and Lesbian Couples," paper presented at the Third National Conference for Family Violence Researchers, Durham, N.H., July 1987.

19. L. Walker, "Battered Women's Shelter and Work with Battered Lesbians," in *Naming the Violence: Speaking Out about Lesbian Battering,* ed. K. Lobel (Seattle: Seal Press, 1986); C. Renzetti, *Violent Betrayal: Partner Abuse in Lesbian Relationships* (Newbury Park, Calif.: Sage Publications, 1992), 21.

20. K. Vacha, ed., *Quiet Fire: Memoirs of Older Gay Men* (Trumansburg, N.Y.: Crossing Press, 1985), 69.

21. M. Adelman, ed., *Long Time Passing: Lives of Older Lesbians* (Boston: Alyson Publications, 1986), 207–9.

22. See A. Kinsey, W. Pomeroy, and C. Martin, *Sexual Behavior in the Human Male* (Philadelphia: W. B. Saunders, 1948).

23. S. Freud, "Analysis Terminable and Interminable," in *Therapy and Technique,* ed. P. Rieff (New York: Collier, 1963), 232–72.

24. Radclyffe Hall, *The Well of Loneliness* (Garden City, N.Y.: Sun Dial Press, 1928).

25. R. C. Pillard and J. D. Weinrich, "Evidence of Familial Nature of Male Sexual Orientation," *Archives of General Psychiatry* 43 (1986): 808–12; R. C. Pillard, J. Poumadere, and R. A. Carretta, "A Family Study of Sexual Orientation," *Psychiatric Annals* 18, no. 1 (1982): 52–56.

26. R. Stall, L. McKusick, J. Wiley, T. J. Costes, and E. G. Ostrow, "Alcohol and Drug Use during Sexual Activity and Compliance with Safe Sex Guidelines for AIDS: The AIDS Biobehavioral Research Project," *Health Education Quarterly* 13, no. 35 (1986): 9–71.

27. J. Kuriansky, *The Complete Idiot's Guide to Dating* (New York: Alpha Books, 1996).

28. For information on Parents and Friends of Lesbians and Gays (PFLAG), write to 1101 14th Street, N.W., Suite 1030, Washington, DC 20005.

29. Don Clark, *Loving Someone Gay* (Millbrae, Calif.: Celestial Arts, 1977); B. Fairchild and N. Hayward, *Now That You Know: What Every Person Should Know about Homosexuality* (New York: McGraw-Hill 1977).

30. Leslea Newman, *Heather Has Two Mommies* (Boston: Alyson Publications, 1989).

Resource Guide

Web Sites

Gay and Lesbian Resources
Everything from outdoor groups, religious organizations, mailing lists, Pink Pages, and magazines to safe sex information and chat sites:
> http://www.3wnet.com/rainbow/gnl.html
> http://www2.baldwinw.edu/~alternet/list/gay-les.htm

Infoqueer
Servers by subject, geographic area, and organization:
> E-mail: queer@server.berkeley.edu
> http://www.infoqueer.org/queer/qis/orgs.html

Arts, culture, and recreation:
> http://www.infoqueer.org/queer/qis/arts.html

Media:
> http://www.infoqueer.org/queer/qis/media.html

E-mail lists, Netnews Group, NetBBSs:
> http://www.infoqueer.org/queer/qis/email/html

Queer Resources Directory
Information and resources from all over the world, including business, politics, and events:
> http://www.qrd.org/qrd

Internet mail lists:
> http://www.grd.org/grd/electronic/
> http://www.lesbian.org

http://www.cyber-designs.com/pride
http://www.peachpit.com/peachpit/titles/catalog/88453.html
http://www.udel.edu/nero/lists/blacklist.html
http://www.ourworld.compuserve.com/homepages/EvaRainbow
http://www.tiac.net/users/sojourn
http://ww2.cruzio.com/~abbyb

Community Centers and Social Services

Arizona
Phoenix: Valley of the Sun Gay and Lesbian Community Center
602-265-7283

Tucson: Wingspan Youth Group
602-624-1779

Arkansas
Little Rock: Women's Project
501-372-0009

California
Culver City: Lambda Youth Network
Pen Pal Program
P.O. Box 7911
Culver City CA 90233
310-216-1316

Garden Grove: Young Adult Program—Gay and Lesbian Center of California
714-534-0862

Los Angeles: Gay and Lesbian Community Services Center
Youth Outreach Pen Pal Program
1625 North Schrader Blvd.
Los Angeles CA 90028
213-993-7400

Los Angeles: Gay and Lesbian Youth Talkline
213-462-8130 or 818-508-1802

Sacramento: Lambda Community Center
916-442-0185

San Diego: Gay Youth Alliance San Diego
619-233-9309

San Francisco: Bay Area Sexual Minority Youth Network
Pen Pal Program
P.O. Box 460268
San Francisco CA 94146-0268
415-541-5012

San Francisco: Lavender Youth Recreation and Information Center (LYRIC)
415-703-6150

Santa Barbara: Gay and Lesbian Resource Center Youth Project
805-963-3636

Santa Cruz: Lesbian, Gay and Bisexual Community Center
408-425-LGBC (-5422)

Santa Rosa: Positive Images
707-433-5333

West Hollywood: Gay and Lesbian Adolescent Social Services (GLASS)
310-358-8727

Colorado
Colorado Springs: Inside/Out–McMaster Center
719-578-3160

Denver: Gay, Lesbian and Bisexual Community Services Center
of Colorado—Youth Services
303-831-6268

Fort Collins: Lambda Community Center
970-221-3247

Connecticut
East Norwalk: Tri-Angle Community Center/Outspoken
203-853-0600

Stamford: Gay and Lesbian Guide Line
203-327-0767

District of Columbia
Washington, D.C.: Sexual Minority Youth Assistance League (SMYAL)
202-546-5940

Florida
Gainesville: Gainesville Gay Switchboard
904-332-0700

Miami: Lesbian Gay and Bisexual Community Center, Inc.
305-531-3666

Orlando: Gay and Lesbian Community Services of Central Florida
407-425-4527

Pinellas Park: True Expressions
813-586-4297

St. Petersburg: Family Resources, Inc./Youth and Family Connection
813-893-1150

Sarasota: PFLAG
941-378-3536

Georgia
Atlanta: The Atlanta Gay Center
404-876-5372

Atlanta: Young Adult Support Group
404-876-5372

Illinois
Chicago: Horizons Community Services, Inc.
312-929-HELP (-4357)

Indiana
Indianapolis: Indianapolis Youth Group
Pen Pal Program
P.O. Box 20176
Indianapolis IN 46220
317-541-8726

Iowa
Des Moines: Gay and Lesbian Center
515-281-0634

Kansas
Wichita: The Center
316-262-3991

Louisiana
New Orleans: The Lesbian and Gay Community Center of New Orleans
504-522-1103

Maine
Portland: Outright
207-774-HELP (-4357)

Maryland
Baltimore: Gay and Lesbian Community Center of Baltimore
410-837-5445

Langley Park: BiNet USA
P.O. Box 7327
Langley Park MD   20787
202-986-7186
E-mail: rain@glib.org

Massachusetts
Boston: Boston Alliance of Gay and Lesbian Youth (BAGLY)
1-800-422-BAGLY (-2459)

Boston: Healthy Boston Coalition for Lesbian, Gay, Bisexual
and Transgendered Youth
617-742-8555

Worcester: Supporters of Worcester Area Gay and Lesbian Youth (SWAGLY)
508-755-0005

Michigan
Ann Arbor: Ozone House Gay and Lesbian Youth Group
313 662 2222

Ferndale: Affirmations Lesbian and Gay Community Center
810-398-7105

Grand Rapids: Windfire
616-459-5900

Lansing: Lansing Gay and Lesbian Hotline
517-332-3200

Traverse: Windfire
616-922-4800

Minnesota
Minneapolis: Gay and Lesbian Community Action Council
612-822-0127

Richfield: Storefront / Youth Action
612-861-1675

Missouri
St. Louis: Metropolitan St. Louis Lesbian, Gay, Bisexual and Transgendered
Community Center
314-997-9897

Nebraska
Lincoln: Gay and Lesbian Youth Talkline
402-473-7932

New Jersey
Asbury Park: Gay and Lesbian Community Center of New Jersey, Inc.
908-774-1809

Convent Station: Gay and Lesbian Youth in New Jersey
201-285-1595

New Brunswick: Pride Center of New Jersey
908-846-2232

New Mexico
Albuquerque: Common Bond
505-266-8041

New York
Albany: Gay and Lesbian Young Adults Support Group (GLYA)
518-462-6138

Bayshore: Long Island Gay and Lesbian Center
516-665-2300

Buffalo: Gay and Lesbian Youth of Buffalo (GLYB)
716-855-0221

New York: Bisexual, Gay and Lesbian Youth of New York (BI-GLYNY)
212-777-1800

New York: Lesbian and Gay Community Services Center
212-620-7310

Rochester: Lighthouse
716-251-9604

Syracuse: Lesbian and Gay Youth Program of Central New York
315-422-9741

Troy: Unity House of Troy, Inc.
518-274-2607

North Carolina
Charlotte: Time Out Youth
704-537-5050

Durham: Outright-Triangle: Gay, Lesbian and Bisexual Youth
919-286-2396

Ohio
Cleveland: Lesbian and Gay Community Service Center
216-522-0813

Dayton: YouthQuest
513-274-1616

Oklahoma
Oklahoma City: The Oasis Gay, Lesbian and Bisexual
Community Resources Center
405-525-2437

Tulsa: National Resource Center for Youth Services
918-585-2986

Oregon
Portland: Lesbian Community Project
503-223-0071

Portland: Phoenix Rising
503-223-8299

Pennsylvania
Lancaster: Gay and Lesbian Youth Alliance
717-397-0691

Philadelphia: The Bridges Project–American Friends Service Committee
215-241-7000

Philadelphia: Penguin Place: Gay and Lesbian Community Center of Philadelphia, Inc.
215-732-2220

Pittsburgh: Gay and Lesbian Community Center
412-422-0114

Puerto Rico
San Juan: Foundation SIDA of Puerto Rico
809-771-7713

South Carolina
Columbia: South Carolina Gay and Lesbian Community Center
803-771-7713

Tennessee
Nashville: Center for Lesbian and Gay Concerns
615-297-0008

Texas
Austin: Out Youth Austin
512-326-1234

Dallas: Gay and Lesbian Community Center
214-528-9254

El Paso: Lambda Services
915-562-4297

Houston: Houston Area Teen Coalition for Homosexuals (HATCH)
713-529-3211

Vermont
Burlington: Outright Vermont
802-865-9677

Virginia
Arlington: Whitman-Walker Clinic
703-358-9550

Richmond: Richmond Organization for Sexual Minority Youth (ROSMY)
804-353-2077

Washington
Bellevue: Youth Eastside Services–Bisexual, Gay and Lesbian Adolescent Drop-In Group (B-GLAD)
206-747-4937

Olympia: Stonewall Youth
206-705-2738

Seattle: Gay, Lesbian and Bisexual Youth Program and Infoline–AFSC
206-632-0500

Tacoma: Oasis Gay, Lesbian and Bisexual Youth Association
206-596-2860

West Virginia
Charleston: New Horizons
304-340-3690

Wisconsin
Madison: "Teens Like Us"—Prevention and Intervention Center for
Alcohol and Other Drug Abuse/Briar Patch
608-246-7606 ext. 142

Milwaukee: Gay Youth Milwaukee
414-265-8500

Crisis Hotlines

Gay and Lesbian Youth Hotline
1-800-347-8336 (Monday–Thursday: 7 P.M. to 10 P.M. ET;
Friday–Sunday: 7 P.M. to 12 A.M. ET)

National AIDS Hotline
1-800-342-AIDS (-2437)
1-800-344-SIDA (-7431) (Spanish language; every day, 8 A.M. to 2 A.M. ET)
1-800-243-7889 (for the hearing impaired;
Monday to Friday, 10 A.M. to 10 P.M. ET)

National Runaway Switchboard
1-800-621-4000
1-800-621-0394 (for the hearing impaired)

Youth Development International
1-800-HIT-HOME (-4663)

Covenant House ("The Nine Line")
1-800-999-9999

Teens Teaching AIDS Prevention (Teens TAP)
1-800-234-TEEN (-8336) (Monday to Friday, 4 P.M. to 8 P.M. ET)

Youth Resources

Lambda Youth Network
P.O. Box 7911
Culver City CA 90233
E-mail: lambdayn@aol.com

!Outproud!
P.O. Box 24589
San Jose CA 95154-4589

Agencies Especially for Lesbian, Gay, and Bisexual Youth
Boston GLASS (Gay and Lesbian Adolescent Social Services)
93 Massachusetts Ave.
Boston MA 02115
Phone: 617-266-3349
Fax: 617-457-8133
E-mail: glass@jri.org

You Are Not Alone. National Lesbian, Gay, and Bisexual Youth Organization
Directory
Hetrick Martin Institute
2 Astor Place
New York NY 10003-6998
Phone: 212-674-2400
Fax: 212-674-8650

Horizons Youth Services
961 West Montana St.
Chicago IL 60614
Phone: 312-472-6469
Helpline every day 6–10 P.M. CT (7–11 P.M. ET) 312-929-HELP (-4357)

LYRIC (Lavender Youth Recreation and Information Center)
127 Collingwood St.
San Francisco CA 94114
Phone: 415-703-6150
Toll-free: 1-800-246-PRIDE

On-line/Internet Address
!OutProud! home page: go to URL http://www.outproud.org/outproud
QueerAmerica database: go to URL http://www.youth.org/outproud/
Planet Out: go to URL http://www.planetout.com/
Youth Assistance Organization home page: go to URL http://www.youth.org/

National Gay and Lesbian Organizations Providing Resources

Black Gay and Lesbian Leadership Forum
1219 South La Brea
Los Angeles CA 90019
Phone: 213-964-7820
Fax: 213-964-7830

LLEGO (National Latino/a Lesbian and Gay Organization)
703 G St., S.E.
Washington DC 20003
Phone: 202-454-0092

Trikone
P.O. Box 21354
San Jose CA 95151-1354
Phone: 408-270-8776
Fax: 408-274-2733
E-mail: trikone@rahul.net
An organization of gay and lesbian South Asians

Asian/Pacific Lesbians and Gays, Inc.
Box 433, Suite 109
7985 Santa Monica Blvd.
West Hollywood CA 90046-5111

National Coalition for Black Lesbians and Gays
Box 19248
Washington DC 20036

American Indian Gays and Lesbians
P.O. Box 10229
Minneapolis MN 55448-3229

The American Educational Gender Information Services, Inc. (AEGIS)
P.O. Box 33724
Decatur GA 30333-0724
Phone: 404-939-0244

Gay and Lesbian Arabic Society
Box 4971
Washington DC 20008

The International Foundation for Gender Education (IFGE)
P.O. Box 229
Waltham MA 02154-0229
Phone: 617-894-8340 or 617-899-2212
E-mail: ifge@std.world.com

National Coming Out Day
P.O. Box 8349
Santa Fe NM 87504

National Gay and Lesbian Task Force (NGLTF)
1734 14th Street, N.W.
Washington DC 20009-4309
Phone: 202-332-6483

North American Multicultural Bisexual Network
584 Castro St.
Box 441
San Francisco CA 94114-2558

Rainbow Alliance of the Deaf
P.O. Box 14182
Washington DC 20044-4182

AIDS
Gay Men's Health Crisis (GMHC)
129 West 20th St., 4th Floor
New York NY 10011
Phone: 212-807-6655 (information line)
Has a young adult project, will send written materials and provide
information and referrals.

Lesbian AIDS Project
129 West 20th St., 4th Floor
New York NY 10011
Phone: 212-337-3532 (information line)
Will provide information, referrals, and written materials.

Runaway Help
National Runaway Switchboard
1-800-621-4000

Psychiatric Abuse Help
The National Center for Lesbian Rights
870 Market St., Suite 750
San Francisco CA 94102
Phone: 415-392-6257
Toll-free: 1-800-528-6257

Antiviolence
Gay and Lesbian Anti-Violence Project
647 Hudson St.
New York NY 10014
Phone: 212-807-0197

Book Resources

Lambda Rising Bookstores
1625 Connecticut Ave., N.W.
Washington DC 20009
Phone: 202-462-6969
Toll-free: 1-800-621-6969
Fax: 202-462-7257
E-mail: lambdarising@his.com (via Internet) and keyword
GAYBOOKS (via America Online)

Further Reading

Fiction

Andersen, Hans Christian. *Michael Hague's Favorite Hans Christian Andersen Fairy Tales.* New York: Holt, Rinehart & Winston, 1981.
Bauer, Marion Dane, ed. *Am I Blue: Coming Out from the Silence.* New York: HarperCollins, 1994.
Brett, Catherine. *S.P. Likes A.D.* Toronto: The Women's Press, 1989.
Brown, Rita Mae. *Rubyfruit Jungle.* New York: Bantam Books, 1973.
Garden, Nancy. *Annie on My Mind.* New York: Farrar, Straus & Giroux, 1982.
Guy, Rosa. *Ruby.* New York: Viking, 1976.
Miller, Isabel. *Patience and Sarah.* New York: Fawcett Crest, 1983.
Mosca, Frank. *All American Boys.* Boston: Alyson Publications, 1983.
Walker, Kate. *Peter.* Boston: Houghton Mifflin, 1993.
Winterson, Jeannette. *Oranges Are Not the Only Fruit.* New York: Atlantic Monthly Press, 1985.

Nonfiction/Biography

Beam, Joseph, ed. *In the Life: A Black Gay Anthology.* Boston: Alyson Publications, 1986.

Bosche, Susanne. *Jenny Lives with Eric and Martin*. London: Gay Men's Press, 1981.

Carnes, Patrick. *Out of the Shadows: Understanding Sexual Addiction*. Minneapolis: CompCare, 1985.

Caster, W. *The Lesbian Sex Book*. Boston: Alyson, 1993.

Chandler, Kurt. *Passages of Pride: Lesbian and Gay Youth Come of Age*. New York: Random House, 1995.

Cowan, Thomas. *Gay Men and Women Who Enriched the World*. Boston: Alyson Publications, 1992.

Deitcher, David, ed. *The Question of Equality: Lesbian and Gay Politics in America Since Stonewall*. New York: Scribner, 1995.

Duberman, Martin Bauml. *About Time: Exploring the Gay Past*. New York: Gay Presses of New York, 1986.

Fricke, Aaron. *Reflections of a Rock Lobster: A Story about Growing Up Gay*. Boston: Alyson Publications, 1981.

Grahn, Judy. *Another Mother Tongue*. Boston: Beacon Press, 1990.

Hall, Marny. *The Lavender Couch: A Consumer's Guide to Psychotherapy for Lesbians and Gay Men*. Boston: Alyson Publications, 1985.

Harris, Robie H. *It's Perfectly Normal: A Book about Changing Bodies, Growing Up, Sex, and Sexual Health*. Cambridge, Mass.: Candlewick Press, 1994.

Heron, Ann ed. *Two Teenagers in Twenty: Writings by Gay and Lesbian Youth*. Boston: Alyson Publications, 1994.

Hutchins, Loraine, and Lani Kaahumanu. *Bi Any Other Name: Bisexual People Speak Out*. Boston: Alyson Publications, 1991.

Larsen, Earnie. *Stage II Relationships: Love beyond Addiction*. San Francisco: Perennial Library, 1987.

Loulan, JoAnn. *The Lesbian Erotic Dance: Butch, Femme, Androgyny, and Other Rhythms*. San Francisco: Spinsters Ink, 1990.

———. *Lesbian Sex*. San Francisco: Spinsters Ink, 1984.

Mishima, Yukio. *Confessions of a Mask*. New York: Harcourt Brace Jovanovich, 1992.

Natalie, Andrea. *StoneWall Riots* (cartoon). East Guttenberg, N.J.: Andrea Natalie, 1990.

Newman, Leslea. *Heather Has Two Mommies*. Boston: Alyson Publications, 1989.

Perry, Rev. Troy, and Charles Lucas. *The Lord Is My Shepherd and He Knows I'm Gay*. Austin, Tex.: Liberty Press, 1987.

Pollack, Rachel, and Cheryl Schwartz. *The Journey Out: A Guide For and About Lesbian, Gay, and Bisexual Teens*. New York: Penguin Books, 1995.

Reid, John. *The Best Little Boy in the World*. New York: Ballantine, 1976.

Schaef, Anne Wilson. *Escape from Intimacy*. San Francisco: Harper San Francisco, 1989.

Silverstein, C., and E. White. *The Joy of Gay Sex*. New York: Crown, 1977.

Singer, Bennett L., ed. *Growing Up Gay/Growing Up Lesbian: A Literary Anthology*. New York: New Press, 1994.

Sisley, E., and B. Harris. *The Joy of Lesbian Sex: A Tender and Liberated Guide to the Pleasures and Problems of a Lesbian Lifestyle*. New York: Crown, 1977. (Out of print.)

Vacha, K., ed. *Quiet Fire: Memoirs of Older Gay Men*. Trumansburg, N.Y.: Crossing Press, 1985.

Music

Ladyslipper

P.O. Box 3124

Durham NC 27715

Phone: 919-683-1570

Toll-free: 1-800-634-6044

Fax: 919-682-5601

Family Resources

Parents, Family, and Friends of Lesbians and Gays (PFLAG)

1101 14th St., N.W., Suite 1030

Washington DC 20005

Phone: 202-638-4200

Fax: 202-638-0243

E-mail: pflagntl@aol.com

Books/Pamphlets

Berstein, Robert. *Straight Parents, Gay Children: Keeping Families Together*. New York: Thunder's Mouth Press, 1995.

Clark, Don. *Loving Someone Gay*. Berkeley: Celestial Arts, 1990.

Fairchild, Betty, and Nancy Hayward. *Now That You Know: What Every Parent Should Know about Homosexuality*. San Diego: Harcourt Brace, 1989.

School Resources

Books/Pamphlets

Harbeck, Karen, ed. *Coming Out of the Classroom Closet: Gay and Lesbian Students, Teachers, and Curricula*. Binghamton, N.Y.: Haworth Press, 1992.

Massachusetts Governor's Commission on Gay and Lesbian Youth. *Making Schools Safe for Gay and Lesbian Youth: Breaking the Silence in Schools and Families*. Boston: The Commission, 1993. Available from: Massachusetts Governor's Commission on Gay and Lesbian Youth, State House, Room 111, Boston, MA 02133, (617) 828-3039.

Minnesota Department of Education. *Alone No More: Developing a School Support System for Gay, Lesbian, and Bisexual Youth.* Saint Paul: Minnesota Department of Education, 1994. Available from: District 202, 2524 Nicollet Ave S., Minneapolis, MN 55404, (612)871-5559; fax: (612)871-1445.

Sherrill, Jan-Mitchell, and Craig A. Hardesty. *The Gay, Lesbian, and Bisexual Students' Guide to Colleges, Universities, and Graduate Schools.* New York: New York University Press, 1994.

Videos

Both of My Moms' Names Are Judy. Lesbian and Gay Parents Association (LGPA). 1994. GLPCI.
> P.O. Box 43206
> Montclair NJ 07043
> Phone: 202-583-8029

Gay Youth: An Educational Video for the Nineties. Pam Walton. 1992.
> Wolfe Video
> Box 64
> New Almaden CA 95042
> Phone: 408-268-6782

Just for Fun. Gordon Seaman. 1994.
> Direct Cinema Limited
> P.O. Box 10003
> Santa Monica CA 90410 1003
> Phone: 1-800-525-0000

Spirituality Resources
Affirmation (Mormon)
P.O. Box 46022
Los Angeles CA 90046
Phone: 213-255-7251

American Baptists Concerned
P.O. Box 16128
Oakland CA 94610
Phone: 510-530-6562
Fax: 510-530-6501

Dignity/USA (Roman Catholic)
1500 Massachusetts Ave., N.W., Suite 11
Washington DC 20005
Phone: 202-861-0017
Toll-free: 1-800-877-8797
Fax: 202-429-9808

Evangelicals Concerned
311 East 72nd St., Suite 1-G
New York NY 10021
Phone: 212-517-3171

Friends for Lesbian and Gay Concerns (Quakers)
143 Campbell Ave.
Ithaca NY 14850
Phone: 607-272-1024
Fax: 607-272-0801

Integrity, Inc. (Episcopal)
P.O. Box 19561
Washington DC 20036
Phone: 718-720-3054

Presbyterians for Lesbian/Gay Concerns
P.O. Box 38
New Brunswick NJ 08903-0038
Phone: 908-249-1016
Fax: 908-932-6916
E-mail: jda@mariner.rutgers.edu

San Francisco Zen Center
300 Page St.
San Francisco CA 94102
Phone: 415-863-3136

Unitarian Universalist Office for Lesbian, Bisexual and Gay Concerns
25 Beacon St.
Boston MA 02108
Phone: 617-742-2100
Fax: 617-523-4123
E-mail: bgreve@uua.org

United Church of Christ Coalition for Lesbian, Gay,
Bisexual and Transgender Concerns
800 Village Walk #230
Guilford CT 06437
Toll-free: 1-800-653-0799
Fax: 203-789-6356
E-mail: mnecoalition@snet.net

United Church of Religious Science
3251 West Sixth St.
Los Angeles CA 90020
Phone: 213-338-2181

Universal Fellowship of Metropolitan Community Churches (MCC)
5300 Santa Monica Blvd., Suite 304
Los Angeles CA 90029
Phone: 213-464-5100
Fax: 213-464-2123
E-mail: UFMCCHQ@aol.com

World Congress of Gay and Lesbian Jewish Organizations
P.O. Box 3345
New York NY 10008-3345

Books/Pamphlets

Aarons, Leroy. *Prayers for Bobby: A Mother's Coming to Terms with the Suicide of Her Gay Son.* San Francisco: HarperSanFrancisco, 1995.

Anderson, Sherry Ruth, and Patricia Hopkins. *The Feminine Face of God: The Unfolding of the Sacred in Women.* New York: Bantam, 1991.

Balka, Christie, and Andy Rose, eds. *Twice Blessed: On Being Gay and Jewish.* Boston: Beacon Press, 1989.

Boswell, John. *Christianity, Social Tolerance, and Homosexuality.* Chicago: University of Chicago Press, 1980.

Cherry, Kittredge, and Zalmon Sherwood, eds. *Equal Rites: Lesbian and Gay Worship, Ceremonies, and Celebrations.* Louisville: Westminster John Knox Press, 1995.

Women of Reform Judaism. *Covenant of the Heart.* 1995.
Women of Reform Judaism
838 Fifth Ave.
New York NY 10021
Phone: 212-249-0100 ext. 352

Community Resources

Civil Rights

Gay and Lesbian Alliance Against Defamation (GLAAD)
150 West 26th St., #503
New York NY 10001
Phone: 212-807-1700
Fax: 212-807-1805
E-mail: glaadny@aol.com

Lambda Legal Defense and Education Fund
666 Broadway, 12th Floor
New York NY 10012-2317
Phone: 212-995-8585

The National Gay and Lesbian Task Force (NGLTF)
6030 Wilshire Blvd., Suite 200
Los Angeles CA 90036
Phone: 213-934-9030

Special Interest
Digital Queers (DQ)
584 Castro St., Suite 150
San Francisco CA 94114
Phone: 415-252-6282

Gay and Lesbian Association of Choruses (GALA)
P.O. Box 65084
Washington DC 20035

Lesbian Herstory Archives
P.O. Box 1258
New York NY 10116
Phone: 718-768-3953
Fax: 718-768-4663

Books/Pamphlets
Community United Against Violence (CUAV). *Lesbian/Gay Speakers Bureau Training Manual.* San Francisco: CUAV, 1993.
  CUAV
  973 Market St., #500
  San Francisco CA 94103
  Phone: 415-777-5500
  Fax: 415-777-5565

About the Author

Linda Handel is a certified clinical mental health counselor in Providence, Rhode Island, and a practicing therapist to gays, lesbians, and others. An experienced speaker and workshop leader, she co-hosted *The Company We Keep*, a public-television series on issues in the gay and lesbian community that was nominated for an Emmy.